LAND AND POWER IN LATIN AMERICA

LAND AND POWER IN LATIN AMERICA

Agrarian Economies and
Social Processes in the Andes

Edited by

Benjamin S. Orlove
and
Glynn Custred

HOLMES & MEIER PUBLISHERS, INC.

NEW YORK • LONDON

First published in the United States of America 1980 by
Holmes & Meier Publishers, Inc.
30 Irving Place
New York, N.Y. 10003

Great Britain:
Holmes & Meier Publishers, Ltd.
131 Trafalgar Road
Greenwich, London SE10 9TX

Library of Congress Cataloging in Publication Data

Main entry under title:
Land and power in Latin America

Bibliography: p.
Includes index.
1. Andes region—Rural conditions—Addresses,
essays, lectures. I. Orlove, Benjamin S.
II. Custred, Glynn.
HN253.5.L36 1980   301.35′098   79-26598

ISBN 0-8419-0476-6

Manufactured in the United States of America

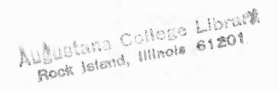

Rising at cock's crow, setting forth at first light,
I wander the long road, I walk the turning path.
Along many rivers, past the high lakes,
In the warmth of the sun, in the chill of wind,
Speaking I say, "Where are you, my brother," calling I say,
    "Where are you, my sister?"

The dove sings of my longing, the owl tells of my dying.
Through the corn fields, through the wheat fields,
Through the valleys, across the mountains,
I wander the long road, I walk the turning path.
I will see your face, soon my brother; I will hear your voice,
    soon my sister.

From Celestino Aguilar, *Fragmentos de una poesia quechua* (Cochabamba: Editorial Voz del Pueblo, 1970, p. 17)
Translation by Sebastián Bocaverde

Contents

Acknowledgments

This book is the product of many conversations and discussions that have taken place between the two editors, the other contributors, and colleagues in the United States, Latin America, and Europe. The sources consulted in the preparation of each chapter are acknowledged in the footnotes. However, we would also like to thank those individuals who have contributed to this volume in a more general way. As the introductory chapter discusses in more detail, the book grew out of a symposium held at a meeting of the American Anthropological Association, and the chapters were greatly improved by the comments of the anthropologists, sociologists, and historians present in the audience. Anthony Leeds, as discussant, offered a number of sharply pointed comments that made us aware of the need for theoretical precision in our statements and that oriented us in our revisions. Eugene Hammel, William Woodcock, and Daniel Chirot suggested changes of organization and content that have helped to unify the volume.

Other individuals have given less immediate but equally valuable assistance. We wish to express our gratitude to John Murra, who has consistently reminded us of the importance of viewing Andean societies in their own terms, rather than through categories imposed from outside. We are also influenced by Enrique Mayer and Jorge Flores, who through their publications, correspondence, and conversations have offered exemplary models of detailed ethnographic studies and rich analytical investigations. Henri Favre and Magnus Morner have helped us reconceptualize the nature of peasant communities and landed estates and their complex historical interaction. We would also like to thank the Conjunto Velille de Chumbivilcas, whose records made the tasks of editing the chapters and preparing the bibliography considerably more enjoyable than they would have otherwise been.

We would also like to thank Cecelia Odelius for her assistance in typing various drafts of this volume and in helping us maintain our correspondence with contributors and editors. A great deal of the work was done on short notice, and we appreciate her efforts greatly. Joan Hellen also provided us with much help, offering us her skills, cartographic and other.

LAND AND POWER IN LATIN AMERICA

CHAPTER 1

Agrarian Economies and Social Processes in Comparative Perspective: The Agricultural Production Unit

Benjamin S. Orlove and Glynn Custred

The Concept of the Agricultural Production Unit

The agrarian economies of the world present wide variation in many dimensions. Crops, soils, climates, technologies, land tenure, labor organization, credit institutions, and marketing systems are arranged in seemingly endless combinations. A number of social scientists, specializing in different disciplines and studying different areas of the world, have developed a vocabulary centering on the concept of the agricultural production unit to organize this diversity in a way that can facilitate analysis. They use several terms, derived primarily from ordinary English usage, to refer to a set of relatively well-defined concepts. This unity of vocabulary does not imply a uniformity of theory. These concepts are integrated into different frameworks and used to explain different activities and behaviors. However, there are certain analytical problems which these concepts can frequently produce. This book examines two of these concepts, the community and the hacienda, in detail; by implication it questions them all. It discusses the difficulties which the use of these concepts has generated in one particular region, the Andes, and proposes an alternative to them.

A number of terms in the vocabulary refer to particular kinds of agricultural production units, each with its characteristic pattern of ownership and control of land, labor, and capital. "Plantation," "ranch," "hacienda," and "community" are examples of such terms. The other terms, such as "peasant," "serf," "slave," and "sharecropper," refer to roles within these units. The terms often occur in conjunction to specify certain sorts of agrarian production units; "slave plantation" and "sharecropper estate" are two examples. The central foci of this book, the hacienda and the community, are only two of these terms, although they are among the most important. The large landed estate and the village of freehold peasants have been reported on by students of agrarian economies on five continents, and appear frequently in the comparative literature on agrarian economies. Before addressing the specific significance of these terms in the Andes, however, it is important to examine these concepts more generally to see how they have been applied. They form a basic part of many different theoretical viewpoints which have been applied to different economic, political, and social phenomena throughout the world. However, there are certain underlying similarities in the manner in which these concepts are integrated into broader analytical frameworks. Because of their wide intellectual and geographical distribution, these terms are of importance outside the Andes.

Two recent comparative studies of political change in agrarian societies illustrate the use of the concept of the agricultural production unit and the incorporation of this concept in a larger explanatory framework. Eric Wolf's *Peasant Wars of the Twentieth Century* (1969) reviews six national revolutions in which peasants play an important role: Mexico, Russia, China, Vietnam, Algeria, and Cuba. He shows that general similarities underlie the individual characteristics of each case. The spread of capitalism from Europe and the United States brought many areas of the world into an economic system which turned land, labor, and capital into commodities. National, regional, and local elites were affected by this process, but the freeholding peasants, living in communities with personalistic social relations, were transformed most drastically. They lost much of their land. Mutual aid associations, reciprocal labor exchange, and other traditional community-based forms of social organization that had protected them against natural and economic crises were severely weakened. An increasing reliance on cash sale of goods made the peasants vulnerable to price fluctuations. They became particularly liable to exploitation by landlords, tax collectors, and traders. Wolf argues that these people, whom he terms "middle peasants" (291), are the ones who provided the backbone of the six revolutions that he studied. They were the ones who were most threatened by the penetration of capitalism, and they were also the ones with sufficient economic and social resources to resist it successfully. By contrast, rural proletarians were too poor or too desperate to mount a significant attack against capitalism. A particular type of agricultural production unit, the peasant community, plays a central role in Wolf's argument. This unit determined the way in which individuals experienced the penetration of capitalism and shaped their response to it.

Jeffery Paige's *Agrarian Revolution: Social Movements and Export Agriculture in the Underdeveloped World* (1975) also examines the influence of capitalism in agrarian economies on political movements. Like Wolf, Paige stresses the importance of agricultural production. He limits his cases to export agriculture and eliminates political movements in which nonagricultural people, such as industrial workers and urban dwellers, play an important role. The period of his study, 1948–1970, is briefer than Wolf's. However, the geographical range is broader. Paige uses survey research methods to examine seventy countries, many of which have more than one export-oriented agricultural sector.

Paige's theoretical model is more elaborate and more systematized than Wolf's. He examines the relations of what he calls the cultivating and non-cultivating classes in export agriculture, and develops a typology of agricultural production units on the basis of the income sources of these two classes. For example, the case in which cultivators draw their income from control of land and noncultivators from control of capital would correspond to small holdings as the agrarian production unit. The noncultivators would dominate credit, processing machinery, and transport. Paige correlates five types of agricultural production units with four types of political conflict. The constraints of different types of agricultural production units lead both cultivators and noncultivators to adopt certain types of economic behavior. These economic strategies shape political behavior and determine the sort of conflict which characterizes each type of agricultural production unit. Statistical surveys using correlations and multiple regressions and close examination of three cases (Peru, Vietnam, Angola) support these hypotheses.

The similarities between the two books go beyond their interest in a world-wide examination of the political correlates of economic change in agrarian societies. They share a broad analytical framework composed of three levels: the global economy, the agricultural production unit, and the rational actor. World capitalism, with its insatiable hunger for raw materials and investment opportunities, offers new alternatives and possibilities for the participants in agrarian economies throughout the world while eliminating many old ways of life. Individual actors attempt to balance profit and security in changing economic and social conditions. Wolf and Paige view their responses as rational. The different ways in which the stimuli from the world economy are mediated explains the differences in the behavior of individual actors. The agricultural production units are the principal mediator. In one sort of unit, revolution is a rational response for individual actors; in another, passivity; in a third, the organization of pressure groups such as unions. Both authors assume that the upper and lower levels in their system of explanation, the global economy and the rational actor, are essentially the same throughout the world. The differences in the particular cases can be explained by the differences in the middle level of the agricultural production unit, that is, the peasant community (Wolf) or the five types (Paige).

This sort of explanation might be called the three-level structural model. The three levels are the global economy, the agricultural production unit, and the individual. The models are structural since they explain variation in economics and political activity by the form of relations between several social sectors. Wolf, for example, would not explain similarities between the Mexican and Cuban revolutions by the countries' common Latin American culture or by their common history as former Spanish colonies, but by similar structural relations of peasants to each other and to wider society. Wolf and

Paige may differ on the specific details of their analyses, but they agree on this general model. For example, Wolf suggests that landownership makes peasants willing to fight to preserve their holdings, and Paige argues that landownership leads peasants to avoid taking risks so that they will not lose this resource. Each cites specific cases to buttress his position. Despite this apparent contrast, they are in close agreement that peasants are rational actors, that the growth of world capitalism demands a response from them, and that the agricultural production unit, the peasant community, is the key link between the two.

This emphasis on the agricultural production unit as part of the three-level structural model is also found in a number of different contexts. Two of these will be explored: the Marxist literature on agrarian economies and comparative studies of agrarian reform.

A large portion of the Marxist literature on agrarian economies also shares this three-level structural model and the emphasis on the nature of the agricultural production unit. Marx set a precedent for this perspective in several of his writings. He emphasizes the organization of the manorial estate in his discussion of the transition from feudalism to capitalism (1947:11–13). In his famous analysis of the conservatism of the nineteenth-century French peasant, he stresses the isolation which small independent household farms generate, comparing the peasants to "potatoes in a sack" (1963:124). In both of these instances, Marx argues that a certain type of agricultural production unit corresponds to the dominant mode of production in the economy. The relations of production characteristic of these units shape rural society in politics. Medieval serfs and nineteenth-century peasants act in different ways because of the differences between manorial estates and small freehold plots.[1]

Some recent research in comparative agrarian economic history follows this Marxist approach. Witold Kula's *Théorie économique du système féodal* (1970) demonstrates that the feudal manor imposed strong constraints on the economic choices of landlords, peasants, and artisans in Poland from the sixteenth to the eighteenth centuries. He uses the nature of the agrarian production unit to explain apparently irrational responses to economic stimuli, such as the increasing Western European demand for wheat. In other words, he also sees the agrarian production unit as mediating between the wider economy and rational actors. Other recent comparative studies of feudal economies in different parts of the world and in different historical periods are based on Kula's analysis (Kay, 1974).

The recently revived interest in a minor theme of Marx and Engels, the Asiatic mode of production (Sofri, 1971; Hindess and Hirst, 1975), shares this analytical viewpoint. The relatively static character of many non-Western economies, such as those of precolonial India and China, is explained by the manner in which the agricultural production units characteristic of the Asiatic mode of production limit the extraction and reinvestment of economic surplus. The autonomous and self-sufficient nature of agricultural villages precludes the emergence of separate artisan or merchant classes. Communal landholding and cooperative labor eliminate the possibility of economic differentiation within the village.

Economists who are somewhat more conventional also practice this line of analysis. Recent studies of the economic behavior of agricultural workers and landowners in sharecropping estates in underdeveloped nations illustrate this point (Cheung, 1969; Hsaio, 1975; Newberry, 1975). These individuals respond to economic stimuli from the national and international level in a manner which does not accord with the predictions of conventional neoclassical economists. Their utilization of factors of production, for example, would appear inefficient and irrational. However, these economic responses can be explained as rational when the risks and incentives which are associated with the institutional context of sharecropping are taken into account. It is not the individual but the agricultural production unit that is different from the cases ordinarily encountered in standard economies.

In a similar vein, much of the extensive literature on agrarian reform also shares this emphasis on the agrarian production unit and the three-level structural model. A number of economists and policy makers of varying orientations would agree that "the main obstacles to agricultural development [are] to be found in the institutional arrangements governing land tenure systems and relations of production of the land" (Stavenhagen, 1975:228). A number of economic problems are due to the organization of agricultural production units, rather than to a lack of capital, inadequate technology, or an absence of cultural values favoring work and investment (Chonchol, 1965).

In his comparative analysis of eight cases of agrarian reform programs, Tuma breaks agrarian production systems into three major variables: the kind of land tenure, the pattern of cultivation, and the scale of operation (1965:12). Agrarian reforms change one or more of these variables in a rapid and dramatic fashion. This change in the organization of the agricultural production unit greatly alters the manner in which individuals participate in national-level economic, social, and political institutions. Tuma covers a large number of cases in different historical periods and geographical areas. Other studies, based on fewer cases, frequently present similar arguments. The system of large, privately owned estates tilled by resident peons and day laborers does not provide incentives to landlord or worker to increase efficiency and productivity as rapidly as demand for foodstuffs grows. The consequences are insufficient food supplies, inflation, chronic unemployment, and unequal income distribution. Agrarian reform is needed to remedy this situation; the change must take place in the agricultural production unit, rather than in the global economy or the individual actor (Barraclough, 1970).

These examples illustrate the range of literature that utilizes the three-level structural model and emphasizes the importance of the agricultural production unit. Wolf, Paige, Kula, Stavenhagen, and Tuma examine different empirical phenomena and rely on different theoretical positions, but they share a common analytical stance. They view the agricultural production unit as determining the manner in which individual actors in rural settings respond to national and international economic and political systems. The organization of these agricultural production units is considered to be relatively unproblematic. A relatively small number of types are assumed to reoccur in a number of different settings.

Because of its generality, this analytical stance facilitates comparison between different societies, geographical areas, and historical periods. It permits specialists in particular areas to strengthen their explanations of local phenomena by examining parallelisms with other areas where similar agricultural production units are found. This procedure is a fundamental part of research in some areas. Caribbean specialists have long argued that the plantation has given rise to basic economic, social, and cultural forms on the islands, such as strong union movements, the matrifocal family, and emphasis on personal reputation (Mintz, 1966).

The debate over the nature of Japanese feudalism allows parallels to be drawn between Japan and medieval Europe to clarify the nature of historical processes in each area. These similarities bring a more precise understanding of the response of Japanese peasants and landlords to changing economic and political conditions in Japan and the West. Historians, anthropologists, and political scientists who study India have engaged in fruitful debates over the applicability of the concepts of feudalism and the Asiatic mode of production to their area. This reexamination of the organization of agricultural production units in India has helped explain the relations among landlords, peasants, and artisans in village settings, and the response of these individuals to changing national economic conditions.

The hacienda and the peasant community, the principal foci of this book, are two of these basic types of agricultural production units that have a wide distribution. Neither type is restricted to the Andean highlands. The rest of Latin America contains numerous examples. The fertile irrigated valleys of coastal Peru, treated only sketchily in this book, are also characterized by a mix of communities of small peasant holdings and large haciendas or plantations. In most cases, the latter dominate the former or have completely replaced them (Hammel, 1969; Horton, 1973; Burga, 1976). A review of Peruvian coastal agriculture divides the countryside into haciendas and communities (Matos Mar et al., 1969). The haciendas own the best land, have easier access to credit, and control the valley-wide irrigation systems; the more densely populated communities have a relative surplus of labor. The book argues that the economic and political activity of peasants and landlords can best be explained by the way in which these institutions constrain the responses of individuals to growing demand for agricultural products and increasing population pressure on the land. Although the recent agrarian reform has led to significant changes in the ownership, control, and management of these units, the current agrarian situation cannot be understood apart from its past (Lowenthal, 1975).

Mexico and Guatemala bear strong geographical and historical similarities to the Andes, and their rural areas are dominated by the hacienda and the peasant community. There have been numerous studies of both of these and of the interrelationships between the two (Adams, 1970; Chevalier, 1963; Miller, 1973; Womack, 1969). Wolf has stated:

> Much of the recent history of Middle America may be summed up as a major effort to disestablish the twin foundations of the old social order, represented by Indian community and hacienda, and to ring in a new order, unhampered by the narrow social boundaries and unbreachable cultural barriers of the past. Each Indian community, supported in its autonomy by a grant of land, charged with the autonomous enforcement of social control, constituted a small, closely defended island, securing the social and cultural homogeneity of its members within, struggling to maintain its integrity in the face of attacks from without. The other integrative institution of the past, the hacienda, similarly exercised a monopoly of the labor force within its social and economic precinct. Using the mechanism of peonage to turn community-oriented peasants into a disciplined labor force capable of producing cash crops for a supercommunity market, the hacienda nevertheless imprisoned its workers in a tight little social world, circumscribed by its boundaries, lorded over by the hacienda owner who, concentrating in his hands social, political, and judicial power, became chief arbiter of their life and chief buffer between them and higher levels of integration. Indian community and hacienda both had in common that they interposed institutional barriers between local group and outside, containing their personnel within narrow limits, and causing communication from outside to pass through the hands of special agents, the members of the civil-religious hierarchy in the Indian community, the hacienda owner or his managers on the hacienda. (Wolf, 1967:299)

Many other writers share this opinion. The closed corporate peasant community of villagers engaged in subsistence agriculture on freehold plots and communal lands is an important element of the writings on Mesoamerica in anthropology, history, economics, and political science. Less frequently studied but equally important is the large landed estate or hacienda, with permanent tenants, sharecroppers, and peons working small fields for themselves and larger extensions of land for the hacendado. The attempts of the former to encapsulate themselves from the hostile forces outside them and of the latter to dominate regions economically and politically provide much of the dynamic of rural Mesoamerican society and account for the actions of different sets of individuals. Elsewhere, Wolf generalizes this description to other parts of Latin America, such as Colombia and Venezuela (Wolf and Hansen, 1972: 71–99; 135–150). The Brazilian fazenda exhibits a number of similarities to the hacienda elsewhere in Latin America, including private ownership of land, a work force of resident peons, and domination of credit facilities by the landlord (Johnson, 1971). The haciendas included bear strong structural resemblances to their counterparts elsewhere in Latin America, despite the differences in local cultural traditions (Bauer, 1975). In brief, the hacienda and the community as agricultural production units are seen as dominant elements in the entire Latin American countryside (Furtado, 1970; Duncan and Rutledge, 1977).

The hacienda and the peasant community are by no means unique to Latin America. Kula's treatment of the large landed estate in Poland has already been mentioned. The combination of the estate and the peasant community is found elsewhere in Eastern Europe before the advent of socialist regimes. Russia is a notable example. The Russian *mir* resembles the Latin American peasant community, with the strength of the village as a corporate group. The large landed estates in both areas had similar land tenure patterns and labor arrangements. The conflict before the Russian Revolution between the two generated by increasing foreign demand for Russian agricultural produce, population pressure, and changes in national politics shares a number of elements with other cases of agrarian conflict. North Africa also contains similar agricultural production units. Precolonial Algeria had tribal lands which correspond to peasant communities, with strong corporate ownership of land combined with individual usufruct rights. Although the Turkish rulers and administrators retained ultimate sovereignty over all other land, individual estates controlled by officials, military rulers, and the elite families resembled haciendas. The lands were worked by sharecroppers, leaseholders, or laborers from nearby tribes. Patterns similar to Algeria and Turkey are found in parts of the Middle East with a generally similar environment and history of external domination, such as Lebanon.

Recent reviews of rural society and politics in Southeast Asia also show the importance of peasant communities and large estates, particularly in the precolonial period. The Vietnamese villages and lowland Philippine estates, for instance, bear strong similarities to their Latin American counterparts, and it has been suggested that they influence the economic and political behavior of peasant and landlord in similar ways (Scott, 1972). Discussion of the negative influence of the large estate on agricultural development and the need for agrarian reform also parallels the literature on Latin America.

The hacienda and the peasant community, then, are not social and economic forms whose distribution is limited to the Andes. They are found in many areas of the world. The principal motive for examining them, however, is the important role that they play in certain systems of explanation. Like other agricultural production units, they have a central position in the three-level structural model that characterizes many current studies of agrarian economies. It is this assumption of the small number of types of agricultural production units and the uniformity within each type that has led us to review closely two of these types, the community and the hacienda. The different instances of the three-level structural models focus on the relations between levels, but do not closely examine the middle level. Their readiness to undertake intersocietal comparisons, however, rests on this procedure. A reassessment of the nature of the hacienda and the community calls into question the solidity of analytical frameworks of which they are a fundamental part. For this reason, a reconsideration of the hacienda and the peasant community in the Andes has considerable theoretical as well as empirical significance for scholars in a range of disciplines and geographical areas of specialization.

The Community-Hacienda Model in Andean Studies
and the Development of an Alternative Model

A persistent set of ideas based on the concept of the agricultural production unit has served not only as a theoretical base for research in the social sciences in the Andes, but also as a framework for political theories and national literatures. Despite its wide acceptance, it has often remained partially or wholly unstated. This set of ideas or implicit model, which will be referred to as "the community-hacienda model," emphasizes the peasant community and the hacienda as the crucial institutions of agrarian society. It consists of the following propositions: Each plot of productive land and every peasant belong either to a community or a hacienda. Both institutions are types of corporate groups which are attached to specific extensions of land. The members of the community own some land as individuals and have corporate rights to the remainder; land ideally cannot be sold to outsiders. Certain community institutions, such as hierarchies of posts associated with religious fiestas, increase the solidarity of the community. By contrast, the hacienda or landed estate is owned by a member of a nonpeasant elite, the hacendado. The peasants who live on the hacienda work the hacienda land in exchange for rights to cultivate plots of their own. Because of the domination of the hacendado, the hacienda peasants do not have a strong internal organization. In this manner, these two agricultural production units affect the social organization of their members. Both isolate peasants from the wider world, the community by directing social ties inward rather than outward, and the hacienda by channeling ties through a single individual.

There are a number of other notions which are often associated with this community-hacienda model. The communities are characterized by solidarity, cooperation, and consensus. Haciendas, on the other hand, have been viewed as devices which permit an unproductive elite to extract wealth by exploiting the peasantry. They exist at the expense of the community. The opposition of community and hacienda parallels other oppositions which recur in Andean studies; Inca and Spanish, Indian and mestizo, highland and coast. The community becomes the repository of traditional culture; the hacienda is viewed as the source of change, conflict, and domination. The origins of the community are usually traced to the pre-Columbian *ayllu* or local kin group, and the hacienda is seen as a modification of colonial instructions, particularly the *encomienda*. Unsurprisingly, most studies of local-level organization have focused on highland communities and coastal haciendas. This model has brought attention to these contending social and economic forms and the drama of their struggle, rather than leading to an examination of the great variety in the relations of peasants to each other and to local elites in the

broader context of the national economy and politics. A number of inac-
curacies have resulted from the use of the community-hacienda model. The
model has underemphasized the complex processes which have generated
present social structure and economic relations, and led to the neglect of
peasants who do not fit neatly into easily definable communities. Though it
stressed the importance of haciendas as critical social and economic entities,
the community-hacienda model has not stimulated investigation of the internal
functioning of haciendas and their links with the broader society. It has also
failed to consider fully a range of other elite-peasant relationships outside the
hacienda context. Before outlining a more comprehensive model, however, a
brief review of the rise of this particular approach is in order.

It should be stated that this traditional perspective is not wholly unjustified;
it represents a selective emphasis of certain features of certain regions within
the Andes. In some areas peasant communities and haciendas exist as
observable entities. They consist of well-defined sets of individuals attached to
clearly bounded territories. Local residents recognize the integrity and the
importance of these social units. One can indeed observe communities in many
parts of the Andes in the form of village clusters; in a similar vein, haciendas
are massive houses with associated fields and outbuildings. The ties which
bind peasants to nonpeasant landowners are a matter of simple observation
and of a few readily answered questions. However, this approximate fit to
certain aspects of Andean reality is not the only reason for this emphasis on
these social forms in Andean areas. Incorrect theory has misled writers more
than incomplete information has biased them. The basis for the traditional
community-hacienda model can be found in Western intellectual history. The
relation between this foreign intellectual tradition and Andean social reality is
a complex one. On the one hand, this tradition influences the categories into
which outside observers classify social forms. On the other hand, the
dominance of foreigners and foreign education has led to the formulation of
policy based on these ideas. Andean society has often accommodated,
whether under pressure or willingly, to this model which is based on a
misinterpretation of it.

This complex interaction of theory, policy, institutions, and behavior is
traced in chapter three of this volume. A number of intellectual traditions,
including Spanish corporativism, economic liberalism, and *indigenismo*, are
shown to converge on a series of variants of the community-hacienda model.
The Andean countryside and its inhabitants are seen as neatly and unambiguously partitioned into a collection of haciendas and communities.
Ideological connotations and historical associations are linked with each of
these two institutions. This selective emphasis on the community and the
hacienda has led to a distortion of Andean social and economic reality.

The editors of this volume believe that there are several major elements of
this distortion: a neglect of the peasant household as a social and economic
unit, a view of the peasant as tradition-bound and passive, and a presentation
of the Andean countryside as static and unchanging. This book has been

written to present and support an alternative view of agrarian economies and social process in the Andes.

Most of the chapters in this book are based on papers given at a symposium in November 1974 at the annual meeting of the American Anthropological Association in Mexico City. This book constitutes a highly reworked version of the symposium. The participants prepared their contributions after they had read an introductory statement or "preliminary working paper" which reviewed standard analyses of the community and the hacienda in the Andes and proposed a new household-centered view of rural social and economic organizations. These papers have been extensively revised and updated for publication. Several papers which were presented at the symposium are not included in the volume, because they focused on ritual or land-use patterns at the expense of social organization. The preliminary working paper was extensively revised, and sections of it have been incorporated into this chapter and the next one.

The book retains the most basic structure of the symposium. The introductory chapters review the discussion of agricultural production units, particularly haciendas and communities in the Andes, and propose an alternative model. They emphasize the importance of the household and the variety of different forms of organization, including corporate groups and networks. These different forms are presented as adaptations to environmental, economic, and political constraints. The model uses a processual point of view to clarify the range of social organization in the Andes and the manner in which corporate groups and networks constitute adaptations to wider systems.

This introductory chapter reviews the use of the concept of agricultural production units generally and its specific application to the Andes in what is termed the community-hacienda model. The second chapter presents an alternative model in detail. It argues that the household, rather than the hacienda and the community, should be considered the basic unit of social and economic organization in the Andes. Common features of the developmental cycle of domestic groups, the division of labor by sex and age, patterns of descent, alliance and adoption, and rural-urban migration support this point. It develops a general framework for the description and analysis of interhousehold links, showing how they form networks and corporate groups. The chapter applies this model to data from the four southernmost provinces of the department of Cuzco, Peru. Interhousehold links include several forms of reciprocal labor exchange, patron-client relationships, and trading partnerships. Ties between peasant households and local elites are also described. Communities and haciendas are presented as corporate groups composed of households; it is emphasized that not all households belong to one or the other form. Examples of corporate groups on other scales are also presented, filling an important gap in the descriptive literature by showing the variation in forms of social organization. These examples also encourage a revision of current analytical understandings of Andean peasant society by indicating its flexibility. Communities and haciendas are the product of peasant social and economic activity, rather than of the context which limits such activity, as the three-level structural models would suggest. There is a wide variety of forms of utilization of land, labor, and capital, rather than a small number of types of agricultural production units.

The third chapter provides an historical overview of Andean rural communities and a framework for analyzing their relations to governments and elites. In this chapter, Yambert examines the relationship between the actual organization of the communities and the images of them which are found in social theory and policy. The details of the interaction between social reality and ideology have varied in different historical periods, but this interaction has been consistently linked to the efforts of different groups to gain economic and political power. Social scientists participate in this process as well as comment on it. The following chapters tend to support this alternative model, although Primov and van den Berghe argue for the advantages of a macrosociological rather than a household-based approach. In many cases the data show the same range of forms as are found in southern Cuzco; in other cases, they demonstrate different aspects of interhousehold networks and groups. There are two chapters written by historians, two by sociologists, and five by anthropologists. Several chapters examine what has been for a long time the core area of Andean studies, the central and southern Peruvian highlands populated by Quechua-speaking peasants; other studies are based on field work in the northern Peruvian highlands and Colombia.

Chapter 4, by Spalding, offers a synthetic description of the development of agrarian systems of production and class relations in the Andes. She shows the complex historical development of the region before the major impact of incorporation into the modern world economy in the twentieth century. The third and fourth chapters provide a context for the remaining eight, which offer more detailed and localized studies of the region in the twentieth century. These two chapters share the perspective outlined in the introduction: they have a processual point of view, and they link social, economic, and political organization and activity. Local groups of peasants are shown to change their forms of social and economic organization in response to changing political and economic structures on the regional and national level. It is the articulation of the peasants with the wider economy and society, rather than their isolation from it, that shapes their organization. Spalding reviews and rejects the community-hacienda model, what she calls "the traditional dichotomy of hacienda and village, huge estate and minifundia." She shows that the desires of peasants and hacendados to participate in production and cash sale of wool and agricultural crops, and their efforts to establish links with governmental institutions, led to a striking differentiation and diversification: local populations were stratified and organized along more complex lines than the standard models would suggest.

Maltby's chapter is among the recent research to come out of the rich archival material contained in the Archivo del Fuero Agrario, which has collected the records of many haciendas which were expropriated under the Peruvian government's agrarian reform program. Her detailed case study revises a number of standard conceptions of the hacienda. The common themes associated with the community-hacienda model, total domination of the peon by the hacendado and the isolation of the peon from the wider society and economy, are shown to be false. The social relations of the peon households are more extensive than has generally been supposed, so that they have considerable freedom to manipulate the landowners and engage in independent economic activities. There are dense social networks linking the hacienda with nearby communities. The peon households establish wide networks linking them with traders, officials, and other peasants. The social and economic organization of the hacienda is quite fluid and flexible; peon households adapt readily to changing economic and political opportunities.

Chapter 6, by Orlove, on Surimana and Quehue, is a controlled comparison of the historical development of relationships between peasants and elites in two adjacent areas in the department of Cuzco, Peru. The two areas were virtually identical throughout the nineteenth century, but the elite of one area gained more direct access to the national government when the village in which they lived was granted the status of district capital. Their current power depends more on their position as representatives of the government than on their original landholdings. These areas now have distinct patterns of land use and labor relations. These differences in relations between peasant households and elites in the two areas can be accounted for by this historical explanation. An analysis of the two areas in terms of the distribution of haciendas and communities does not provide as thorough an explanation. The case further demonstrates the adaptability of peasant social organization by showing its responses to different sets of political circumstances.

Ortiz's material from Colombia, Chapter 7, demonstrates that remote populations are as strongly affected by their links to markets and the central government as less isolated groups are, even though their forms of social and economic organization are very different. A number of traders and government officials have personal ties to peasant households in both cases. She examines a variety of social networks which are mobilized for different purposes. Her discussions of interhousehold exchange of goods and services parallel the case material from Peru. This chapter strengthens the view of social organization as adaptation to structural constraints rather than as the continuity of cultural traditions, because the populations whom Ortiz studies are historically and linguistically distinct from the Quechua-speaking peasants studied by Maltby, Orlove, Primov, and van den Berghe.

In Chapter 8, Primov's study of the changing role of schoolteachers in a particular community examines linkages between local and regional levels of organization. He argues that the importance of the schoolteachers lies as much in their ability to bypass certain blockages in the regional power structure as in their activities in providing skills for the young. The use that peasants make of the schoolteachers varies in different periods, as regional political institutions

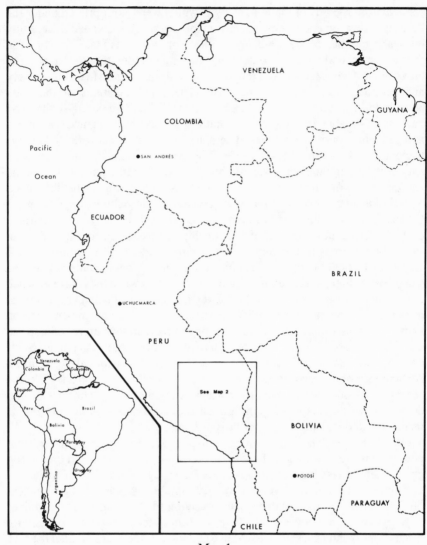

Map 1

change and alternate avenues of access to them become available. The description of forms of political decision-making in the community shows the variability of local-level social organization.

Van den Berghe's examination in Chapter 9 of the processes of transformation in the hacienda Ccapana near Cuzco correlates changes in hacienda organization with shifts in regional economic and political systems. The peasants reorganize themselves on a subhacienda and hacienda level when these wider systems favor these changes. The structured relations of inequality between peasant and elite are shown to be drawn from regional and national

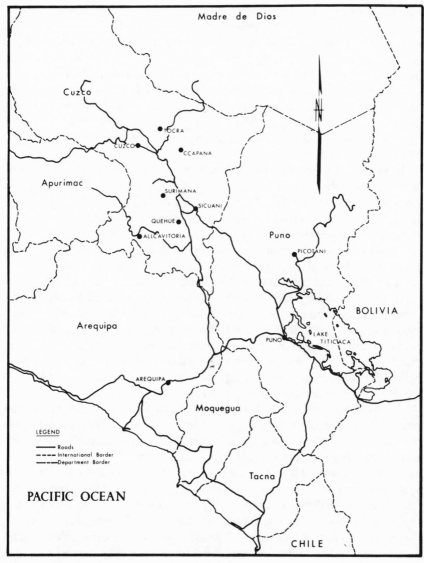

Map 2

systems of stratification, rather than depending solely on the internal organization of the hacienda.

In Chapter 10 Orlove examines the position of rustlers in a province in the department of Cuzco. He supports Maltby's contention that peon households have a range of options open to them. The rustlers develop extensive networks with a variety of individuals in order to carry out their attacks. Their tendency to steal from landlords rather than peasants is explained in terms of their need to maintain these networks. The chapter shows that peasants have a variety of adaptations and responses to the structural constraints under which they live.

Custred's discussion of peasant ritual, Chapter 11, takes a different approach to rural social organization from that of the other chapters and arrives at similar conclusions. He demonstrates that a series of rituals, including patron-saint festivals, masses, and offerings to the hills and the earth, correspond to a series of levels of social relations. The household is the lowest and most fundamental level; higher levels include interhousehold alliances, communities, and regional systems. The ritual is as flexible as the social organization. Custred documents changes in ritual which follow shifts in local-level social organization.

In the final chapter Brush discusses a little-studied topic, migration from one rural area to another. He examines a region in the northern Peruvian highlands since 1900, systematically describing the variety of economic and social strategies available to peasant households in areas with different degrees of scarcity of land. Different economic strategies translate into different forms of social networks and different types of interhousehold links. Through the use of controlled comparison of two villages, he shows that there is considerable variation within the categories of "community" and "hacienda."

All the contributors to this volume examine legally titled haciendas and officially recognized communities and they all show them to be less isolated, rigid, and static than the community-hacienda model would suggest. These studies do not argue that communities and haciendas do not exist. They do say that they are not as ubiquitous, fundamental, or homogeneous as has been believed. Important processes operate at higher and lower levels, generating a number of other forms of social organization.

The book, then, offers a coherent and detailed alternative view of Andean rural society. It presents a general model and a number of studies which apply this model to specific situations. The historical articles demonstrate the variety and adaptability of peasant social organization in the past, and argue that the ideal types of community and hacienda are inadequate tools for analyzing the agrarian society and economy. The subsequent chapters all share this concern for processual analysis. The emphasis on the household as the fundamental social and economic unit is particularly strong in the chapters by Brush, Custred, Orlove, and Ortiz, but all chapters show the flexibility of peasant organization and its adaptation to external constraints. All the articles adopt a processual point of view, and Primov and van den Berghe carry this analysis to the period of current military government in Peru. Drawing from different disciplines, field sites, and research topics, the authors collectively argue for the reconstruction of an alternative model. By implication, similar reanalysis in other parts of the world could also offer powerful insights. The simple typology of agricultural production units does not appear to be valid under close examination in the Andean case, and analyses based on three-level structural models are therefore also suspect. The alternative approach, to build up from the much lower level of peasant households, can account for a wide range of social, economic, and political activity in a number of settings.

Notes

1. From a Marxist perspective, each mode of production has a corresponding form of ideology and thought, and Marxists would thus not be disposed to accept an argument solely based on the universality of rationality. Formal rationality in a pure form would be found only in capitalist economies. However, there are also common elements to ideology and thought in different modes of production because of common elements in material practice, and these are sufficiently important to justify the addition of the three-level structural model.

CHAPTER 2

The Alternative Model of Agrarian Society in the Andes: Households, Networks, and Corporate Groups

Benjamin S. Orlove and Glynn Custred

The Alternative Model: A General Statement

The presentation[1] of the alternative model of Andean social organization consists of two related parts: a general description and justification of the model for the entire Andes, and a more detailed application of the model to a region in the southern Peruvian highlands. The first part describes features of social, economic, and political organization which are found over wide areas; the second concentrates on forms which are found in a particular region, although there are similar forms in many other regions as well. The model differs from a theory in that it does not present hypotheses which can be tested. Instead, it establishes categories which can be used in a description and analysis of Andean social organization.

A brief digression is necessary, however, since a reexamination of Andean agrarian society requires a firm position on a thorny issue. The extensive literature on stratification in the Andes is characterized by extreme controversy. As a recent article demonstrated (van den Berghe, 1974a), there are a number of contradictions between different analyses of status groups in the Andes with regard to their number, their relative economic and political positions, and the relations among them. Two rather cautious conclusions may be drawn: there is considerable local variation in stratification systems and many individuals occupy ambiguous status.

Nevertheless, an analysis of rural society is somewhat less complex. Two sets of individuals, peasants and elites, can be distinguished fairly easily. This separation is often striking in particular cases, and it seems generally applicable to most regions and historical periods. There are a number of households whose members are directly involved in production as agriculturalists, herders, and artisans. We will term them "peasants" as a rough translation of the Spanish term *campesinos*, since the alternative possibility, "countrymen," seems dated and artificial. This lumping of small-scale freeholders, tenants, sharecroppers, peons, seasonal laborers, and day laborers is justifiable only as a general approximation. There are other individuals who do not engage directly in production. They earn their livelihood either through ownership and control of land and capital, or through power allocated to them by national institutions. We will term them "elites," recognizing again that a number of different sorts of positions are being crudely lumped into a single category. Both sets of people show high internal differentiation with regard to wealth, power, and status. There may be a certain degree of overlap between them with regard to these dimensions. Some peasants who own large herds and extensive fields, for instance, are wealthier than some back-country priests, assigned to poor, remote, and unresponsive parishes. However, such anomalous cases are infrequent. The people who occupy intermediate and ambiguous statuses tend to be found in the towns and cities. There are relatively few of them in the countryside, aside from the important category of petty trader. Because of their small numbers, they do not warrant an extensive treatment.

To return from the digression to the principal theme, the alternative model offers a series of categories which can be used to describe and analyze rural Andean society. Stated in its simplest terms, the model consists of four propositions:

1. The household, rather than the community or the hacienda, is the fundamental unit of agrarian society and economy in the Andes.
2. Households establish links with other households to form networks and corporate groups.
3. These networks and groups constitute adaptations to environmental, economic, and political constraints; they change as these constraints change, and in turn they may influence these constraints.
4. The nature of these networks and corporate groups may be specified by three variables: content, organization, and stratification.

Our alternative model may be distinguished from the community-hacienda model and the three-level structural model in the following ways. Although we accept the importance of communities and haciendas in many cases, and we acknowledge the three levels of global economy, agricultural production unit, and rational actor, we argue that agricultural production units are complex and changing, and should be examined through their component households. We see actors and institutions as mutually interacting and influencing each other rather than as sharply separated levels, as the three-level structural model presents them. We suggest the importance of additional levels, such as the nation-state and the region. Finally, we view rationality somewhat differently than the adherents of the three-level structural model do. Defining rationality as the consistent allocation of scarce resources to a ranked hierarchy of goals or ends under conditions of constraints, we would tend to find the origins of goals and the nature of constraints as more problematic than the followers of the other models would.

The alternative model considers the household, not the community and the hacienda, as the fundamental element of peasant society for a number of reasons. Firstly, the household is the basic unit of economic activity. Although many goods are individually owned, and rights to land and irrigation water are frequently based on membership in larger corporate groups, the household is the locus of decision-making with regard to production, exchange, and consumption. Its component members engage in economic activities as part of the overall budgeting and allocation of household resources to meet the needs and goals of the household.

A second reason stems from patterns of social organization. Other peasant social aggregates are composed either of households or of individuals acting for other households. Other researchers concur on this important role of the household (Bolton and Mayer, 1977). This central position of the household is reinforced by the fact that in the Andes, unlike certain other areas of the world, household membership is rarely ambiguous. It would be inaccurate to deny either that individuals are social actors in the Andes or that relationships exist between particular individuals as well as between households. However, we have chosen not to examine in detail these relationships, since friendship, cooperation on work projects, trading partnerships, and other such relations which link two individuals tend to become relationships between households. This change may be recognized informally, or it may be formalized through mechanisms in which the household is emphasized. Such mechanisms include the establishment of ritual kinship ties (*compadrazgo*) between couples, repeated participation in work groups in which male and female roles are complementary and necessary, and participation in ritual systems such as fiesta cycles, in which only members of fully established households may participate.

Certain features of Andean kinship and demography reinforce this pattern. Virtually all adults marry and very few are separated or divorced, so that most adults are married and living with their spouses and children. Orphaned children are adopted by other kin, godparents, or, less frequently, other peasant households. The strong corporate character of the peasant household does not permit responsibility for children to be diffused among a number of households; every child must be unambiguously associated with a specific household.

In addition, other aspects of Andean kinship stress the autonomy of the household. Lambert states that "a clue to the locus of solidarity is the treatment of affines, especially siblings-in-law. When a married couple is treated as a unit in economic and legal affairs, sibling ties between adults serve to connect nuclear families, not individuals" (1977:3). These ties appear in ritual contexts as well (Isbell, 1977; Mayer, 1977). Inheritance patterns, despite their variations according to region, population density, and subsistence base, rest on the household as the fundamental corporate group (Lambert, 1977:12–15).

The extensive rural out-migration and growth of cities have also reinforced this pattern of the completeness of households. Peasants typically migrate to cities between the ages of fifteen and thirty, either as unmarried adolescents or as relatively young people recently married. Households are rarely split by the migration of only one adult member. Furthermore, the networks of interhousehold relations are disrupted much less by the out-migration of young couples than they would be by the loss of older, more well-established couples.

Even though households are relatively autonomous units, they are not wholly self-sufficient and they do not exist as social isolates. Cooperation in agricultural tasks, management of collectively owned resources, relations with political authorities, and a number of other activities lead households to establish networks and corporate groups. Communities and haciendas are two such types of groups, but they are not the only ones. Indeed, a great variety of social forms can be observed throughout the Andes. These forms are the results of the operation of specifiable factors which affect the relations between households.

It is necessary to distinguish among a variety of social forms encountered in the Andean countryside. A simple typology, however, is a poor device for grasping the basic processes which underlie this variety. The clearly bounded nature of typological categories forces similar but slightly different phenomena into a rigid set of classes and subclasses. Furthermore, such categories would be too static for the highly flexible social forms under examination. Such variability within types may be of importance when seen from a processual point of view. A typology would tend to mask these nuances and cause important processes of change to be missed.

The model elaborated in this essay involves what might be termed "building from the bottom up." The household is considered the fundamental unit of rural Andean social organization. The links between households form networks.[2] A variety of corporate groups are also composed of households. Haciendas and communities are two examples of such corporate groups, but there are a number of others. In addition, many households belong to neither an hacienda nor a community. External social, economic, political, and environmental conditions act as constraints on the choices which individual households make in entering into relations with each other.

There are three variables by which interhousehold relations may be distinguished. The first is the content of the relation, that is, the activities in which the related households jointly engage. This variable refers to overt functions and observed regular behaviors which the households carry out. Frequent important aspects of content include the exchange of goods and services, utilization of commonly owned resources, and representation in local and regional political systems.

The second variable is organization. It includes the different features of social organization commonly studied by anthropologists: the set of different positions that hold between related households, the stability and duration of the relations, and the procedures of establishing and terminating relations. This variable does not refer only to the internal organization of sets of linked households. The relations of any particular set to other sets of households, organizations, and institutions, which might be termed its external articulation, are complementary to the internal organization of the set; the two influence each other reciprocally.

The third variable is stratification. It measures the position of different households on scales of wealth, power, and prestige. The variable measures the degree of inequality among households along objective scales. The three variables are analytically separable: the first examines what the households do, the second how they are organized, and the third where they stand in relation to one another.

An examination of a particular set of interhousehold links known as *ayni* demonstrates the utility of this tripartite system. This form of organization is one of the most familiar elements of Andean ethnography. *Ayni*, also known as *waje-waje*, has generally been described rather loosely and briefly as reciprocal labor exchange, in which two parties perform equal amounts of labor in each other's fields on different occasions. To take only one of many examples from the anthropological literature:

> Symmetrical exchange [*ayni*] takes place between equals: what is received corresponds to what is given.... The peasant who offers his labor—his effort and his time—is assured of receiving adequate compensation, and he clearly does receive it when the return is equal in quantity and effort.... Symmetrical exchange generally requires units which are organized in the same fashion and which have the same amounts of productive resources. It is obvious that a peasant would be interested in having his labor repaid with labor only if he also owned land. Symmetrical exchange is not only utilized for agricultural labor, but it is also extended to other services. (Alberti and Mayer, 1974:22–23; our translation)

Reference to the three variables permits a more accurate and precise analysis. The content of an *ayni* relation is a labor exchange as described above. One individual organizes a work group by calling another to help him. The organizer later repays this individual with an equal amount of time spent in the same kind of work. The assistant must be provided with food, coca leaf, and home-brewed barley or maize beer. The organization of the relation is somewhat more complex. Work teams are often composed of more than two people representing two households, so that an individual will call several people to help him on a given day, incurring a number of obligations. If the task to be performed requires a large labor input, the same set of individuals may be assembled on successive days. *Ayni* workers tend to be chosen from kin, friends, and neighbors, so that pairs of households will have many labor exchanges over a number of years, and regular *ayni* partnerships will be established. Some individuals in a given area may have more *ayni* partners than others because they have more work to be done, because they have arranged for workers through *ayni* rather than through other mechanisms, or because they choose *ayni* for still other benefits that accrue to them through it. The external articulation of certain *ayni* partners will affect their relations with others. A peasant who is heavily involved in selling in markets will be likely to work his lands through wage labor and sharecropping arrangements, rather than *ayni*, because he will have more available cash and less disposable time.

The stratification variable clarifies certain difficulties in the analysis of *ayni*. *Ayni* labor exchanges need not take place between equals, and there may be large gaps in wealth, power, and prestige between *ayni* partners. A household with four hectares of land may sow and harvest it with the help of *ayni* workers who each own half a hectare apiece. *Ayni* involves exchanges of equal quantities of labor. However, *ayni* relations may allow some individuals to have a number of partners and others to have few; they may take place despite large disparities in wealth and prestige. The standard anthropological view tends to merge the three variables which are distinguished here. In a number of cases, anthropologists present the equivalent of *ayni* exchange as the basis for egalitarian relations between *ayni* partners, confusing the variables of content, organization, and stratification.

Ayni may be viewed as an adaptation to certain constraints. The environment and technology require the formation of sizable work teams, since certain tasks must be performed at specific times in the agricultural or pastoral calendar (Brush, 1977). The chronic scarcity of cash and the frequent low opportunity cost of labor favor this sort of labor exchange. The quality of the labor is guaranteed by the anticipation of receiving labor in return and by the long-term nature of the tie.

This alternative model, then, permits a more exact and thorough description of interhousehold relations. It attempts to isolate the basic features involved in all agrarian social forms. Households and the dynamics of their relations are made the starting point for an investigation of the social system. In this manner it becomes possible to emphasize similarities in process rather than differences in structure, and to show the coherence of a society whose main characteristic would otherwise appear to be endless diversity. The variety of forms of social and economic organization can be accounted for by a single scheme: the adaptations of sets of peasant households to different environmental, economic, and political constraints.

The Alternative Model: A Specific Application

This section examines several specific cases from the southern provinces of the department of Cuzco and adjacent portions of the department of Arequipa in terms of this model, in order to illustrate the manner in which this approach may be developed to deal effectively with the entire range of Andean agrarian social forms. A brief discussion of the peasant household, the fundamental unit of the model, will be followed by presentation of interhousehold networks and multihousehold corporate groups. These examples refer to the period immediately prior to the implementation of the Agrarian Reform program; however, the present tense has generally been retained in the discussion. The underlying constraints to which these forms are adapted will be discussed briefly in the final portion of this chapter.

The Peasant Household

An individual household is defined by the common residence of its members and by the pooling of their resources to form a single unit of production and consumption. It is the locus of decision-making with regard to production and exchange. Households are based on the nuclear family, but they may also contain unmarried siblings or aged parents of either marriage partner, as well as adopted children. Less frequently, other relatives, such as widowed siblings of parents, are also included. Post-marital residence tends to be neolocal; virilocal residence is infrequent and brief. Roles within the household are determined by age, sex, and kinship relationships. Men and women have their respective tasks, as do children according to their sex and age. Parents exercise authority over their children. In certain economic and political contexts, the man of the household acts as an intermediary linking the household to other social groups. He arranges interhousehold labor exchanges and represents the household at local political assemblies.

Although households are relatively autonomous with regard to economic decision-making, child rearing, and a number of other activities, they are not totally self-sufficient. Certain environmental constraints favor cooperation for production tasks. The establishment of linkages between peasants and political and economic structures on regional and national levels also encourages coordination between households. These interhousehold relations show considerable variety and complexity.

The specific forms of interhousehold relations are affected by variation in the composition of the household itself. The balance between the material resources available to a household and the personnel which constitute it is not constant. It changes for each household at different times. These two characteristics are thus important to consider in somewhat greater detail. This discussion is influenced by the work of Chayanov (1966) and Sahlins (1972).

The developmental cycle. The developmental cycle of the household is strongly affected by demographic variables, particularly rates of fecundity, mortality, and migration. It may generally be considered to begin with the marriage of a couple and the distribution of resources to form the capital base of the new household enterprise. Marriage in the Andean countryside generally, and in southern Cuzco specifically does not, however, involve a single change in status from unmarried to married. A couple has an informal understanding that they will form a household. After contacts and negotiations between their parents, they enter into the relationship of *servinakuy*, as a newly constituted couple bound by a legitimate conjugal union. No priests or state officials are concerned with this agreement or with the simple peasant ceremonies which mark it. It is nonetheless a binding contract which triggers the division of property which forms the capital base for the new household, thus initiating the new production and consumption unit. The man can now attend political assemblies and hold certain local political offices. Formal marriage recognized by the state or the church may occur much later, or be omitted altogether.

Upon the formation of a recognized conjugal union, the parents of both bride and groom present the new couple with their share of the household capital. Details of inheritance differ even within the area of southern Cuzco under consideration here. In the most common pattern, though, each spouse receives a portion of his parents' property equal to that of each of his siblings. A couple with three children and adequate resources, for example, divides its property into four equal parts, one for each of the offspring upon his marriage and one for themselves. This last part is given to the child, often the youngest son, who cares for the parents in their old age. In the case of livestock, some animals are assigned to each child at birth. The offspring of these animals are used by the household as a unit until the child in question marries, at which time he takes possession of his animals. Environmental and economic constraints affect this pattern. In conditions of scarcity, male offspring have priority in the division of property. Furthermore, this pattern of anticipatory inheritance may be subject to some limitations when the parents give their child a smaller share of the household goods upon his marriage than would otherwise be allotted to him, and indicate that they will compensate any deficit later on.

The development cycle of this basic unit of production and consumption, therefore, begins with two people with limited production potential and low consumption requirements. Another definable stage in the cycle obtains in the case of households with young children; the offspring increase the consumption needs of the unit without adding to its labor potential. When the children are old enough to help in production and exchange activities, the household has reached its peak of production potential, but its consumption needs are also at their highest. The next stage in the cycle is marked by the segmentation of the household into new household units, as the children, one at a time, marry. This process brings about a gradual reduction of labor power and a corresponding reduction of resources through inheritance. The parental household is then reduced again to two people, with close ties to the new households of their married children.

The final stage in the cycle is the retirement of the parents from basic agricultural, herding, and trading activities. They retain control over their property; however, their offspring now contribute the labor needed for their support in a cooperative manner, and often a young grandchild is sent to live with them. If an aging widowed parent becomes unable or unwilling to manage his resources properly, he is absorbed into the household of one of the children who then takes the responsibility of caring for the parent. This shift ends the once autonomous household through merger.

The changing labor capabilities and consumption needs of a household as it moves through this developmental cycle shape the selection of economic strategies and the establishment and mobilization of interhousehold links. For example, the close relationships of siblings and their spouses form the basis of *ayni* arrangements. The care of aged parents strengthens this cooperation and affects the decisions of individual households in their own economic strategies since it entails a prior commitment of labor and cooperation by each household in the support of parents. Kinship linkages as they change through the development cycle are therefore a very important basis for a number of coalitions and groups of varying content and organization.

Resource distribution. In addition to this variation based on the development cycle, differences between households are based on their relative wealth. Some households are so poor that they do not control enough resources to produce food to meet their consumption needs. The wealthier households own resources that provide a great deal more than their subsistence needs; they require considerable outside labor to utilize them. Between these two extremes fall households which operate adequately in normal years within the constraints set upon them by the environment and wider society.

Households tend to shift along this scale of relative wealth. One reason for this is the many risks inherent in peasant production. The resources that a household controls may be diminished or eliminated through theft, disease, drought, earthquakes, or other such disasters. A peasant household may thus be reduced from abundance to poverty in a short time; the reverse process is slower.

The differences in wealth between households, and the degree of correspondence between the labor of a household's members and the other resources which it controls, are thus subject to greater variation than would be expected on the basis of developmental cycle alone. This variation strongly affects interhousehold relations particularly but not exclusively along the dimension of stratification. It shapes the formation of work teams and the establishment of patron-client relationships and retainerships. The economic strategies of social networks of poor households are quite different from those of prosperous ones. These social networks will be examined in greater detail in the following sections of this chapter.

Links Between Peasant Households

Although households are autonomous units with regard to economic decision-making, they are not wholly self-sufficient. Many activities require the coordination of several households. For instance, without outside help it is virtually impossible for a single household to shear its sheep and alpacas, or to harvest, thresh, and winnow its grains. Other tasks such as house construction and irrigation canal maintenance require the effort of sizable work teams. These constraints strongly influence the formation of groups and networks.

Households tend to join work teams even when this is not strictly imposed by the nature of the task: a peasant couple would prefer to get two others to help them plant their maize in one day than to spend three days doing it by themselves.

The labor deficits at certain points in the developmental cycle and the unequal distribution of productive resources described in the previous section also favor the participation of different households in joint activity. The household with more property than its members can manage must use outside workers, and the one whose holdings do not meet its members' needs must look to others for sources of income. There are a variety of possible arrangements, but all involve the coordination of different households.

Cooperation between households is therefore a necessity which gives rise to networks and groups of households which differ in content, organization, and stratification. Links between households are as important to each household as are the internal kinship bonds which define the individual household unit. In this section we will briefly discuss five types of interhousehold links which result in coordination of activity and in the formation of action-sets and coalitions. They are: (1) primary kin alliance, (2) *ayni*, (3) *mink'a*, (4) patron-client relations, and (5) trading partnerships.

Primary kin alliances.   Every individual plays different roles in two or three different households, first as offspring and sibling in his parents' household, later as spouse and parent in his own, and, in some cases, finally as aged dependent in the household of a married son or daughter. At times, two individuals who at one time had lived in the same household may find themselves living in different households. The link between them, particularly when it is across generations rather than within one, forms the basis for a link between households. The man who had once been cared for by his parents when he was a young child, will later care for his aged parents when they are unable to carry out all economic activities. Adult offspring who have formed their own households help their parents in a variety of economic activities. These primary kin alliances occasionally extend to godparents and to more distant relatives, such as uncles, aunts, and grandparents. They are symbolically extended after the death of the members of the senior household on *Todos Santos* (All Saints' Day) through the offering of meals to the spirits of the dead.

The content of primary kin alliances is the performance of economic tasks, such as working land, herding animals, and marketing goods. It is an important factor in the economic decisions households must make, since a husband and wife must consider the labor needs of their parents in planning their own activities. The organization of primary kinship alliances thus not only links directly a senior and a junior household, usually that of parent and offspring, but also indirectly coordinates the activities of other households. In particular, households of siblings must cooperate in the execution of shared tasks. Since primary kin alliances join closely related households, the variable of stratification is not as important as in other interhousehold links. Although great inequalities of wealth between such households do exist, they are not common. Although primary kin alliances involve only small numbers of households, they are the most binding links between households and produce a number of coalitions created to deal with problems of production and exchange.

Ayni. This form of interhousehold relation has already been described in the first section of this chapter.

Mink'a. Like *ayni, mink'a* relationships are used to organize work teams for different tasks. In the enthographic literature, *ayni* and *mink'a* have been portrayed as similar sorts of reciprocal exchange. However, the two differ sharply. They can be distinguished along the variables of content, organization, and stratification.

The content of a *mink'a* relation is an exchange which involves labor and goods, rather than labor only as in the case of *ayni*. An individual organizes a work team by calling others to help him. He provides the assistants with food, coca leaf, and home-brewed barley or maize beer. The repayment can be in two forms.

One form of *mink'a* is festive. There is better food in greater quantity than in an *ayni*, and *aguardiente* or alcohol as well as beer is liberally supplied. Festive *mink'a* are used for nonseasonal labor. They can be used for certain herding tasks, such as earmarking and examining ewes for pregnancy, especially if the animals are numerous. The workers are then repaid with a feast rather than with goods they can consume later. Festive *mink'a* can be used for tasks which occur so infrequently as to make *ayni* exchange unfeasible.

The other form is nonfestive, with repayment in goods or cash. An individual might arrange for other people to help him shear his sheep by giving each one a fleece for every ten shorn. In other cases the payment would be by the day, rather than by the piece; workers at a potato harvest might each be given a quarter of a sack of potatoes for a day's work.

The organization of *mink'a* relations is different from *ayni*. As in *ayni*, *mink'a* teams tend to be drawn from the same set of people. However, the roles of organizer and assistant are not inherently reciprocal. One individual may call another to help him on a number of occasions without working in the *mink'a* that the latter organizes. An individual expects that the people he invites to his festive *mink'a* will invite him to theirs, but this practiçe is not followed with the precision that characterizes *anyi* teams. Finally, it is not unusual to see two men working together in *ayni*, but *mink'a* are held only for projects which require more than three or four men.

This content and organization influence the variable of stratification. *Mink'a* may take place between equals, much as in *ayni*. It occurs commonly between unequals, though; a relatively prosperous household will arrange to have much of the labor in its fields performed by poorer households. The external articulation of a *mink'a* organizer affects his choice of work team formation. If he engages in activities outside the local area which consume a good deal of his time, he may be too busy to repay *ayni* partners in labor.

Patron-client relations.   The content of patron-client relations may be based on land use. The poor family may work as peons, in which case they are granted a plot of land to cultivate. This grant may be made in exchange for a certain number of days of their labor each year, or they may become sharecroppers, in which case they perform all the labor on a given field belonging to the superordinate household and retain a portion of the harvest. In other cases, the content may center on domestic service. The members of the attached household perform a variety of agricultural work, domestic chores, and other services in exchange for food and shelter.

The organization and the stratification variables are closely linked. The attached households may be impoverished families taken on in time of drought or famine; in some cases they are kin or *compadres*. On other occasions, adopted orphans remain in the status of client after they marry and bear children. The head of the superordinate household and, to a lesser extent, his wife demand a large variety of services from the subordinate ones. The rights of the subordinate household are much more limited.

Trading partnerships.   Trading partnerships constitute a fifth form of interhousehold links. The content is the barter of products from different ecological zones. A peasant from a herding area may have a partner whom he regularly visits in a maize-producing valley. He will barter dried meat and wool for maize and other agricultural products. The rates of exchange may shift slowly from year to year. In some cases one peasant may help his partner in the harvest through *mink'a* as well as by bartering his own products.

The organization of these trading partnerships involves a number of pairs of households. One peasant household may have several households in other zones with which it exchanges, and they in turn may have several partners who come to trade with them. Although it is generally the men who travel, the relationship exists between households. The bond is often strengthened by the exchange of ritual gifts and the establishment of *compadrazgo* links. The ties are often maintained for several generations; they are usually but not exclusively inherited patrilineally.

In terms of stratification, the partnerships usually take place between equals. However, as in *ayni*, equal exchange (in this case, goods for goods rather than labor for labor) can be consonant with inequality. A number of poor herders may come from a high grassland zone to barter with a rich agricultural peasant household in a river valley. In a similar fashion, a wealthy herder might visit a number of different agricultural households in different areas to acquire a variety of products.

Ties Between Peasant Households and Local Elites

Peasant households maintain important ties with local elites. In some cases the ties are direct; in others, one peasant household acts as an intermediary between local elites and a set of peasant households. The relations involve different activities or content, and they vary in organization, but they are never altogether lacking. They are found among peasants who do not reside on elite-owned land as well as those who do.

Different local elite positions may be distinguished by the resources which they control and by their other sources of power. Four important types are landowners, traders, political authorities, and clergy. The variation in the organization of elite-peasant relations is too complex to describe fully here. A few illustrative examples will indicate the range of types.

The ties between peasant households and landowners may take the form of wage labor, rental, peonage, and sharecropping. A specific peasant household may combine these relations for varying periods with one landowner or with several different ones. The ties with traders involve cash sale and barter. Regularized trading relations often occur; at times they are maintained by debts. As political authorities, local elites may require performance of labor services or payment of fines. They settle disputes among peasants and between peasants and elites. They may be representatives of national governmental agencies which offer services to the peasant population. Church personnel, especially priests, also enter into contact with peasants. They perform certain rituals basic to local political and religious systems. They also may control land and require certain labor services. In many cases these different elite positions are combined in single individuals, as in the landowner who is a *juez de paz* or the trader who is *gobernador*.

As will be elaborated later, relations among peasant households and peasant-elite relations cannot be considered in exclusion from one another. The political and economic constraints may operate in close coordination. The internal organization of sets of peasant households is affected by their articulation with local elites; the control and domination of local elites also is related to local peasant social organization. This point is examined in more detail in following sections.

Small-scale Groups

Networks and groups are essentially different orders of social phenomena, even within specific sets of persons. Groups possess important characteristics which networks and action-sets do not, notably corporate existence beyond the tenure of specific members, defined membership rules and boundaries, and corporate rights and resources. In short, they are more than mere statistical regularities which emerge from social networks of actors. Our empirical investigations have led us to note that links between households such as those described in the previous two sections extend outward in some cases without becoming divided into clearly demarcated groups, and that in other cases they conform to group boundaries.

We wish to stress the variety of forms of small-scale and local groups which are composed of peasant households in southern Cuzco. In this section we will examine several examples of them with regard to content, organization, and stratification; in the next section we will discuss communities and haciendas as groups of households. We will argue that they constitute adaptations to certain constraints. It is important to bear in mind, however, that many households do not belong to these sorts of groups.

Sectores. The officially recognized peasant community of Tortorani in the province of Canchis, is divided into seven subcommunities. This subcommunity unit is called *sector* in Spanish and *ayllu* in Quechua. We will use the former term, since the word *ayllu* has a number of different meanings, both in Quechua colloquial usage and in the ethnographic and historical literature. Illakuyu is one of these *sectores*. It has a population of about one hundred in twenty households. Like the other *sectores*, its lands are contiguous rather than scattered. In the case of Illakuyu, the lands lie along both sides of a stream and occupy most of its rather small drainage. The households also own land in other *sectores* and members of other *sectores* own land in Illakuyu, but virtually all the lands are owned by local residents, and they have most of their plots in Illakuyu. Their dwellings are dispersed throughout Illakuyu. There is private ownership of agricultural land, both the stretches of irrigated land along the stream and the *temporales* or unirrigated land at higher elevations. The pastures on the slope above the stream belong to the community of Totorani. However, most of the households whose animals graze on these lands are from Illakuyu rather than from other *sectores*.

Work teams are formed of the households in Illakuyu for a number of purposes. Peasants tend to choose *ayni* partners from kinsmen and neighbors in the *sector*. On a *sector*-wide basis, work teams clean certain irrigation canals along the stream. They also built a *sector* chapel and cemetery. Local politicking by some of the more numerous kindreds led to the informal consensus that supported the formation of these work teams and the collection of money for these projects. The chapel was built in 1970 and the cemetery in 1972. These buildings serve as a symbolic and an empirical focus for *sector* activity.

Membership in Illakuyu is determined by birth and residence. Like the other *sectores*, it is not endogamous. Those households consisting of persons born in Illakuyu or persons married to Illakuyu residents are considered members, and their membership is affirmed by participation in work teams and by sponsorship of the fiesta at the chapel. In addition, Illakuyu households participate in community-wide work projects and fiestas. They also work in the work teams of other *sectores* where they own land, or arrange for someone to work in their stead. Illakuyu also acts as a unit with respect to larger groups of households. Like the other *sectores*, it sends a representative (*teniente*) to the community assemblies. There is a certain degree of variation in wealth and power between Illakuyu households based on size of landholdings, number of residents, and influence within the relatively unstructured power system of the *sector*.

Environmental constraints, especially topography and hydrography, favored the formation of Illakuyu as a *sector*. *Sector* organization is also found in other places where geographical factors are not so crucial, as in the wider parts of the Río Vilcanota valley of Canchis. Economic and political constraints are also important. *Sector* work projects such as irrigation canals, schoolhouses, and chapels, seem to provide the major focus of organization.

Retainerships. In the community of Phawsiri, in the province of Espinar, one wealthy peasant owns approximately two thousand sheep and three hundred cattle. He started his wealth by defaulting on an advance from a wool merchant. He used this capital to establish himself as a trader, carrying *aguardiente* from the Río Majes valley, in the department of Arequipa, on donkey trains. He invested money in a truck and a large store in Yauri, the provincial capital. His business activities occupy so much of his time that he no longer cares for his animals personally. Several of his shepherds are close relatives whom he maintains without a wage, giving them food, clothing, and a place to live. Some of them are known locally as *internados*. In exchange for cancellation of debts or loans of money, some parents have given him effective authority over their children indefinitely, and these child laborers now herd his animals. The number of retainer households changes every few years, as an old family leaves or a new one moves in. The total is usually six or seven. These families are all dependent on the wealthy *comunero* for their livelihood. They cooperate with each other in *ayni* and *mink'a* in certain tasks. His strong political influences makes it difficult for them to break away.

In a similar way, many households of agricultural peasants in other areas have one or two families attached to them as sharecroppers and peons. The retainer families own no land. In some cases they also work as domestic servants. These ties occasionally last two and even three generations. They represent a more stable and permanent relation than the patron-client relations described in the previous sections.

Localized descent groups. In Huaracopalca, in the province of Castilla, department of Arequipa, which lies at and above the upper limits of arable land, close-knit groups of three to ten households are found. All households belong to one and only one such group. They are made up of related households, linked usually though agnatic ties; frequently the household heads are brothers and patrilateral cousins. The residences are located in named population nuclei separated from each other by distances of over a kilometer. These groups are sometimes three generations deep. In short, the organization of these localized descent groups resembles a lineage system.

The principal aspect of the content variable is that the households are bound together by common ownership of land. Each localized descent group owns some of the scarce permanent pasture land along with huts and corrals located on it; this resource supplements the seasonal grasses which appear during the rainy months. Individuals have grazing rights both on these permanent pastures and on the rainy-season pastures by virtue of membership in a localized descent group.

The localized descent groups which have access to portions of the limited arable land have modified the more common system of bilateral partible anticipatory inheritance. The localized descent group retains the agricultural land. Each household uses a portion of the land for its own maintenance, but ownership remains corporate with the senior household head acting as executor. In such cases, only sons and unmarried daughters may lay claim to the land. Offspring who marry out receive a cash settlement in exchange for renouncing inheritance rights to land; they take their animals with them. Because of the residence pattern and the density of kinship ties within the localized descent group, there is a high degree of mutual cooperation in such groups. Ties of primary kin alliances, *ayni*, and *mink'a* unite the groups further. These localized descent groups show considerable variation in the dimension of stratification. In some cases households are relatively equal in terms of wealth and power. In others, one household owns a disproportionately large portion of the animals and enjoys much closer ties with traders. This position permits it to dominate the other constituent households.

The local descent group, therefore, is an adaptation to a set of several constraints. The steppelike conditions of the upper portions of the *puna* or high-altitude grasslands of the south central Andes permit extensive herding but only very limited agriculture, leading to a low population density. Interhousehold links tend to be strongest between closely related households. The scarcity of permanent pasture and agricultural land leads to corporate control of these resources.

In many high puna zones where these conditions hold, localized descent groups rather than the more commonly described peasant communities form the locus of the highest concentration of interhousehold cooperation. Territories and corresponding political organization are not the basis for social cohesion; the communities which form a part of the traditional model of Andean agrarian society do not exist in these areas. Nachtigall describes a similar situation in the department of Moquegua (1966:194).

Estancia   The hacienda[3] of Añumarca in the province of Canchis, which was expropriated by the Agrarian Reform in 1974, contains two sets of dwellings: the central *caserío* where the administrator and the two *mayordomos* live with their families, and the eight outlying *estancias*, where the peon families live and keep their herds at night. In addition to this permanent dwelling, called a *cabaña*, each *estancia* has an *astana* (a smaller house and group of corrals located on higher ground) for use during the rainy season

The hacendado and his employees have assigned a shepherd and his nuclear family to every *estancia*; they would prefer each *estancia* to contain only one household. The administrator assigns the shepherd a portion of the hacienda herds to care for. He is also permitted to keep a herd of his own animals, called *waqcho*. The total of the peons' herds is about as large as the hacendado's. The shepherds are also required to provide other labor services for the hacendado and his employees, such as carrying hacienda produce to market, performing occasional domestic service in the *caserío*, and maintaining *caserío* buildings.

Several *estancias* are composed of only one household, but others have two or three. One is composed of two married brothers, with their wives and children; others have married offspring with children of their own still resident on the *estancia* on which they are born. The different married couples live close to each other in separate households. The animals of the different individuals are usually herded together. *Estancia* herds are often large enough to provide a livelihood for all the different members. The different labor tasks are shared among the residents of the *estancia*, providing greater flexibility in the organization of activity. For instance, one individual can herd hacienda animals, while a second cares for the *waqcho*, a third works at the *caserío*, and a fourth goes to a market place to sell *estancia* wool. The *estancias* form well-bounded groups. Every peasant is identified with one and only one of them. The hacendado and his employees treat the *estancias* as units; *waqcho* rights are assigned to *estancias* rather than to individuals. The main shepherd on the *estancia*, who is usually the oldest male household head, acts as an intermediary between the hacienda employees and the other *estancia* residents in terms of distribution of labor tasks and resolution of disputes. The administrator requires one individual from each *estancia* for certain routine tasks, although he will call for more labor service on other occasions, such as the annual shearing. The main shepherd, in consultation with the other members of the *estancia*, decides which member will be sent to perform the tasks.

Although there has been a certain degree of out-migration, there have been no cases of entire *estancia* groups leaving Añumarca. There have been a number of marriages of members of different *estancias*. As a consequence of the stability of residence and a certain degree of endogamy, all the peons are related to others on other *estancias*. Peon households establish *ayni* and *mink'a* exchanges for the formation of work teams. The peon households also have ties of kinship in other haciendas and to peasants in nearby communities.

The hacendado would prefer to reduce the size of the *waqcho* herds, since they compete directly with his own animals. One means of achieving this goal would be to reduce the number of individuals on each *estancia*, so that the *estancia* could have the same per capita income with a smaller number of *waqcho*. The loss of workers would be more than compensated for by the increase in the size of the hacienda herds, permitting the hacendado to make up any labor deficit through the occasional use of wage labor. However, he has been unable to make the number of peons smaller, since the peons, linked by ties of kinship, coresidence, and reciprocity, exert strong pressure against him. His only measure of control is to refuse to build more *estancias*; the peons respond by maintaining multi-household *estancias*.

Estancia organization is found on other haciendas in the province of Canchis, and quite probably in other areas as well. It constitutes an adaptation to the economic and political domination of the hacendado. Each household resident on the hacienda does not necessarily deal directly with the hacienda administration as an isolated individual, but may do so as a member of a larger localized kin group.

Local Groups

Communities. Many anthropologists, sociologists, historians, and political scientists engaged in research in the Andes have focused their studies on communities. Because of the abundance of this literature, the communities are a particularly difficult subject to discuss briefly. We refer the reader to Fuenzalida (1970b) and Yambert (this volume) for an excellent summary of community organization in Peru, and to Leeds (1973) for a useful theoretical treatment of the concepts of community and locality. In this section we will restrict ourselves to a discussion of how the model proposed in this essay can be applied to this wealth of data.

A community may be defined in terms of a bounded territory and a recognized set of households who have rights to that territory. Like other peasant households, those households which are members of communities are autonomous economic decision-making units. The activities which communities perform include the protection of community lands from usurpation by outsiders; the use of community-wide work teams to maintain community property such as irrigation canals, chapels, schoolhouses, bridges, and trails; the regulation of crop rotation on certain lands with long fallow periods; and interaction with government agencies and local elites. In a few cases, community elders redistribute land among constituent households.

These activities involve larger numbers of households than are found in the small-scale groups. Most communities have populations of several hundred to one thousand. Their internal organization is more complex than that of the small-scale groups. The coordination of the activities of a number of different households for the completion of community tasks and the management of the community treasury are carried out by elected political officials who also act as agents of conflict resolution within the community. In addition to these roles, other political positions interdigitate with ceremonial offices connected with the celebration of certain saints' days. The particular structure of official positions changes widely from community to community, as does the degree of factionalism.

Recruitment to community membership is chiefly by birth. Outsiders can join if they marry a community member or if they are adopted by community members. Many communities are not exogamous, and some individuals own land in more than one community. They may participate in more than one community, but they are primarily identified with only one. Primary kin alliances, *ayni*, and *mink'a* occur more frequently between *comunero* households than across community boundaries.

The external articulation of communities is a crucial aspect of their organization. Communities have some form of recognition by local, regional, and national authorities. Certain community officials act as intermediaries, representing the community to outside groups and external political authorities to the community. They are particularly important in handling boundary disputes with haciendas and other communities and in dealing with the claims of local elites for irrigation water and unpaid labor services. The seemingly endless litigation in which many communities are involved is carried out chiefly by the community officials.

Communities differ greatly in the extent of internal stratification. Some communities have relatively small inequalities in the size of land holdings, and virtually all adult men hold some political offices during their lifetimes. Age is the principal basis of authority. In other communities, some households own large extensions of land and herds numbering in the thousands; they dominate community politics quite thoroughly. Not all communities are the egalitarian communes that many anthropologists have described.

Community organization, then, depends on a number of external constraints. Certain environmental conditions, particularly the availability of irrigation water, favor community activities. Pressure on land frequently leads households to band together to defend their fields. The presence of government agencies which serve a clientele of communities also encourages the formation of communities. In areas where all these factors are found, such as the lower sections of the province of Canas, many communities are found. Where they do not, as in certain portions of the puna in the province of Espinar, community organization is weak or absent.

Changes in external constraints lead to changes in the nature of communities. One detailed example will illustrate this point. It is important to note that the strength of community organization is not due to the survival of traditional culture in isolated regions, but results from the acceptance of new economic and political influences in less remote areas.

Many of the *comunidades campesinas* officially recognized by the state do not correspond to the earlier traditional peasant communities but only to portions of them. The split has taken place in the last fifty years under the influence of changing national administrative structures and market conditions.

In the 1920s wool prices in international markets increased; this rise trickled back to herders in the southern sierra. The value of puna land with respect to valley agricultural land increased as wool became relatively more valuable than foodstuffs. Herders began to sell their wool for cash more frequently, rather than trading it in barter exchange.

In the province of Canchis, many communities had had land in both the valleys and the punas. Households in one zone had access to products in the other. Puna herders owned fields in the lower zone, and agriculturalists from the valleys had grazing rights and took their animals to the puna. As wool prices rose, it became more profitable for herders to sell their wool and purchase foodstuffs, rather than working fields themselves. They also wished to block access of others to their pastures. At the same time, the Leguía administration (1919-1930) brought a number of bureaucratic and administrative changes. The 1920 constitution provided for official recognition of Indian communities. Older traditional communities began to split up as groups in the punas established themselves as independent. The bureaucratic channels favored this split; it was advantageous to representatives of government agencies to have as many communities as possible under their administration. Officially recognized communities could make some headway in prohibiting non-*comuneros* access to community land. They were also in a better position to receive state aid for different projects such as schoolhouse and road construction and eucalyptus forestation. In short, political as well as environmental constraints favored the division of communities.

In this context, other sources of conflict which had been present for long periods emerged as bases for splits. Irrigation canal maintenance led to divisions. The groups higher up preferred to keep more of the water and not to help those lower down in cleaning and repairing the canal, and so larger irrigation units split up. Households in general preferred to work on local *faenas* or collective work groups. By comparing old documents, particularly colonial church records in the case of Canchis, with current lists of communities, it is possible to document the split. The community of Seneca in the district of Sicuani, for instance, split into six communities: Trapiche, Huitacca, Uscapata, Chauchapata, Pumaorcco, and Chectuyoc.

Haciendas.   Like communities, haciendas are composed of groups of peasant households with rights to specific lands. The difference between the two lies in their relations to elites. Though subject to a variety of authorities and power holders, communities retain ownership of their lands. Hacienda lands are formally owned by individual hacendados or by institutions such as a convent or a legal corporation. In many cases, as we have attempted to stress, peasant households belong neither to communities nor to haciendas.

Haciendas vary considerably with regard to their content. The resident peasant families, known as peons or *colonos*, receive various rights in land in exchange for a set of obligations. In agricultural haciendas, households are granted fields to cultivate; in pastoral haciendas, they are given grazing rights for their animals on hacienda land. Many haciendas have these two types of production, and peon households get both sorts of rights. In addition, the hacendado often gives them small sums of money. The obligations vary as well. The most frequent one is a certain number of days of labor on the hacendado's fields or with the hacendado's herds, but other services are common, particularly transporting the harvest to market, performing domestic chores in the hacendado's house, and maintaining hacienda buildings. Peon households may also be required to give the hacendado a part of their harvest. There is a wide range of rights and obligations on different haciendas. In some cases the hacendado receives a small annual payment of hides, wool, and potatoes from virtually autonomous peon households; in other cases peon households work over 180 days per year in exchange for small plots of land. In most cases, the content is relatively fixed. It changes little from year to year.

The organization of haciendas also varies considerably. In some cases peon families remain on the same hacienda for a number of generations; in others, the labor turnover is much more rapid and the typical length of stay is under a decade. There is usually a dense network of relations between peon households, generally similar to that of other peasant areas. Ties of primary kinship alliance, *ayni*, *mink'a*, patron-client relationships, and trading partnerships link households. These networks are mobilized for cooperation between households, especially for productive tasks on peon fields or with peon herds. The corporate character of haciendas is affirmed through patron-saint fiestas.

The relations between the peons and the hacendado can differ widely. Some hacendados, especially ones who own small areas of land, reside on their properties and manage them directly. Absentee landlords are more common, though, and they rely on a variety of administrators, representatives, and foremen to organize the peons into large work teams for tasks which require the labor of a number of households. The hacendado or his employees may appoint some peasants to be straw bosses.

The external articulation of haciendas can include a number of forms. In some cases the hacendado acts as an intermediary for all interaction between peon households and wider society; he becomes trader and advocate as well as landlord. However, peon households often market their goods independently, and establish their own relations with other authority figures. Kinship ties often bridge the hacienda boundary. Other sorts of relations with other peasant households may be formed; for instance, many peons will graze the animals of a *comunero* household with their own herd, claiming to the foreman that they own all the animals. They will receive cash or a number of young animals in return for this arrangement.

The stratification of peon households is a fascinating and little-studied topic. On the hacienda of Añumarca mentioned earlier, the herds of peon households ranged from 2 to 259 animals. Counting them in sheep units, or the amount of pasture they consume relative to an adult sheep (a horse equals ten sheep; a lamb, one-third of an adult sheep; and so forth), they range from 20 to 622 with an average of 352. This striking variation would appear to occur on many other haciendas as well.

Wider Links

Haciendas and communities, therefore, do not constitute maximal groups of households. As we have endeavored to show, the organization of groups of households is not limited to internal arrangements, but includes external articulation. They form parts of economic and political systems on regional and national levels.

Many interhousehold ties cross community and hacienda boundaries. One important set of links, partnerships, has already been discussed. Local exogamy and bilateral inheritance have led to a common pattern in which households own lands in different areas and work them through *ayni* and *mink'a* partnerships in different communities. The massive out-migration mentioned earlier also establishes networks between households in rural areas in the highlands and other households in large cities, coastal plantations, and colonization areas in the lowlands. However, the composition of work teams on haciendas illustrates this point most simply. The peon households resident on a hacienda are frequently not sufficient to perform all the labor required by the hacendado. When the hacendado needs large work groups at seasonal peaks, he hires day laborers from communities close to the hacienda. The payment, whether in cash or in kind, supplements the budget of the *comunero* household.

This general relation takes a number of different specific forms. The relations between the hacendado and the *comunero* households are often relatively long-lasting. The same *comuneros* are contracted year after year. Other economic ties may develop. In the province of Espinar, especially in the northern districts, many hacendados rent out some of their grazing lands, and the *comunero* households that work for them as day laborers receive preference in being allocated land. In other areas, *comuneros* pay for use of the hacienda grist mills.

A variety of regional and national formal organizations link groups of households into wider systems. Some of them are associated with national politics. In different parts of the highlands there are peasant leagues and federations associated with national political parties such as APRA and PCP. Hacienda-based unions and community associations often form the local chapters of these organizations. Recent government policy has weakened them while favoring the organization of communities and haciendas (reestablished as cooperatives or adjudicated to adjacent communities) through its agrarian reform program. In all these institutions, however, representatives, whether chosen by election at assemblies or appointed from above, articulate communities, haciendas, and other groups of peasant households with various national organizations.

It is important to see that this model does not propose a system of hierarchical levels of social organization, with households, small-scale groups, communities and haciendas, and regional systems constituting four successive levels, each incorporated into the next higher ones. Peasant households have different sorts of ties which cut across the boundaries of these groups. These groups are only one set of organizational forms generated by interhousehold links.

Summary and Conclusion

This chapter has proposed a new model of social and economic organization in the Andean countryside as an alternative to the community-hacienda model, and applied this new model to a region in southern highland Peru. Its value should not rest in the particular details of the proposed model, but in the general nature of the description, analysis, and explanation, and in its ability to stimulate further inquiry.

Stated in its most general form, the model builds up from the peasant household, with its particular developmental cycle and variation in wealth. Households are linked into networks through different sorts of ties: kinship, *compadrazgo*, residence, labor exchange, trading partnerships. These ties also form the basis for corporate groups composed of a number of households. As units of production and consumption, households have certain social and material resources and needs. They operate in the context of a set of external constraints which affect the outcome of their decisions. Given their resources and these constraints, households mobilize these networks and participate in these groups for a variety of ends. These networks and groups constitute adaptations to these constraints.

This point of view is in opposition to the ones that depict Andean agrarian society as static and unchanging. It emphasizes the flexibility of its forms and the variety of adaptations which its constituent households have produced and criticizes the view that two institutional arrangements, the hacienda and the community, dominate the life of all peasants. It suggests that the numerous instances in which social organization remains constant for long periods of time can be explained by stable external constraints rather than by habit, inertia, conservatism, or tradition. Changing external constraints would permit changes in the ties between households, both in the configuration of inter-household networks and in the nature of corporate groups. Political and economic constraints have undergone dramatic changes in recent times; environmental constraints have been relatively fixed. Peasant households have used those changing conditions in a variety of ways. The model proposed here should not be evaluated solely on the basis of its success in accounting for the range of forms of social organization in the southern part of the department of Cuzco, nor on the general appeal of its emphasis on the relation between local-level social organization and wider society. The measure of its strength should be its ability to generate further research, to provoke a reexamination of familiar themes, and to open new lines of inquiry. The following chapters present more fully what could not be attempted in an introduction. They contain richly detailed studies of Andean agrarian society based on recent field work and archival research. There are sociologists and historians among the authors as well as anthropologists. They cover a variety of social, economic, and political phenomena. There is a considerable range in the geographical areas and historical periods covered. Nevertheless, a unity runs through this diversity. The chapters collectively affirm the value of replacing old explanations and understandings with a new conception of a complex, contradictory society. They stress its openness rather than its closure, its adaptability rather than its fixity. Its coherence, they argue, lies in the process of a people's attempt to deal with their poverty and their weakness, rather than in the brevity of a catalogue of structural forms which this process has generated. The following chapters demonstrate what the introduction has proposed: peasants in the Andes create their world rather than passively and impotently inheriting a tragic past that offers them no choice but to continue it.

Notes

1.   The authors are grateful to Gordon Appleby, Mario Dávila, Tulio Halperín, Eugene Hammel, Bernd Lambert, Anthony Leeds, Natalio Mamani, Sutti Ortiz, and Richard Schaedel for helpful suggestions and criticisms. Above all we are indebted to Daniel Maltz for his extensive and penetrating review of an earlier version of this chapter. We remain solely responsible for the views presented here.

2.   The concept of network has taken on considerable importance in social anthropology in the last ten years. It allows investigators to see human social activity as based on individual choice and decision rather than as the outcome of a well-defined set of rules. By focusing on the links between individuals, it moves away from the notion of social structure as the study of corporate groups. In one of the first of the current wave of network studies, Barnes stated that both individuals and groups could be at the nodes of networks (Barnes, 1954: 43). Virtually all the work has studied only individuals as nodes, which avoids certain logical and epistemological problems. In this section we will use the network concept but study the links between households. Since the household is the basic unit of production and consumption, it can enter into economic relations with other households. For our material, there is little danger in overextending the concept of network.

3.   The discussion of haciendas and *estancias* is written in the ethnographic present.

CHAPTER 3

Thought and Reality: Dialectics of the Andean Community

Karl A Yambert

Introduction

Rural society in Andean South America has long been characterized by haciendas and communities. It is not surprising that the hacienda and the community, as widespread and apparently perdurable agrarian structures, have been crucial to conceptualizing the nature and dynamics of agrarian economies. Their presence in the rural landscape, unavoidably evident in many cases, has provided an obvious point of departure in the formation of both social theory and public policy. Furthermore, the relationship between agricultural structures and the ideas about them is a dialectical one. Images or conceptions of rural society are not simply reflections of existing arrangements but also play an active role in social change when they guide the behavior of concrete groups of people. This chapter outlines a history of Andean communities in the light of the mutual influences that policy and theory, on the one hand, and social organization, on the other hand, have exerted on each other. This dialectic will provide a focus for analyzing changes both in communities and larger social structures. Though the emphasis here is on communities, it is strongly implied that haciendas can be viewed profitably from a similar perspective.

The term "community" in Andean studies is not to be used casually. It often has fairly specific meanings in particular contexts. For example, as one pole in the widely used "community-hacienda model," it implies the existence of a recurring configuration of socio-cultural features. These include Indian ethnicity, corporate control of land and irrigation systems, and strong internal organization that is reinforced by the participation of adult males in

I owe a special debt of gratitude to Benjamin Orlove for his patient encouragement and careful editing of this chapter. Arnold Bauer, Richard Curley, William Davis, and Thomas F. Love also offered helpful suggestions. Errors of fact, omission, or interpretation are entirely the author's responsibility.

hierarchical civil-religious posts and sponsorship of public fiestas. Other characteristics that are often adduced are reciprocal (or even communal) labor on major projects, such as preparing fields for planting, harvesting crops, or building houses. Inwardly directed social relationships based largely on ties of actual or ritual kinship are also features of the "community-hacienda model."

In other instances, the community concept has been accorded special significance by national governments when official administrative and representative structures are expanded to incorporate formerly isolated regions and social groups. Thus in Peru the organization of officially recognized *comunidades indigenas* (now called *comunidades campesinas*) implies that the *comuneros* share diagnostic social and cultural traits, at least in the eyes of the government, and are also entitled to a legally specified set of administered privileges and resources.

Nor do these understandings of what is meant by "community" at all exhaust the numerous meanings and implications of the term. If we consider just the efforts to organize communities from above, it is apparent that colonial and national governments have metamorphosed profoundly over time in their ability and inclination to mobilize institutional and material resources on the behalf of client communities. Further, many communities are not even recognized officially as corporate entities. Just as the material and ideological commitments of governments to rural communities have varied, so also may it reasonably be hypothesized that the essence of the concept of community has been considerably transformed as it was carried by different social groups in diverse sociohistoric circumstances. Indeed, it is this very assumption that unifies a history of the interaction of theories of the community with actual local-level situations.

In order to avoid the false impression that the succession of images of the community has proceeded exclusively under its own dynamic and that its trajectory is subject to entirely arbitrary and convulsive reversals, it is necessary to locate the implementation of ideas, successful or not, within a universe of social groups acting on the basis of their competing material interests. Hence, the study of Andean communities is bound to considerations of demography and human ecology and their effect on the ability of interest groups to pursue and achieve their perceived interests. In addition, it is an enlightening research strategy to analyze the impact of ideologies on local-level situations. These ideologies can in turn be related broadly to transformations of national and global economies, while yet managing to avoid the implication that fluctuations in world markets directly and mechanically determine social thought and political power. Institutions of colonial or national states are especially important for mediating the impact of international economic forces as well as for establishing and enforcing legislation affecting community organization. In particular, at least three major dimensions of the state might profitably be examined in order to assess their consequences for communities: the state's ability to win legitimacy and compliance from significant segments of the social order; its command of administrative and material resources; and its commitment to institute and maintain particular conceptions of community structures.

Precolonial Period

Our knowledge of early Andean communities derives mostly from archaeological evidence, which shows that the earliest settlements of any kind were no more than the temporary camps of bands of hunter-gatherers. Standard evolutionary interpretations of the course of sociocultural change would anticipate that the development of agriculture would be the breakthrough that would permit, or require, permanent settlements. However, Peru appears to be rather exceptional in that many of the characteristics of civilization have been found without an intensive agricultural foundation. It was not farming but maritime fishing which first supported stratified societies with complex sociopolitical organizations that transcended the level of villages and even single coastal valleys (Lanning, 1967:59). Coastal fishing communities cultivated primarily such plants as cotton and gourds for industrial purposes, though they also grew food plants. The familiarity of coastal Peruvian societies with cultivated plants and river-mouth irrigation constituted a preadaptation to intensive irrigation agriculture in valley interiors. Though the first states grew out of a maritime economy, their elaboration and the consolidation of their authority rested on the transition to farming (Moseley, 1974, 1975).

A number of civilizations rose to predominance and then fell or were absorbed by other powers in the Andean region. Chavín, Huari, and Tiahuanaco are three such states which have left their imprint on the archaeological record. However, the nature of the record is such that it is difficult to arrive at a comprehension of even the general pattern of the expansion and operation of these states. Our picture of the details of local-level community organization is likewise very limited.

For more recent periods of the precolonial Andes, archaeological evidence can be augmented by inferences from later historical sources. Using this research method, Murra presents a plausible model of Andean agrarian communities which he claims is based on a widespread and ancient ideal of "vertical control of a maximum of ecological levels" (Murra, 1975:66). He postulates that a typical arrangement involved nuclear settlements, each of which had peripheral colonies in higher and lower ecozones. Different nuclei might send colonists to the same peripheral settlements so that residents in any colony might be of different ethnic origins, but colonists retained rights of membership in their original nuclear village. Thus there was apparently no neat correspondence between ethnic groups and territories. The point to such dispersed residence was to ensure a supply of materials from many ecozones through the exchange of goods by members within each "vertical archipelago."

The Incas adopted major elements of the verticality model as they set about conquering and unifying an empire for themselves. Inca communities were composed of local kinship groups, or *ayllus*, which owned agricultural land corporately. Settlements tended to be located on slopes between the fertile valley bottoms and the pastures at the highest elevations. Terracing and irrigation permitted intensive agriculture in the highlands, which was complemented by stock raising. The combination of production strategies served to diversify the risks of production and was also a means of satisfying an understandable inclination toward variety in foodstuffs. These agrarian communities were frequently divided into "halves," or moieties, for reasons which are not altogether obvious. Further, there seems to have been some variation in centralization of political authority within the communities, some maintaining a fair degree of autonomy by ruling themselves informally through family heads, and others ruled by hereditary chieftains known as *curacas* (Métraux, 1969:64–69).

However, the Incas also instituted some important modifications of previous landowning systems and community organization. For example, to the established obligations of community members to support their chiefs and gods through labor on specially designated lands were added services to benefit the Inca state. Another way community organization was affected by Inca domination was that rebellious groups were liable to have all their lands confiscated. Some property could also be made private by grants from the Inca to favored nobles. In these ways, "the Incas attacked the territorial integrity of communities" to such an extent that had it not been for the interruption brought by the Spanish conquest, the Inca state would have ceased to be a group of mainly autonomous agricultural collectives and would instead have become a "prefeudal empire," with huge estates owned by nobles and officials, and worked by serfs or even slaves (Métraux, 1969:97, 104–5).

The Incas also used colonization in a sense quite different from that of the verticality model. Loyal subjects were often established as colonists, or *mitimaes*, among actually or potentially rebellious peoples. The *mitimaes* served as models for the troublesome groups, and as spies for the Inca. The rather local and ecological functions of vertical colonization were supplanted in the case of *mitimaes* by the political intent to maintain the Inca conquest state, though of course the two sets of functions are not mutually exclusive.

Some mutual influences of community organization and various aspects of centralized states can be ascertained from the preceding discussion. It is evident that a sizable and structured population is required to sustain enormous and highly centralized empires. Communities were an accessible and useful unit of empire. Those communities with a history of relative autonomy nevertheless had traditions of communal obligations and service that could be redirected in part to maintaining institutions of the state. Where communities had been accustomed to rule by *curacas*, and to subordination to earlier states, it made administration of policies and extraction of surpluses that much easier for later empires. Thus the structure of the community was seized upon by states as a convenient organ of rule and administration. In fact,

Marx's sketchy classification of ancient Peru as an example of an "Asiatic mode of production" suggests that communities were entirely self-sustaining and contained within themselves all necessary conditions for the production of agricultural and manufactured goods. In such a view, the domination of the state is secondary and derivative from institutions of tribal or communal property (Marx 1964:68–71; Espinoza Soriano, 1978).

Yet the presence of an overarching state is certainly important in determining the functioning of its constituent communities. The very incorporation of communities into the larger organism of the state ensured that new political and economic constraints were imposed on activity within the communities. The Incas, for example, managed not only to adapt existing community patterns of tribute and communal labor to their own ends, but also subordinated the community structure to state interests by establishing new communities of colonists to consolidate their political control over an area. Since community and state structures do rely to such an extent on each other, an understanding of one requires consideration of the other.

The Spanish Conquest State

Pizarro's conquest of the Inca empire indisputably redirected the course of Andean history. Yet in many ways the initial stages of this new epoch involved a less considerable impact on community social organization than the drama of the conquest and succeeding civil wars might imply. In fact, the "Spanish conquest state," dating from the capture of Atahuallpa in 1532 to the defeat of Tupac Amaru and the Neo-Inca state in 1572, was based on indirect rule and thus preserved to a great degree the political and administrative structures of the Incas (Steward and Faron, 1959).

Indians were made official wards of the Spanish crown; their interaction with Spaniards was to be tightly regulated. The care and protection of Indian villages was entrusted to certain Spaniards as a reward for their service to the crown. Such responsibility was a reward because it entitled the *encomendero*, as he was called, to claim tribute from his charges. The royal intent was that the tribute be in the form of native goods, but *encomenderos* were able frequently to exact it as labor service.

Curacas, the native chieftains, remained a powerful group even after the conquest. Their claims to nobility were recognized by the Spanish (Rowe, 1957) and, without the authority of higher Inca officials to keep them in check, *curacas* often managed to increase their power and authority under the colonial system of indirect rule (Spalding, 1974). For instance, in the confusion after the conquest, they often convinced the Spanish that lands belonging to the community as a whole were in fact their own private estates. They were charged by their Spanish overlords with seeing that Indians in communities provided their share of labor and tribute, an authority which the *curacas* in many instances invoked for their personal benefit as well.

Encomenderos and *curacas* were principal elements of a powerful provincial elite that challenged royal authority in the viceroyalty of Peru. Rebellious *encomenderos* killed the first viceroy to arrive in Peru and were subdued only after a long series of civil wars, and even then the king was forced to grant certain concessions concerning the heritability of grants of *encomienda*. The Spanish state was politically vulnerable in the early stages following the conquest and won compliance from colonial elites only with great difficulty.

In its economic orientation, the Spanish conquest state was more concerned with redistributing wealth than with creating it; it relied much more heavily for revenue on the collection of tribute from native subjects than on the reorganization of productive processes, as might have occurred through promoting the development of commercial agriculture. Dependent as it was on indirect systems of economic exploitation, Spanish colonial society at this time encountered little inducement to reorder Indian populations in any fundamental fashion. Neither the human ecology of native pastoral and agricultural producers nor the cultural identification of Indians with their homeland territories seems to have been radically disturbed (Fals Borda, 1957:351; Dobyns and Doughty, 1976:78).

However, there are two principal exceptions to this idyllic portrait of smooth transition: the rapid and often devastating decrease in the Indian population of many areas in the new colonies and the widespread decay of preconquest irrigation systems (Kubler, 1952). Smallpox killed a great many Indians: for example, the last native of the Zaragoza region in Colombia died in the epidemic of 1588, which necessitated the importation of slaves to work the mines there (Parsons, 1949:44). Depopulation of natives was especially pronounced on the coast, caused by the natives' contact with Europeans and consequent exposure to malaria and yellow fever. The development of coastal plantations and commercial agriculture later in the sixteenth and early in the seventeenth centuries would involve importation of slaves here as well to offset the scarcity of labor. This is in contrast to the strategies employed by highland manorial haciendas which, surrounded by denser Indian populations, frequently encroached on Indian lands as a means of artifically creating a shortage of land, thereby impelling natives to earn a livelihood by working on neighboring estates.

Closely related to the reduction of the Indian population was the partial disintegration of irrigation networks. In many instances traditional bureaucratic structures collapsed during the turbulent post-conquest years, with the result that allocation of water became more narrowly a local affair than formerly. Settlements tended to consolidate into larger towns in the lower valleys. In addition, food markets in urban and mining centers were as yet quite limited and contributed little stimulus to commercial agriculture. This in turn diminished the need for rigorous regulation of water by the Spanish (Keith, 1976:49, 124).

In sum, it is evident that both the higher order maneuverings of certain sociopolitical groups and local-level ecological and demographic factors were influential in shaping community organization. The Spanish state supplanted the Inca state as sovereign over the Andean region. Yet in order to establish control over its newly won territory, Spain parcelled out responsibility for administration to *encomenderos* with a consequent reduction in its power to exact compliance with its edicts. The system of indirect rule also enabled native officials, the *curacas*, to gain power in the absence of higher Inca nobles. The relatively autonomous provincial elites capitalized on the labor and tribute they could exact from members of the Indian communities. These elite groups were all too capable of gaining de facto control of Indian land and labor despite regulations designed to keep Indians separate and protected. The potential was manifest early for the massive intervention of non-Indians into Indian communities.

The different impacts of native depopulation on the coast and in the sierra served to heighten the contrast between those major ecozones. The distinction grew beyond purely ecological considerations and functioned also to set apart production within plantations from that in haciendas and communities. In general, it served to distinguish the non-Indian from the Indian. This distinction between the acculturated coast and the traditional Indian highlands continues even today to be an elementary principle of the sociology of Peru to such an extent that although a significant number of official indigenous communities are in coastal valleys at the edge of the Pacific, most studies have been of sierra communities (Dobyns, 1964:5). This is so despite certain objections that might be raised against too neat a discrimination. For example, in several areas of the supposedly mestizo coast, several pre-Incaic languages survived until late in the past century (Rivet, 1949). In the "Indian" highlands, on the other hand, ethnic ascription and self-identification have been shown to be comparatively context-specific, thus precluding absolute categorization of individuals as either Indian or mestizo (Fuenzalida, 1970a; Tschopik, 1947; van den Berghe and Primov, 1977). The confusion between races or ethnic groups is compounded by the fact that non-Indians sometimes have sought to be classified as residents of Indian communities, that is, as Indians, in order to hold title to community land. Fals Borda (1957:342) tells how racial intermixture in colonial Colombia makes difficult the legal distinction between communities of Indians and communities of Spaniards.

The Colonial Period

The administration of Viceroy Toledo (1569–1581) marks an important turning point in Andean colonial life. The crucial elements in redirecting the economics of colonialism were the discoveries of silver at Potosí in 1545 and of mercury eighteen years later at Huancavelica. Mercury could be used to separate silver from its ore, and the availability of major quantities of both minerals revolutionized the mining industry. It also increased suddenly the value of Indian labor in mines and intensified the contest between royal officials and private entrepreneurs over the right and ability to command native work forces.

In order to strengthen the crown's position against *encomenderos* and gain the benefits of a surging silver industry, Toledo instituted numerous reforms. One of these was the regulation of the *mitas de minas* in 1574, which compelled Indian communities to provide a quota of laborers to work in the mines. Service in the mines, as well as the travel to and from them, was exceedingly onerous, even fatal. One recurring indictment against the Spanish colonial system revolves around charges that *mita* was instrumental in dramatically reducing native populations in the communities. Labor drafts also contributed to a greater geographic mobility among Indians than had been evident previously. Not only was there movement to and from the mines but many Indians opted to leave their home communities for more distant parts. Though their access to land was more precarious as *forasteros*, or outsiders, in their new communities, they were not subject to recruitment to meet *mita* obligations.

In order to govern the natives better, to facilitate efforts to Christianize them, and to protect them from unscrupulous speculators and entrepreneurs, Toledo decreed that Indians were to be concentrated into new settlements, or *reducciones*. This concentration of the native population, where it occurred, was a significant departure from previous Andean settlement patterns of dispersed households and hamlets. Its ecological orientation was quite different in that it usually established new population centers in valley bottoms rather than on mountain slopes. In some valleys officials reserved upstream lands for Indians to guarantee them water (Keith, 1976).

Another effort at reform involved establishing a system of local government whose features are often evident even today. Lower-rank Indian leaders, known collectively as *varayoc*, were patterned in their organization after officials in peninsular Spanish municipalities. As in Spanish communities, a council (*cabildo*) of elders (*regidores*) appointed mayors (*alcaldes*) and constables (*alguaciles*), and served as a court of justice (Simpson, 1966:93). The community maintained corporate ownership of agricultural and pastoral lands as well as of woodlands and water for irrigation. Spaniards and other non-Indians were forbidden to dwell in Indian communities. Indians were wards of the crown, and the communities in which they resided were protected by law from the encroachment of outsiders. *Encomenderos* and *curacas* were excluded from holding municipal office. The intent was thereby to limit the power that these provincial elites could exercise in community affairs.

The policy of *reducción* involves some central issues in the contemporary study of Andean communities. One of these is the immediate question about the indigenous or borrowed nature of the community. On the one hand, it is possible to select numerous elements of community organization that appear to have endured relatively unchanged from preconquest or even pre-Inca times. As will be discussed in a later section, it is a common theme to emphasize the persistent qualities of Andean communities and to attribute to them special adaptive or even moral significance. Thus, the division of many communities into moieties is taken to represent the survival of ancient *ayllus*, or groups of related families (Fuenzalida, 1976; Matos Mar, 1976). This is both plausible and straightforward, though it seems at least possible that dual organization of communities might have resulted in certain cases from the forced coresidence of two or more different groups of people in colonial *reducciones*.

On the other hand, several features of any given community, including its location and hierarchy of municipal officials, seem to reflect strongly a Hispanic model for the community. Operating from that assumption, it is a valid research procedure to undertake studies of communities in Spain and to extend generalizations to the Andes in order to gain insight into the workings of Andean communities (Arguedas, 1968; Hurtado, 1974). This approach apparently ignores the problem of explaining how and why Indian communities throughout the Andes adjusted so rapidly and apparently with so little difficulty to the Spanish model of municipal authority. It is likely that the differences between Andean and Spanish authority systems were not so great as might be supposed, or at least that natives adopted the Hispanic model as in some ways advancing their own self-interests.

It is of course a fruitless endeavor to insist too strongly on either the autochthonous or European character of Andean communities. A wiser and certainly more practical course is to recognize the type of situation which, appropriately, the very word *varayoc* can symbolize. The root *vara* is Spanish and denotes the staff of office with which incumbent authorities are invested. It is combined with a Quechua possessive suffix. The word was thus originally a combination of two distinct traditions and has been employed since its coining in contexts that at once retain important elements from the past and also have undergone significant modification. Likewise, the features of the community were an amalgam of Andean and Hispanic institutions and they also have changed over the centuries in response to transformations in the life conditions of community members.

To return to the colonial community, the simultaneous rise in Spanish demand and the growing shortage of Indian producers through depopulation combined to create a relative scarcity of foodstuffs available to the Spanish population, especially in urban areas. Indirect control of Indian production through *encomienda* began to lose its attractiveness viewed against the possibility of managing directly private estates on which could be produced the crops and livestock required by cities and mining centers. Whether the connection between the *encomienda* and the hacienda is one of direct, institutional descent or is instead only one of functional substitution is a matter of some debate (Keith, 1971, 1976; Lockhart, 1969; Grieshaber, 1979). It is probable that no single answer is adequate in all cases. However that may be, by the early seventeenth century, haciendas devoted to commercial agriculture were well established through much of the Andes, and the *encomienda* was in sharp decline.

In other words, the demographic circumstance of Indian depopulation, coupled with the growth of Spanish populations, led to a situation in which control of Indian lands, now often vacant, replaced control of Indian labor as the key to agricultural entrepreneurship. Haciendas expanded in the seventeenth and eighteenth centuries by encroaching on lands belonging to badly reduced Indian communities. This process was reinforced by the financial difficulties in which the Spanish state found itself in the eighteenth century. The Bourbon kings of Spain found it expedient to sell lands to which title was unclear, a procedure which tended to favor Spanish landowners over Indian *comuneros*.

The colonial period, then, was one in which the Spanish state was able to limit the power of the *encomenderos*, though they retained in practice a considerable amount of autonomy. In fact, it was as much changes in economic opportunities as the power of the crown that finally brought an end to the *encomienda* and led to its replacement by private landed estates and the institution of *repartimiento*, in which Indian labor was in theory closely regulated by the colonial state. The state's command of resources was dependent on revenues from silver mining and mercantile control of trade. The weakness of this mercantilist state, compared to other industrial ones, was exacerbated in the eighteenth century by Spain's expense of maintaining a far-flung empire and its costly involvement in foreign wars. Financial debility finally forced Spain to compromise its commitment to protect Indian communities. Initially, it had hoped to regulate strictly the contact between Spaniards and Indians, who were royal wards. Spain now found it necessary to sell lands that were often claimed by communities of Indians. Processes of hacienda expansion were accelerated by this decision.

The fact of Indian depopulation is also central to understanding changes in official policies and in the communities themselves. The precipitous drop in the native population also seriously undermined the power of those provincial elites, the *encomenderos* and *curacas*, who relied most immediately on Indian surpluses to maintain themselves. Royal grants of rights to Indian tribute were replaced by direct production of commercial products on private estates as the principal means of wealth. These haciendas frequently acquired land by appropriating it from weakened Indian communities.

Colonial policies of *reducción* and *mita de minas*, and the great numbers of *forasteros*, are clear evidence of large-scale movements of people that altered the "vertical" orientation of the human ecology in many communities. Such movements broke many of the links holding communities together by undercutting old authority structures and abolishing traditional titles to the land. It may be postulated that there was a breakdown of old regional ethnic identities because of these movements. The hardships of forced labor, combined with onerous taxation, which often continued to be levied against communities at preestablished levels despite the sharp decline of taxable Indian populations, eventually spurred Indians in communities to join their complaints with those of other social sectors in a series of eighteenth-century revolts.

The Early Republic

Creoles became increasingly discontented with their exclusion from civil and ecclesiastical posts and chafed against the barriers to trade imposed by Spanish mercantilism, especially with the temptation of British free trade before them. Bourbon administrative reforms had disaffected numerous social groups, including provincial governors, miners, traders, and Indians of various occupations (Cornblit, 1970). It is difficult to trace exactly the flow of intellectual movements, but there is no doubt that Enlightenment ideas were a powerful influence on restless Creoles in the colonies. With the examples of the North American War of Independence and the French Revolution before them, it took no great leap of imagination for Creoles to consider the possibility of political independence. That possibility was greatly strengthened by the Napoleonic invasion of Spain and the consequent weakening of ties between metropole and colonies.

Of importance also were the principles of liberal economics which advocated policies of *laissez-faire* in place of colonial restrictions, and stressed the autonomy of individuals and the fundamental importance of private property. Thus, at independence, or even before it was finally attained, both San Martín and Bolívar acted to end the legal distinction of Indians from other classes of citizens and to institute formal equality in the new nations. Their efforts were directed at establishing Indians as part of a citizenry composed of independent yeoman farmers. In the eyes of the liberators, the pivotal procedure in effecting this social revolution lay in abolishing the reservation of special lands to Indians and their communities. The community was seen as a holdover from the hated colonial epoch, preserving the castelike separation of Indians from other groups, and maintaining land in communal *mortmain* rather than making it available for rational exploitation. Thus, the liberators acted immediately to end the legal recognition of communal lands. They divided lands of the community among its individual members; land was now partible and alienable.

However, formal equality only opened the way to even greater exploitation of the Indian and usurpation of his land. "In a less than perfect world a simple increase in freedom does not necessarily yield an increasing well-being" (McGreevey, 1971:140). Lacking the protection formerly provided him by communal ownership of land, the individual Indian was much more vulnerable to being duped or coerced into parting with his land. Hence the period from roughly the 1820s to the middle of the nineteenth century is frequently seen as one of expansion of large estates.

This rather standard interpretation of the growth of haciendas in the first half of the nineteenth century has much to recommend it, but some qualifications are in order. First, as Chevalier (1966) and Spalding (chapter 4) argue, in regions such as the highlands of Bolivia and southern Peru the hacienda became preponderant only at the end of the nineteenth century, or even later. The expansion of great estates in these cases is related to the increased importance of commercial exchange economies and demand for raw materials for export. Infrastructural developments such as the construction of railroads to link areas of production with ocean ports also promoted the growth of commercial haciendas after about 1880.

Second, the expansion of large estates did not necessarily occur at the expense of indigenous communities. Estates frequently grew by expanding the area devoted to agriculture within estate boundaries. This was accomplished by cultivating lands formerly left vacant or used for grazing (Bauer, 1972). In addition, the land that haciendas did incorporate from outside their previous bounds often belonged to one of the several other rural structures of landownership besides the community. Among these were *baldíos,* or lands in the public domain, and lands expropriated from Loyalists during the struggle for independence. A little later, in 1861, Colombia began a policy of disamortization that principally affected lands owned by the Catholic church but also included municipal *ejidos.* There was yet another source of land for haciendas: other haciendas. In the rush to indict hacendados for the evils they have perpetrated against the peasantry, it is common to attribute to them a capacity for concerted and conspiratorial action that they could not actually have lived up to. Their cohesiveness as a group is open to question. All too often the possibility is ignored that hacendados might sue and war among themselves, or buy up one another's property, in order to augment their real estate holdings (Favre *et al.,* 1967).

Haciendas were not always the only units to benefit from the division of community lands. In Colombia, again, hacendados did indeed have an interest in opening the communities in order to obtain access to the labor they represented. However, land speculators also stood to gain if they could buy and sell Indian land on the open market, and *municipios* resented the status of communities as privileged properties that paid no land tax. Hacendados, speculators, and *municipios* each had reasons of their own for desiring to divide community lands and they competed for the former community lands that did become available (García, 1952:13–14). It is worth pointing out also that communities often disintegrated under the weight of their own impracticality and internal problems rather than because of assaults from outside (McGreevey, 1971:127).

A final point concerning the expansion of haciendas at the expense of Indian communities in the nineteenth century: communities were in some regions successful in defending themselves against loss of their lands. García (1951:14–15) indicates briefly some factors in their success. Laws designed to dismantle the community were not always carried out, and in some places local administrators sought to protect the Indians. Indians displayed active resistance and a "will to survive" rather than submitting or relying passively on external aid. Perhaps community solidarity was strengthened in the face of encroachment (Wolf, 1957; Métraux, 1959:230). Also, some lands reserved to Colombian Indians (*resguardos*) were outside of the areas most affected by capitalist penetration. Cauca and Nariño in southern Colombia are examples of regions where persistence of the *resguardo* coincided with weak capitalist markets and elites.

The middle third of the nineteenth century was generally one of political instability and fiscal crisis for the Andean nations. If rapid turnover of chief executives can be used as a simple indicator of instability, it is evident that Peruvian and Colombian leaders must have had difficulty unifying their countries and formulating coherent policies with a chance to be implemented. No fewer than thirty-four men headed the Peruvian government between 1826 and 1865, and in Colombia there were thirty-two administrations in the years 1830 to 1866. Ecuador also experienced a succession of weak leaders in the same period.

A predictable result was an inconsistent attitude toward indigenous communities and the Indian population. The head tax levied on Peruvian Indians is a case in point. San Martín had terminated Indian tribute in 1820 only to have the first Peruvian Congress reinstate it in 1826 because it was an essential source of revenue. According to Bollinger (1977:27–8), it was alternately instituted and abolished throughout the century as an incipient industrial bourgeoisie struggled to convert the Peruvian economy to one based on protectionism and promotion of national industry, but was not yet strong enough to prevail completely over the "comprador bourgeoisie" and its reliance on pre-capitalist forms of expropriation, such as the tribute tax. The tax was finally ended in 1895.

Even a boom in mineral exports did little to stabilize governments. Much of the profit from nitrates and guano in Bolivia and Peru, for example, accrued to the foreigners who oversaw the mining and marketing of the products. The revenues that the respective national governments did obtain induced them to increase their foreign debts and thus to avoid developing any sound fiscal policies (Cotler, 1978).

To summarize the mutual influence that state and community exerted on each other during the period of the early republics, the importance of the break from Spanish colonialism must be noted. With independence, newly powerful groups were in a position to put their ideas into effect and to abolish colonial remnants, including the institution of communal ownership of property. The national governments were actually quite unstable and were unable to win the support of large segments of society for any length of time. Their political problems were made even worse by their financial difficulties. There was a decentralization of power, represented by the disintegration of large confederations, including the confederation of Peru and Bolivia as well as one comprising Colombia, Ecuador, and Venezuela. Furthermore, federalist principles tended to win out over centralist ones within each of these nations. As a result, provincial elites were able to achieve considerable autonomy.

The inability of ruling groups to maintain the longstanding compliance of contending groups or to command reliable and substantial sources of income prevented them from pursuing any cohesive policy toward Indian communities. An end was proclaimed to the head tax, to personal services required of Indians, and even to the concept of *indio* itself; yet these were in fact not seriously threatened and continued unabated throughout the nineteenth century. Corporate ownership of land by communities was declared abolished, according to the principles of liberal individualism, yet community organization very frequently persisted, largely because of lack of enforcement of the state's laws and also because of the defenses adopted by the communities. The policy of *laissez-faire* under which haciendas were able to expand their territory was due as much to the inability of the state to intervene as it was to commitment to liberal ideas.

There are few social histories of Indian communities during this period but some presumptions may be set forth. The communities' embattled defense of their lands, on those occasions when it appeared that they had been abandoned by any and all protectors, not only enabled them to keep much of their land but would eventually win them the sympathy of several indigenist groups in the latter part of the century. Also, the growth of the native population on community lands that had been reduced by encroachment, the continued taxation of the Indian as an important source of state income, and the perpetuation of forms of forced labor, led to indigenist revolts, such as that in 1861 in Colombia (García, 1952:31), the tax revolt in Huancané, Puno in 1866, and the Atusparia revolt in Ancash in 1885. These movements, and their violent suppression, called attention to the plight of Indians and eventually gave pro-Indian forces a strong moral and legal position from which to launch efforts at reform of the conditions in which the Indian communities found themselves.

The Epoch of *Indigenismo*

The period beginning about 1875 and lasting until 1930 marks an important transition in Andean economies to production geared to world markets. Groups attuned to the possibilities and requirements of modernized production of agricultural and mining products for export began to achieve political power. The disastrous War of the Pacific undermined the legitimacy of military rule and helped clear the way for civilian sectors to take command. Thus groups connected to the tin mining industry benefited both from the infusion of new technology and sources of capital, as well as from the military's loss of prestige, and were able to capture political control of Bolivia. In Peru, merchants and the owners of cotton and sugar plantations established an era of civilian rule. About the same time, the growing involvement of Ecuador in the cacao, sugar, and rice markets of the world helped enable liberals there to gain power.

Areas which once were provincial backwaters were drawn ever more intensively into participation in world capitalist markets. The building of railroads was especially important in ending the isolation of many regions and in promoting the sale of primary products, just as education and military conscription expanded the horizons of many ruralites. Migration from the highlands to coastal cities and plantations began to increase to significant levels in this epoch.

It is in this context that the intellectual movement of *indigenismo* must be understood. Its glorification of the denigrated Indian was a form of critique of old forms of society, which were perceived as capable of only slow and inadequate response to the disruptive intrusion of capitalism and foreign entrepreneurs. Influenced by the example of the recent Mexican Revolution, and then by the Russian Revolution, *indigenismo* incorporated a strong current of socialism, as evidenced by Baudin's (1928) study of the Incas. He viewed the preconquest *ayllu* as the basis of Andean collectivism and peasant welfare, and the Inca empire as a socialist state.

In the place of liberalism with its emphasis on individual economic action came a focus on collectivism as articulated not only in Marxism and Marxist-influenced interpretations, but also in more nationalist traditions which looked to the peasant community as a typification of a pre-industrial past. The basis of economic action was now considered the group, and the peasant community was seen as the ideal locus of such action. This view was further supported by the work of intellectuals such as Joaquín Costa (1915) who were rediscovering communal traditions in Europe.

In conjunction with the first stirrings of urban poor and industrial workers, reformist voices were raised first by González Prada and then by his followers. Later, in the early decades of the twentieth century, José Carlos Mariátegui amplified many of the same themes in his reinterpretation of Peruvian history (Mariátegui, 1965 [1928]). He believed that peasant communities retained their organizational strength in spite of colonialism and local elites, which led him to emphasize the central importance of this unit of Andean rural society. In a similar vein, Castro Pozo (1924; 1936) took a closer look at the peasant community and described in more detail what he considered its communal nature. He also saw in contemporary communities and in the preconquest *ayllus* the same basic communal qualities, and for that reason he argued that they held a fundamental place in peasant social organization. Moises Saénz (1933) was another prominent voice crying for recognition of the Indian's true place in society.

The pro-Indian movement served certain ideological ends: by making the Indian the essence of national reality, a support of the Indian became an attack on existing economic and political structures. *Indigenismo* took on political functions independent of the social reality of the peasants to whom it referred. Rising middle classes used it to undermine the political influence of the traditional elites. It was adopted by APRA, a political party whose strongest base was in the plantations and towns of the north coast of Peru, far from the more Indian areas of the southern sierra.

Political consequences of *indigenismo* can be seen in Peru in the enactment of laws. The 1920 constitution made provisions for the legal recognition of communities, and in 1926 the actual process of adding *comunidades* to official registration lists began. A number of agencies, such as the Sección de Asuntos Indígenas, were established to provide communities with support; in some cases they created client communities. Though less well studied, similar processes might operate in the case of haciendas. The political strength of hacendado associations and credit policies that favored haciendas might have led to their formation where they had not previously existed.

Yet the passing of laws in Lima cannot be presumed to have determined the actual state of affairs in the provinces. During the Leguía administration of 1919 to 1930, the impact of *indigenista* legislation was uneven. Despite community registration policies, only a small proportion of potentially eligible communities were actually registered in this period. Decrees were issued under Leguía to assure Indian communities their proper share of irrigation water and their right to administer their own finances. However, the same administration also implemented the program of *conscripción vial* which obligated able-bodied males to work on construction of roads. The bulk of the labor fell on Indians. Many of the charges leveled against the colonial *mita* were revived for use against *conscripción vial* before it was abolished in 1930.

The contradictory tendencies of Leguía's presidency were due largely to the pragmatic politics of implementing proclaimed reforms. "Simply stated, Leguía's *indigenismo* may have been a shield behind which he could aid small landowners and proadministration *hacendados* at the expense of the traditional landed oligarchy....It is likewise probable that Leguía used *comunidad* recognition to reward or to punish *hacendados* and may have manipulated many Indian revolts to achieve the same end" (Davies, 1974: 92–93).

In whatever terms the Leguía regime is assessed, it is certain that Peruvian communities had begun to be more tightly integrated into official administrative structures than ever before. As this process of incorporation advanced in succeeding decades, it increased the significance of institutional resources administered by the national government and consequently promoted the dependence of communities on them (Montoya *et al.*,1979:202–29). Orlove's discussion (Chapter 6) of the different social conditions of Surimana and Quehue focuses on the important effect exerted on each community by its official status within a set of administrative units and its connections to the national government.

Recent Perspectives

Indigenismo incorporated several overtly political themes into its reevaluation of society and the place of the Indian community in it. Another perspective, which may be called the functionalist approach, is less concerned with restructuring the social order than with establishing universal or at least general categories of behavior with which to conduct scientific comparisons of social phenomena. The "community" is one such fundamental typological unit. Though it is an independent intellectual tradition, the functionalist approach to Andean rural society parallels the *indigenista* view and originated partially from the same European source. Richard Adams writes that the European thinkers Tönnies, Maine, Durkheim, and others "set forth the community as a mode of human life peculiar to a period or to a portion of human evolution" (Adams, 1962:412). Heinrich Cunow's work constitutes an early example of this thinking as applied to the Andes (Cunow, 1927). This tradition shaped Robert Redfield through the Chicago school of sociology, and Redfield in turn influenced such North American anthropologists as John Gillin, Harry Tschopik, Allan Holmberg, and their North American and Peruvian students.

Redfield (1956) felt that the community was an "integral entity" whose characteristics made it ideal for the ethnographic method of investigation. Communities were characterized by small size, distinct boundaries, internal homogeneity, and self-sufficiency. Their basic *Gemeinschaft* qualities made them central aspects of peasant society and contributed to the long-term persistence of community institutions (Goins, 1967). Village ethnographies and programs of community development in other parts of the world served as models for anthropologists and agents of planned social change. Often working in close collaboration, these two sets of professionals shared theoretical and practical concerns which placed further emphasis on the community. They applied the term "community" to a wide range of forms. Theoretical and methodological considerations in anthropology, therefore, supported an existing leitmotif of intellectual social thought in the Andean republics to produce a very influential conceptualization of Andean agrarian society.

The community development literature is concerned to demonstrate its distance from Redfield's functionalist model of the perdurable community by emphasizing change rather than continuity in its models of peasant society and by applying itself to the practical problems of implementing progress in actual development projects. Emphasis is given the fact that peasants not only undergo change but often initiate it, either on their own or by seeking appropriate agencies for assistance (Núñez del Prado, 1973; Whyte and Alberti, 1976).

However, there are strong affinities connecting Redfield and his followers with many of the theoreticians of community development or applied anthropology (Carter, 1964; Buitrón, 1966; Bourque *et al.*, 1967; McEwen, 1969; Dobyns *et al.*, 1971; Escobar, 1973; Whyte, 1975). Chief among these is the assumption that the community, as fount of solidarity and common interests, provides a ready-made basis for action. Furthermore, despite a certain focus on institutional links to regional and national political structures, development studies tended to be overly optimistic about the ability of communities to organize themselves effectively in the context of structural constraints on behavior. This optimism was perhaps fueled in the 1960s by the support of the Agency for International Development and the Alliance for Progress for projects such as those sponsored by Cornell University. In turn this optimism rested on a confidence in the feasibility and mutual support of economic growth and participatory democracy in Latin America, which the events of the last decade have cast into doubt. The well-known Vicos project, put forth as a model of effective agrarian reform, required substantial external inputs and failed to spawn a series of successful imitators. This was due to unwarranted expectations of great community solidarity and cohesion during work projects, and to insufficient recognition of both the individualism within the community and the social and institutional hindrances to continued and efficacious action at the local level. A series of dissertations by Cornell graduate students during this same period provided some of the recognized classics in Andean community studies yet shared these same limitations (Andrews, 1963; Barnett, 1960; Dobyns, 1960; Doughty, 1963, 1968; Snyder, 1960; Stein, 1955).

The use of "community" by *indigenistas*, functionalists, and community developers is in several fundamental ways similar to concurrent uses of the "tribe" and other related entities such as "ethnic group." Concepts such as these were originally appropriated by social scientists because they seemed intuitively to be natural units of organization, embodying primordial sentiment and solidarity. The boundaries of these units have been viewed from this perspective as essentially discrete and unambiguous. Furthermore, there is a marked tendency in this framework to attribute the patterning of behavior within the community and the tribe to the adherence by individuals to a shared set of customary values and beliefs.

These concepts have continued to evince parallel evolutions within social science. Rather than being fixed and unproblematic, the boundaries of communities, tribes, and ethnic groups are increasingly recognized to be subject to negotiation and redefinition. Individuals are often capable of claiming or disclaiming membership in these groups according to their manipulation of symbols in different social contexts. They pursue self-interested strategies and frequently are in competition with one another. There is a growing recognition also that the structure of these groups, and perhaps even their origin, is due in large part to conditions imposed by colonial and national governments (Friedlander, 1975). "Tribes" were often formed by colonial regimes in Africa which desired to deal with ordered sets of people and to maintain a clear line of authority. So, too, has the organization of Andean communities been bolstered or even created by the policies of state institutions as shown by cases such as the establishment of *reducciones* in the colonial epoch, or the official recognition and material benefits accorded to client communities in more recent times. Looked at in this way, communities do not appear to be "integral entities" but instead are the result of a conjunction of local and regional or national forces.

The functionalist view of communities rested on certain ideological influences and on specific types of political relations between peasants and other social sectors. As both of these began to change, new approaches to the Andean communities emerged. These changes, though related, can be considered separately. New ideologies and theories entered Peru in the 1960s. The Cuban Revolution and the evident difficulties which troubled the Belaúnde regime by the mid-1960s led to considerable discussion in military and civilian circles about the possibility of alternative forms of government. The Peruvian left, with its strong roots in the universities, underwent an expansion and fragmentation in both organizational and ideological aspects. Those political events generated a questioning of North American social science and favored an experimentation with ideas of other origins. This openness to new ideologies characterized community studies as it did many other areas of thought.

The ties which linked rural communities to national systems also increased and diversified. Some national and international institutions made efforts to establish direct connections with rural communities, often in relatively remote parts of the highlands. Political parties became active in the 1960s, with the presidential campaigns and municipal elections in the early years of that decade. The Catholic Church became active in the years following the 1959 encyclical *Princeps Pastorum*, which directed religious orders in developed nations to devote a greater portion of their activities to the Third World; these efforts increased after the Vatican II Council. Other government agencies increased the attention which they gave to the peasants. This concern was motivated in part by increasing peasant activism leading up to the land invasions of the mid-1960s. The nature of this activism and the directions which it might take provoked a great deal of comment across the political spectrum. This intensification of ties between rural communities and national society created positions for community development agents of a functionalist persuasion, but it also placed other individuals who were sympathetic to other theoretical viewpoints in contact with communities.

Of the new perspectives which appeared during this period, dependency theory is perhaps the most important. Other major ones include British social anthropology, cultural ecology, and French structuralism. One reaction to the view of the community as a natural unit is dependency theory, which challenges the notion of the separateness of the community from the hacienda. It contends instead that the community and the hacienda are intimately connected in terms of both structure and function. Structurally, communities are often bound to or embedded in haciendas; they are captive communities. Hacendados are able to exercise dominion by the political and socioeconomic power they wield over individual *comuneros* and by the influence they have within community administrative structures (Cotler, 1969). Functionally, communities advance capitalist production and marketing through the laborers and commodities they provide to haciendas. From this perspective, it is in the interest of agrarian elites to maintain the communities as reservoirs of cheap labor power. The theoretical inalienability of land serves to bind Indians to their communities (Patch, 1959; Mishkin, 1947; Stavenhagen, 1975). Communities are thus the bottom link in a chain of local, national, and international relations of exploitation and domination (Long and Roberts, 1978).

This revised view of rural communities was prompted at one level by peasant activism, such as the 1952 revolution in Bolivia and the land invasions conducted by Peruvian *comuneros* and peons in the 1960s (Dandler, 1969; Barnes de Marshall, 1970; Simmons, 1974; Guillet, 1974; Whyte and Alberti, 1976). These movements demanded a reconsideration of the functionalist conception of peasants as passive occupants of a static countryside. The persistence of rural structures was regarded as due less to peasant conservatism than to the oppression of peasant masses by landed and capitalist classes (Castillo Ardiles, 1970).

At another level, the dependency viewpoint on haciendas and communities is an outgrowth of Lenin's analysis of imperialism and monopoly capitalism (Lenin, 1939). The Great Depression forcefully demonstrated the limitations of development based on exports as an engine of growth. A new economic strategy was developed after World War II that emphasized import substitution industrialization to produce goods previously provided by imports. Yet, by the 1960s, it had become obvious that these programs had not helped the balance of payments, nor made income distribution more nearly equal, nor lessened dependence to the degree that had been expected. This failure was critiqued by dependency theorists within a general Marxist theory of capitalism, and particularly as an aspect of the theory of imperialism (O'Brien 1975:8–11).

The dependency paradigm represents an advance on Redfield's conception of the community because it introduces as a necessary element of community analysis a consideration of forces outside the community itself. The community is recognized as but one part of an entire set of regional, national, and even international relationships (Casagrande and Piper, 1969; Rodriguez, 1969; Cotler, 1970; Escobar, 1970, 1973; Favre, 1977; Gomez, 1977). Dependency theorists are also more inclined than functionalists to study the relations of social inequality and exploitation that can be found in any community (Celestino, 1972; Degregori and Golte, 1973; Villasante, 1978). However, analysis within the dependency perspective tends to proceed by a series of dualistic contrasts, including those between communities and haciendas, owners and workers, and satellites and metropoles. It thus is rather schematic and confronts data with an insensitive preconception about the structure and dynamics of agrarian society (Orlove, 1977a).

The other approaches which seek to move beyond the functionalist perspective may be summarized more briefly. Drawing on British social anthropology, substantivist economic anthropology, and cultural ecology, John Murra developed a model of the late preconquest native societies which has influenced research on earlier and later periods as well as on the one he originally examined. As mentioned before, his notion of verticality argues that Andean populations attempt to control the largest possible number of ecological zones at different elevations in an effort to achieve their ideal of self-sufficiency (Murra, 1964, 1967, 1968, 1970, 1972). Anthropologists and ethnohistorians have shown the importance of verticality in shaping resource utilization patterns by rural communities up to the present (Flores, 1978). Some writers have claimed that this complex multi-zonal pattern is a key part of a uniquely Andean heritage, while others have drawn parallels to other parts of the world (Rhoades and Thompson, 1975; Brush, 1976a; Sánchez, 1978). A number of such studies (Barrette, 1972; Flores, 1975, 1977a; Fonseca, 1966, 1972a, 1972b; Vallée, 1971, 1972; Webster, 1971, 1973; Concha Contreras, 1975; Brush, 1977; Harris, 1978) have recently been summarized by Brush (1976b).

French structuralism has been another major influence. Some researchers, following the initial lead of Zuidema, have adopted Levi-Strauss' emphasis on mediated dualities in thought and their correspondences in social organization (Zuidema, 1964; Palomino Flores, 1971; Ossio, 1973; Urbano, 1974; Wachtel, 1973). Their studies include analyses of cosmology, ritual, sex roles, agriculture, and village organization (Isbell, 1978; Platt, 1975). In perhaps a less dramatic fashion, British social anthropology has also influenced community studies, as a recent volume on kinship and marriage shows (Bolton and Mayer, 1977). The conceptualization of the developmental cycle of the household and the relation of kinship networks and communities reflect this borrowing (Lambert, 1977). Although both French structuralism and British social anthropology have been criticized as ahistorical, the scholars who apply them to the Andes frequently attempt to use them to show the long continuity of preconquest patterns of thought and organization (Zuidema and Quispe, 1967; Pinto, 1971; Platt, 1976). This fascination with survivals is, in part, itself a survival from *indigenista* days, but it also indicates a rejection of the efforts of dependency theory to explain rural society primarily on the basis of external influences. Some authors have combined those approaches. Brush's study (1977) of land use and kinship in a northern highland community draws on cultural ecology and social anthropology. There have been efforts to link French structuralism with studies of social organization (Albó, 1972; Fiorinanti-Molinié, 1978) and cultural ecology (Ossio, 1978). Some recent work unites all three (Isbell, 1979; Houdart-Morizot, 1976).

In its focus on the household as the locus of decision-making and in its use of an actor-oriented model (in this case the actor is the household), the perspective on rural Andean society that is presented in this volume is a further manifestation of a pattern that typifies recent social science: a concern for typologies is replaced by one for processual interpretation. Rather than limit itself to description of community structures, the household model sets out to analyze the adjustments made by households to their natural and social environments (Mayer, 1977), a range of perspective considerably broader than the functional one of Redfield and his followers and more finely attuned to behavioral variation than are dependency models. It incorporates consideration of units other than the community and the hacienda as important components of the rural environment. This concern for examining a range of forms of social organization and the adaptation to environmental constraints shows the influence of British social anthropology and cultural ecology. Finally, it converges with the dependency paradigm to some degree by recognizing that the strategizing and struggling of households for resources is structurally unequal. In other words, its actors are not the formally free and unconstrained individuals postulated in nineteenth century liberal theory; instead they interact with different interests, perceptions, and resources, which in turn enhance or hinder their ability to compete against other decision-making bodies.

These recent perspectives on the community are less directly determined by the class position of their proponents than were the previous ideas about communities. In part they have this relative autonomy because they are largely the product of the burgeoning of a stratum of intellectuals who are trained to criticize arguments on the basis of abstract properties of logical consistency and completeness as much or more than on the grounds of social utility or impact. It is possible, for example, for a scholar to criticize a functionalist model for its failure to consider adequately the problem of social change without himself either advocating or condemning any change. His theoretical stance is not necessarily translated immediately into political action.

However, it is important to claim neither that an absolutely objective judgment is attainable by intellectuals nor that apparently abstract opinions are devoid of political implications. Even as academic a book as *Reciprocidad e intercambio en los Andes peruanos*, for instance, contains a veiled criticism of the centralized Agrarian Reform program of Peru and suggests a greater incorporation of local forms of organization in government programs (Alberti and Mayer, 1974:30–33). Conceptions of the community, no matter how abstract they may appear, have been shaped under conditions of group competition for material resources and are therefore capable of deeply influencing the direction of life within communities.

Again the state plays a key role in mediating the dialectic between thought and reality. Crucial to its position is the state's command of material and institutional resources. During this century national states in the Andean region have generally not only managed to centralize their control over capital and credit facilities, for example, but have expanded as well the size of their participating sectors by incorporating formerly marginal groups into national politics. The period after 1930 especially has been one of mass political mobilization. The success of participatory democracy has not always been striking, in large part because ruling groups, through a process of "segmentary incorporation" (Cotler, 1969), managed to allow certain marginal groups to have a political voice without altering fundamentally the existing balance of power. Nevertheless, the leverage that sectors such as peasants and Indians have gained in national politics is substantial and is due to a number of factors.

The vast increase in migration from rural to urban areas and from sierra to coast has served to expand the wants of many rural peoples and to increase their knowledge about how to satisfy those wants. Education and military service have accomplished much the same result.

There are, in addition, ruling groups, and groups challenging them, who need to expand their bases of support. Community development schemes tie the community very directly to the state and its effort to strengthen its representation in new areas. Social scientists, no matter how sincere and selfless they are in their attempts to play the roles of impartial observers, often must operate in some way through government agencies and thereby lend an aura of legitimacy to the existing bureaucracy by participating in its studies. The opening of positions in government agencies to graduates of social science programs has reinforced these links of scholars and bureaucrats. For example, several investigations of the social conditions in rural communities conducted under the auspices of the Ministerio de Trabajo y Comunidades of Peru in the late 1960s, after a series of land invasions in the highlands (e.g., Miranda Rocha, 1967; Revilla Corrales, 1967; Gutierrez Galindo, 1967a, 1967b; Gutierrez Galindo and Miranda Rocha, 1967; Revilla Corrales and Báez de Revilla, 1967), can be viewed as part of an effort by the ruling Acción Popular party to co-opt peasant movements by instituting its own structures of participation. Similarly, close ties were established between academic anthropologists from the United States, the Peace Corps, and government agencies.

The strengthening of government ties and the building of national power bases are therefore closely related. The expansion of representative and administrative structures is not simply part of the internal dynamics of a juggernaut bureaucracy but is linked to a larger political process. Different institutional channels are utilized by national and regional power groups to mobilize technology and capital in exchange for local-level political support. The reverse process also occurs in which communities imply a promise of votes and support, or tacitly pledge to remain quiescent, in order to receive desired services or goods.

Conclusion

By examining the dialectical interaction of thought and reality through several centuries, particularly as that interaction is mediated by state institutions, considerable transformations can be seen to have taken place in the internal organization of Andean communities and in their perception by outsiders. At various times, and by different groups, communities have been seen as foci of neighborly compassion and cooperation, as microcosms of a world of class exploitation and struggle, as reservoirs of untapped energy for development projects, as survivals from an autochthonous past, and as a heritage of European colonialism. Life in communities has been dramatically altered by changes in population and in the availability of land, by pressures and inducements emanating from other agrarian structures, including haciendas, and by the kind and degree of support offered by various regional and national groups.

It is evident, then, that the structure, organization, and concepts of the community (and, by similar reasoning, the hacienda) are not in any way given or eternal. They are, instead, an intimate part of the preeminently human activity of creating a world in which to live by putting thought into action and adjusting belief according to experience. Communities are created in a ceaseless process of definition and redefinition, conception and activity, impingement and reaction.

The household model of Andean agrarian society that is the unifying theme of this book possesses a behavioral orientation that can accommodate the dynamism of a dialectical perspective on communities and haciendas. It incorporates the perceptions of actors about the ordering of their natural and social conditions and postulates behavior on that basis. Just as changes in the structure of the environment—perhaps imposed from above by powerful elites through institutions of the state—lead to altered perceptions and behaviors, so also does realignment of household behaviors contribute towards restructuring the larger conditions and thus the thought and activity of elites. Communities are entities, but not "integral" ones. Their structures are not fixed, but are forever being negotiated, as insiders and outsiders alike seek to make of the community a source of benefits for themselves.

CHAPTER 4

Class Structures in the Southern Peruvian Highlands, 1750–1920

Karen Spalding

For generations, scholars and activists seeking to comprehend Peruvian society have pointed to the great estate, or hacienda, as both one of the characteristic institutions of the country and as the source and the manifestation of the sharp class distinctions in rural society. The problem of the Indian, commented José Carlos Mariátegui, founder of the Peruvian Communist Party and one of the major political thinkers of the twentieth century in Latin America, is the problem of land (Mariátegui, 1965:41). From at least the 1920s and '30s, when people critical of contemporary conditions began to look for the origins of those conditions in the past, the importance of the hacienda as a social and political, as well as an economic institution, was an established fact.

Recent Peruvian scholarship has insisted upon the curious alliance between the landed elite of the highlands and the "modernizing" and export-oriented bourgeoisie of the coast as underlying much of the development of the country since political independence. The coastal elite, in control of the political structures in the capital, has firmly defended the highland landlords. The alliance lasted until the 1950s, when the disintegration of the landlord-bourgeois alliance became a publically admitted fact, marked by the open support of the Sociedad Nacional Agraria for agrarian reform in the sierra. But it still required the action of the military government that took power in 1968 to make the agrarian reform a reality and the end of the alliance an accomplished fact. In 1969 the military government, then under the leadership of General Juan Velasco Alvarado, decreed the most far-reaching land reform yet to take place in Latin America outside of Cuba, and in the years following actually proceeded to implement that law. Once decreed, the reform went relatively smoothly. Agrarian reform is a very old issue, in which words and laws have served to obstruct change rather than to implement it. Yet in a country in which the landed oligarchy has traditionally been presented as the ruling class, that group crumpled under the new regime with barely a whimper. The major problem today, as the military government moves steadily to the right under the pressure of near bankruptcy and the budget-balancing exigencies of the International Monetary Fund, is the question of the new power structures and the relations of production that will emerge in the rural areas in a society that, despite the reorganization of formal property relations, remains fundamentally part of the world capitalist system.

The nature of class relations outside of the major urban centers remains an important problem for people seeking to understand both the evolution of Peruvian society in the past and its possible direction in the future. The character of the vast spaces outside of the major urban centers is of major historical importance at least until the 1940s, if not later. The history of rural relations of production in Peru demands study as much today as it did when Mariátegui drew attention to the importance of that problem in the 1920s. Younger scholars, particularly in Peru, are now beginning to respond to that need, and much exciting work on the character of rural society has been done in the past decade (Macera, 1977: 139–228; Burga, 1976).

The following chapter represents an early and very tentative attempt to suggest an hypothesis to explain both the ubiquitousness of the hacienda system in contemporary Peru and its fragility, as indicated by the relatively painless and swift disintegration of the system following the agrarian reform of 1969. The chapter was originally presented as a conference paper in 1975, and that same paper, without revisions or notes, appeared in translation in Peru in 1977 (Spalding, 1977). Much to my surprise and pleasure, the piece drew comments and criticism from both Peruvian and North American specialists (Caravedo, 1978:108; Jacobsen, 1978). It is encouraging to find such evidence of dialogue among historians and social scientists, and I urge those interested in the problem to read the criticisms and other analyses and to join in the effort to devise a satisfactory explanation of the role of the great estate in the political and economic life of Peru.

My own hypothesis was built upon little beyond existing published materials. It rests essentially upon the assumption that economic relationships, if they have any real permanence, are ultimately reflected in political structures. In Peru, where the penetration of capitalist relations of production is relatively late—it is thought by most analysts to date only from the latter part of the nineteenth century, if then—it seems likely that the social matrix of Peruvian society in the rural areas remained heavily influenced by precapitalist relationships. In any precapitalist structure, economic and political factors are not easily separated, for they function intimately together to ensure the extraction and monopolization of surplus by the dominant class. My attention was drawn by the characteristic fusion of the political and the economic in precapitalist systems. I sought to comprehend the impact and the role of that fusion in a model that may well need to be discarded by the time it is printed in this volume, but that I hope will help stimulate the kind of work that will provide us with a more complete and satisfying explanation of the structures of Peruvian society than has been the case to date.

I began my work by asking some questions about commonly accepted categories and definitions. As I began to examine the data on the late colonial period, from about 1750 to the end of the Wars of Independence in 1825, as well as available data on the nineteenth century, I became increasingly aware that the traditional dichotomy of hacienda and village, huge estate and *minifundia*, is an abstraction that covers great variations of power and wealth between haciendas and between villages. A closer look at the variety of social relations subsumed in the categories of village and hacienda can provide the basis for the formulation of a much more dynamic model of change than those commonly presented. It could further provide some insight into the relatively rapid demise of the hacienda system following the ascension to power of the military government.

The following pages contain a largely theoretical model of the pattern of change in highland rural society from the beginning of the nineteenth century to the 1920s. The model emphasizes two major periods: the mid-nineteenth century, when colonial patterns were still predominant, and the early years of the twentieth century, particularly the years from 1919 to about 1930, which I define as the period of the consolidation of hacienda power in provincial society. The data are drawn from the southern highlands, now regarded as one of the poorest areas of Peru. This region is part of what was known as the *mancha india*, which translates as "Indian stain." From the 1940s at least, the *mancha india*, which includes the present departments of Ayacucho, Ancash, Apurímac, Cuzco, Huancavelica, and Puno, was regarded as the most backward area in the country. In 1961 the average income of the population of the region was 39 percent lower than the national average. Sixty-nine percent of the total population was engaged in agriculture and cattle-breeding, as against 42 percent for the country as a whole (Cotler, 1969:162). The population is predominantly rural, and a substantially larger proportion was until recently classified as "Indian," by now a quasi-racial label for the most marginalized and oppressed sectors of the population.

At the same time, the southern highlands were actively involved in commerce with Europe, primarily with Great Britain, within a decade following political independence. The region produced sheep, alpaca, and llama wools, which were exported via the southern coastal port of Islay, and later via the port of Mollendo, to the textile mills of Great Britain. Further, the majority of the peasant mobilizations of the period from 1750 to the present took place in the southern highlands. It was a center of the great revolt of Tupac Amaru II in 1780, and the focus of local revolts from the 1860s to the 1930s (Cornblit, 1970; Piel, 1967; Orlove, 1976). The relatively high degree of conflict should bring many of the underlying structural tensions into clearer relief. It also means that data on the region are more easily available than in less openly conflictive and more isolated areas of the country.

The traditional picture of the history of agrarian relations of production presents the great estate as the predominant institution in the Andean highlands. It was assumed to have expanded steadily from the colonial period forward, absorbing the land and labor resources of the Indian peasant villages which in turn were viewed as corporate and self-sufficient and closed to the European economy. That picture has been modified by later research, but it is still assumed in general that the hacienda, in contrast to the self-sufficient peasant villages, was a product of market opportunities and that the hacienda tended to expand rapidly from the eighteenth or at the least the mid-nineteenth century. Local tax and census records, however, do not bear out this view in the case of the southern highlands. The rather sketchy data currently available suggest that the hacienda was not the dominant agrarian institution in the southern highlands until the early twentieth century. Its growth, and the power commanded by the hacendados, were primarily a product of the alliance of members of the highland political elite with the political elite of the coast, whose wealth in turn was built upon its alliance with foreign capital and its dependence upon foreign markets.

Several stages in the agrarian history of the southern highlands can be tentatively proposed at this point. By the end of the Spanish colonial period in the 1820s, the productive system of the Indian communities had been heavily transformed. The traditional links between land and labor access, both mediated through kin ties, were seriously eroded. The communities themselves had become quite stratified, with local elites that monopolized much of the land, together with local political control. At the other end of the spectrum of village population was a landless or semilandless group that supplied labor to the landowners both inside and outside of the villages. There were few extremely large estates, and the owners of such estates, of both European and noble Indian descent, were not in full control of the political and economic system of the highlands.

While there is considerable evidence that local landowners were appropriating community lands during the half-century following political independence, from about 1830 to 1880, I suspect that the struggle took place between the communities and relatively small landowners, many of them part of the local society. Communities and landowners alike were all directly involved in the production of sheep, llama, and alpaca wool for export.

The consolidation of the large haciendas and the extreme concentration of land gathered momentum later, during the early years of the twentieth century. Political factors played an important role in the rise of the great estate. The hacendados were not able to eliminate the smaller producers and appropriate all or even most of the provincial income generated through the wool trade until an alliance with the coastal bourgeoisie, whose wealth was built upon direct relationships with foreign financial interests, permitted the new elite to transform the pattern of market access in the highlands. The conquest of the political system by the coastal elite after 1895, and the transformation of communication systems brought about by the construction of a railroad from Arequipa to Puno (1876), the establishment of the steamship line on Lake

Titicaca, and, especially, the extensive building of roads after 1910, were factors that threw the balance of power in favor of the local landed elite and permitted it to establish its hegemony over the other sectors of highland provincial society.

The expansion of the hacienda-based elite took place at the expense not only of rural village society and the small farms, but also at the expense of the local town and quasi-urban centers. These latter populations were primarily engaged in activities that were also undermined by the expansion of the hacienda: transport, petty commerce, and minor bureaucratic office. The provincial elite built its hegemony on the basis of its political, not economic, advantages. Its monopoly of force and police power through its alliance with the coastal bourgeoisie, and its growing monopoly of market access through its control of transport—also achieved through political means—were the bases of its economic status. This process was not complete in all areas. In some regions smaller producers were able to resist the encroachment of the large estates, in part through seeking alliances themselves with political forces outside of the region and in part through organizing among themselves. The long history of local revolts and disturbances in the southern highlands is testimony not only to the intensity of the struggle but also to the relative tenuousness of elite control, oppressive as it was.

The first stage in the transformation of highland society was the long-term process of incorporation of the indigenous society into the European productive system, a process most fully realized during the Spanish colonial period in the southern highlands. During this period, from the sixteenth century to the beginning of the nineteenth century, the southern highlands were linked to the silver mining economy of Potosí, in what is now Bolivia. Potosí was the center of a market economy that involved a large area, including not only southern Peru but also the lowland provinces of present-day Bolivia and the area of what is now northwestern Argentina. The southern highlands sent cattle, agricultural products, cloth, and other local manufactured goods to the mines. Through its relationship with Potosí, the entire region was tied into the colonial economic system, oriented around the production of precious metals for export to Spain. The dominant figures in this system were the great merchant houses, members of the trade guild of Lima, which in turn were linked to the trade guild of Seville, which controlled the trade of Spain with her colonies (Sempat, 1972).

While the trade guilds absorbed much of the profit of the trade to Potosí, participation in the patterns of market exchange included people at all levels of the society, down to the local villages. In the provinces of northwestern Argentina that supplied Potosí, the dominant local figures were not only landowners but also merchants, who controlled the local supply of goods to the large-scale merchants or who themselves sent goods directly to Potosí. These same groups controlled much of local government and, through that, the monopolies handed out through political patronage (Halperin, 1972:15–27). Under the Spanish colonial regime, political position and mercantile activities virtually merged at the provincial level. The provincial representative of Spanish authority among the Indians, the *corregidor de indios*, absorbed much of the surplus generated by the members of Indian society by means of his mercantile activities. The Indians were an important market for European and colonial products, especially mules and cloth, although they were for the most part a reluctant one. The *corregidor*, who combined the roles of administrator, policeman, and judge, was in an ideal position to distribute goods to the Indians. He could force them to pay, either in currency or in services, for the goods he assigned them. Legally, the *corregidor* was the bridge between the Spanish colonial bureaucracy and Indian society. In his extralegal capacity as merchant, he ensured the flow of currency and goods from the Indians to the commercial intermediaries, and beyond that, to the representatives of the great commercial houses in Lima. The *corregidor's* monopoly of commercial activity through political power ended with the elimination of the provincial officials following political independence. The link between political and mercantile activities continued, however, well into the twentieth century if not to the present.

Access to labor was also linked to political control. Officially, Indian meant laborer during the Spanish colonial period. The principal division in Andean colonial society was the division between two distinct societies, the Spaniard and the Indian, who stood in the relation of conqueror to conquered. Ideologically at least, this division corresponded to the distinction between those who provided the labor and those who appropriated the products of that labor. Private estates or haciendas of varying sizes did depend upon the labor of Indians, who were either assigned to the estate by the colonial authorities or who were attracted and held through a variety of mechanisms. The Indians were assigned to villages established by the Spanish authorities in a massive relocation program about a half-century after the conquest in 1535. Each village was composed of a number of *ayllus*, or extended kin groups, through which the members of Indian society received access to the resoures in land, water, and the labor of their fellows. From the perspective of the Spanish state, the lands held by the *ayllus* were regarded as corporate holdings, claimed by the community as a whole. The economic system of Indian village society as the Spanish authorities envisaged it was based upon a dual principle. In the first place, the Indians were to retain their traditional forms of access to land and labor, through which they could continue to maintain themselves. In addition, they were to produce surplus, which was extracted by the colonial state through direct levies or through the participation of the members of native society in the European market system either for their own gain, or in order to obtain the goods and/or currency demanded by the members of European society.

From early in the colonial period, the members of Indian society were sending a part of their production to the European market centers. The Indians of the southern highlands provided the mines of Potosí with cloth, coca, and foodstuffs that formerly had been consumed within the society or accumulated by the Inca rulers. By the eighteenth century at least, both individuals and communities devoted part of their lands to the cultivation of market crops, such as cattle, fruits, or European grains. Other individuals or villages rented the excess lands of more fortunate communities and then used those lands to produce market crops. Production for the European market, as well as the conversion of land itself into a commodity that could produce rent for a community or for an individual, permitted the elaboration of considerable economic differentiation within Indian society. To the degree that Indian participation in the market economy exceeded the bare minimum needed to pay their tribute and the other levies to which they were subject, a process began that is familiar to any who have followed the penetration of a commodity economy into a rural area: the internal differentiation of Indian village society into a wealthy group that controls land in excess of its subsistence needs, and a poor group that has insufficient land and must hire its labor out to other members of the community (Spalding, 1975).

In the southern highlands, that process was well advanced by the eighteenth century. On the one hand, local chieftains, known as *curacas*, or other people assigned the position of broker between village society and the Spanish authorities, were in a position to accumulate large quantities of land, sometimes far in excess of the landholdings of many members of European society. Wealthier villages also accumulated land at the expense of other corporate groups or individuals. At the other end of the scale, many members of Indian society did not have access to land, or had less land than they needed to maintain themselves. Almost half of the residents of Indian villages in the southern highlands in the eighteenth century were *forasteros*, or outsiders, migrants to the community from other regions (Cornblit, 1970:26–27). Since access to land depended upon membership in the community by birth, these people had only two avenues open to them. They could become petty shopkeepers and traders. Or they could become laborers, either working as peons for European or Indian landowners, or renting land—whose produce they would have to sell in order to pay their rent—from European landholders or Indian landholders or communities.[1]

The activity of the Indian villages limited the possibilities of accumulation open to the landowner who was a member of European society. There was space for the emergence of a few wealthy landowners, whose wealth depended as much upon their relation to the colonial bureaucracy as it did upon the production of their estates. The wealthy in colonial society tended to throw the net of their activities as wide as possible, dealing not only in agriculture but in commerce and politics as well. But private landowners were in competition with the village producers who were forced to unload their produce in order to obtain money to meet their debts. Throughout the colonial period the available markets were limited, and in the eighteenth century, with the decline of Potosí, they were actually shrinking.

The remaining members of European society faded gradually into the ranks of Indian society in terms of their wealth, and probably in terms of much of their lifestyle as well. This, together with the internal differentiation of Indian society, blurred the legal differences between Indian and European, thus bringing about a reorganization of provincial society into a peasant poor and a mestizo or *cholo* commercial sector. This latter group in turn was tied directly into the system of colonial authority whose local representatives monopolized commercial activity on the provincial level. The social structure of village society in the area of Potosí in 1780, reconstructed from the data on the revolt led by Tomás Catari from the village of Macha, provides an example of this pattern. Catari, an Indian native of the village, was the leader of a faction that was in rebellion against the *curaca* of the province of Chayanta. The *curaca*, an interim appointee and friend of the *corregidor* of the province, was a mestizo. He was accused by Catari of expelling the native Indian villagers from their lands in favor of his own party, which was composed largely of mestizos and *forasteros*. It is clear from the history of the revolt that the village of Macha was by the 1780s a complex mixture of Indian and mestizo, native and outsider, whose legal racial or residential status, while providing some clues to the nature of relationships outside the village, tells us little about relative wealth or social status within the village (Lewin, 1957).

But despite the reorganization of colonial society into a system of large and small landowners, petty merchants and traders, and a growing landless labor force, both Indian and European, racial categorizations largely unrelated to that reorganization still continued to be employed. At the end of the eighteenth century, these provinces, in which Indian and European no longer defined a different relation to the means of production, were still predominantly Indian according to official records. Quispicanchis, near Cuzco, was 81.9 percent Indian in 1791; Azángaro and Puno, both parts of the region near Lake Titicaca, were respectively 94.3 percent and 88.9 percent Indian in 1791 (Kubler, 1952; Table 4–1).

What happens to this picture with political independence after 1825? Throughout the nineteenth century, until the end of the War of the Pacific in 1883, the newly organized government in Lima was largely dominated by members of the army, and the struggle over control of the capital left little

Table 4-1

Percentage of Total Population Defined as Indian in Selected Provinces, 1791–1940

Province	1791	1876	1940
Andahuaylas	41.6%	54.4%	80.1%
Azàngaro	94.3%	94.6%	95.5%
Puno	88.94%	92%	—
Quispicanchis	81.9%	78.6%	79.6%

SOURCE: Kubler, 1946; Perù, Romero, 1928:228.

space and time for any lasting integration of the highlands. There was a period of fleeting prosperity built upon the export of guano from the offshore islands, beginning in the 1840s and lasting until the War of the Pacific. But while the guano income laid the basis of the coastal elite and provided the central government in Lima with an illusion of solvency, the only impact of guano prosperity upon the highlands was the short-lived abolition of Indian tribute in 1854. Even that measure was limited, since the tribute was reinstated sporadically by later governments faced with imminent bankruptcy (Bonilla, 1974). Throughout the period, the political system, while formally centralist, was disarticulated and fragmented.

At the same time, the southern highlands found a new and more profitable market orientation to replace the lost market of Potosí. The orientation of highland production shifted from the mines of Potosí to Great Britain, to which the highlands sold raw wool from sheep, llama, and alpaca herds. The wool trade was the third export in value throughout the nineteenth century. The export curves of llama and alpaca wool, and of sheep wool, are somewhat different (see Figures 4-1 and 4-2). From 1840 to 1920, sheep wool exports remained relatively constant, though there were cycles of expansion and contraction. Save for a slump during the period from about 1845 to 1855,

Figure 4.1   Export of Sheep Wool by Units of 100,000 Pounds, 1840–1919.

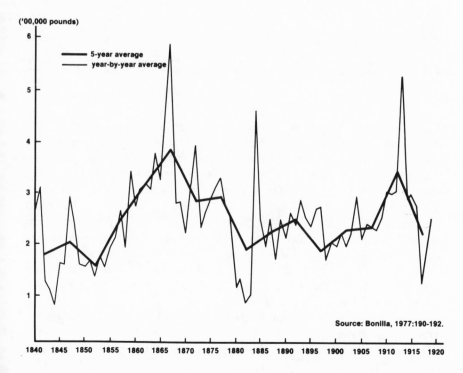

Source: Bonilla, 1977:190-192.

Figure 4.2   Export of Llama and Alpaca Wool by Units of 100,000 Pounds, 1840–1919.

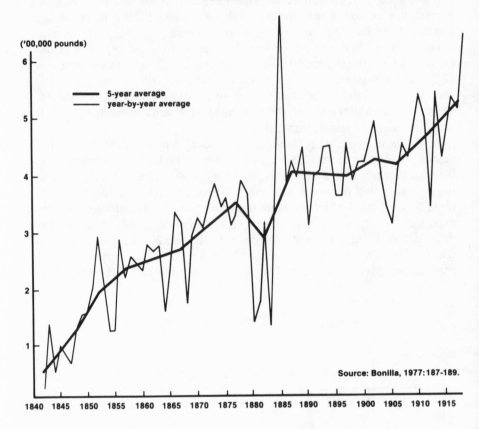

sheep wool exports rose until the late 1860s, then went into a period of sharp decline until 1880 and remained basically at that level, fluctuating between about 1,800,000 and 2,500,000 pounds per year until 1920. Exports of llama and alpaca wool, on the other hand, rose fairly steadily throughout the period from 1840 to 1920, save for a sharp slump between 1875 and 1885, undoubtedly due to the dislocations during and immediately after the War of the Pacific (1879–1883). Another characteristic of both sheep wool and llama and alpaca wool exports is the sharp yearly variation in export volumes. The curve based upon five-year average exports evens out a pattern of continual oscillation, in which exports can vary in volume by as much as five million pounds from one year to the next. Such sharp variations, whatever their cause, probably worked in the long run against producers working close to the margin, for they would find it difficult to absorb the loss of income in one year in expectation of a better year to come.

What was the impact upon the social system of the southern highlands following the change to raw wool and the direct connection with Great Britain? It is difficult to evaluate the impact of the beginning of the wool trade since the only data available on local-level landholding and income patterns during these early years comes from the province of Quispicanchis, in the Cuzco region, which was not incorporated into the wool trade on a large scale until later in the century. Wool exports in the years immediately following political independence were drawn largely from the western part of the highlands, around Ayacucho, Arequipa, and Tacna.[2] It might be noted, however, that the growing incorporation of more distant areas of the southern highlands into the wool trade seems to have had little effect upon the volume of sheep wool exports, though it undoubtedly contributed to the steadily rising export of llama and alpaca wools. This may reflect an internal division in the type of wool produced between the western highlands and the interior region, which in turn could be part of a very different pattern of social relations of production in the highland area around Arequipa on the one hand and the Cuzco-Puno region on the other. But until more data are available, specifically on the Arequipa region and generally on the southern highlands as a whole, such speculation remains totally hypothetical.

Despite these limitations, the available data on Quispicanchis in the mid-nineteenth century provide a useful picture of the region at the beginning of its participation in the wool trade (see Table 4–2). Income does not seem to have been highly concentrated in this province in 1851. Most of the recorded income was in agriculture, which is not differentiated in the records from herding, and incomes were relatively small and evenly distributed. Outside the capital city of Oropeza, home of a few landowners with incomes exceeding 1000 pesos a year, most landowners reported incomes of from 100 to 500 pesos a year, and only 36 percent of the people fell into the lowest range, reporting an income of under 100 pesos a year (Matrícula de Castas, 1851). Incorporated Indian villlage holdings, however, are not included in these records. The distribution of income was less even in the province of Andahuaylas to the north, where 9.4 percent of the landowners reported incomes of 1000 pesos or over, while 62 percent reported incomes of under 100 pesos (Matrícula de Castas, 1841 Table 4–3). But this region, producing primarily sugar cane used for the production of alcohol, does not seem to have participated in the wool trade.

The province of Puno was a center of wool production by the latter years of the nineteenth century, and descriptive materials from that region for the period from about 1850 to 1875 paint a similar picture to that prevailing in the province of Quispicanchis. Travelers described the region as one of relatively small landholdings and Indian villages, all actively engaged in production not only for the local, but for the foreign market as well. The patterns of commercialization are consistent with a system of relatively dispersed landholding and income, in which a small group cannot absorb the wealth and resources of the rest of the population. Until around the last quarter of the nineteenth century, the wool trade was transacted in great fairs, the most

Table 4-2
Declared Taxable Income by Sector and Population: Andahuaylas, 1841

Doctrina	Church		Private Agric.		Merchants		Artisans		State	
	pesos	pop.	pesos	pop.	pesos	pop.	pesos	pop.	pesos	pop.
Andahuaylas	4,277	4	1,077	13	702	7	176	2		
Talavera (urban)	1,750	3	991	11	175	2				
Talavera (rural)			1,468	15						
San Jerónimo (urban)	2,300	3	1,457	15			176	2		
San Jerónimo (rural)			5,672	17						
Cocharas (urban)	1,050	2	3,920	42						
Cocharas (rural)			864	4						
Chincheros (urban)	1,150	1	4,132	49			176	2		
Chincheros (rural)			1,820	16			88	1		
Orcobamba (urban)	1,200	1	2,060	46			176	2		
Orcobamba (rural)			5,608	30			88	1		
Onqoy (urban)	1,200	1	2,112	24						
Onqoy (rural)			6,884	17						
Cachi (urban)	800	1								
Cachi (rural)			550	5						
Huancaray	1,300	1	1,576	15	100	1				
Huayana	800	1	125	1			225	2		
Pampachiri	1,900	1								
Huancarama (urban)	2,100	1	2,760	25	276	3				
Huancarama (rural)			6,254	20			440	5		
Total	19,827	20	51,510	365	1,253	14	1,545	17		

SOURCE: Matrícula de Castas, 1841.

Table 4-3

Declared Taxable Income by Sector and Population: Quispicanchis, 1851

Parish	Church		Private Agric.		Merchants		Artisans		State	
	pesos	pop.	pesos	pop.	pesos	pop.	pesos	pop.	pesos	pop.
Oropeza	1240	3	11,225	38					100	1
Andahuaylas	700	2	3,083	16	100	1				
Huaro	1700	6	4,080	20	270	3				
Mosocllacta			250	3						
Pomacanchi	1000	2	902	8	1400	15	550	6		
Sangarará	1300	3	2,455	19	460	5				
Acomayo	1875	7	1,640	19	336	4				
Papres	650	2	1,119	12	88	1	100	1		
Rondocán	450	3	804	11						
Ocongate	550	2	3,500	4						
Marcapata	550	1	300	3	760	8	100	1		
Quiquijana	1225	4	3,549	25	1870	18	100	1		
Total	11240	35	32,907	178	5284	55	750	8	100	1

SOURCE: Matricula de Castas, 1851.

important of which was held yearly in the town of Vilques, now a tiny village near Lake Titicaca. The permanent population of the town was only a few hundred people, but during the yearly fair thousands of people gathered to exchange mules from Tucumán in northwestern Argentina, *aguardiente* and cane alcohol from the Peruvian coast, and imported European goods, for raw wool. Traders from Argentina, Bolivia, Chile, Great Britain, and other European countries, as well as from Peru, met in this far-away village to haggle over prices and exchange products. Further, communications were limited. Travelers emphasized the lack of mail service and the difficulties of communication (Von Tschudi, 1966; Squier, 1877:376; Romero, 1928:317–319). Under these circumstances knowledge of the local market situation, essential to a merchant seeking to gain the greatest profit, could not be obtained at a distance. Merchants, whether from Bolivia or from Great Britain, had to be on the spot.

In these circumstances a small group of private landowners could not monopolize the trade. Face-to-face contact between merchant and local producer was the rule, and transactions across the market in the fairs set prices. Nor could the large landowner gain an advantage by producing more efficiently, lowering the unit cost of his wool. The technology of production in the haciendas was essentially like that in small farms and villages. Lands were not enclosed; pastures were grazed by the herds of hacendados and Indian villagers alike, and the shepherds attached to the haciendas maintained their own flocks as well (Piel, 1967:391–394; Orlove, 1976). The only advantage held by the provincial elite was its monopoly of local office, which permitted some manipulation of commercial privileges, land claims, and labor obligations. But without a relatively strong central government in Lima and the support of police or military force, even this advantage meant relatively little. Throughout the nineteenth century the control of the central government by any one faction, even within the military, was not strong enough to provide the basis for a political monopoly of any real duration or profit. During this period, I suspect, competition in the market, among both wool producers and purchasers, was the most open of any period before or later. Under these conditions the British merchants, with the capital of their firms behind them, could probably gain an advantage, provided they kept in close touch with local conditions. But the local hacendados, in a competitive market in which they did not control production, did not do so well.

By 1876, the date of the first national census, conditions do not seem to have changed very much. The number of haciendas had grown somewhat, but throughout the region directly involved in the wool trade, the majority of the population lived in dispersed clusters of households defined in the census as *caseríos*, which were neither legally recognized towns nor haciendas. In Azángaro 67 percent of the population lived in 152 *caseríos*; in Puno 68 percent of the population was distributed among 124 of these settlements, which averaged from 200 to 300 people apiece. There were 184 haciendas in Azángaro in 1876, which together accounted for only 25 percent of the total

Table 4-4

Population Distribution by Site Type, Selected Provinces, 1876

Province	Site type	Number of sites	Percent of population	Average size
Andahuaylas	Villa	1	4.9%	2388
Pop=48,769	Pueblo	20	34.5	842
	Aldeia	7	5.5	322
	Caserío	100	35.5	172.9
	Hacienda	116	20.5	86.2
Quispicanchis	Villa	—	—	—
Pop=20,371	Pueblo	8	31.8%	810.8
	Aldeia	2	8.7	889.5
	Caserío	48	36.8	156.2
	Hacienda	73	22.6	63.1
Azángaro	Villa	—	—	—
Pop=45,252	Pueblo	13	7.3%	253.8
	Caserío	152	67.8	201.8
	Hacienda	184	24.9	61.3
Puno	Ciudad	2	6. %	1690.5
Pop=56,018	Villa	—	—	—
	Pueblo	13	5.5	238.8
	Caserío	124	68.4	309
	Hacienda	237	20	47.3

SOURCE: Perú, 1898.

population. There were 237 in Puno, which accounted for only 20 percent of the population (Perú, 1898; Table 4–4). As might be expected, the proportion of the population defined as "Indian" in the census changed little from the earlier period. In Quispicanchis the proportion of "Indians" fell from 79.6 percent in 1791 to 78.6 percent in 1876, hardly a significant decline. In Puno and Azángaro it also remained about the same (Romero, 1928; Kubler, 1952).

The structural transformation of the area from a region of relatively small landholdings, with the majority of the rural population living outside of the haciendas, took place later. These changes, in my opinion, can be more directly linked to political than to economic factors. The War of the Pacific, ending in 1883, devastated much of the highland territory. Reconstruction was linked to the rise of the coastal elite, which finally took control of the political machinery of the national state in 1895. Civilian governments provided means of both market communication and of repression, both essential elements in the rise of a hacendado elite. The railroad line linking Arequipa with Cuzco was completed in 1876 under an earlier civilian government, which disintegrated in the War of the Pacific. It was extended to Ayaviri, in Puno, around 1897. During the second decade of the twentieth century the road network was enormously expanded. The government of Augusto Leguía in particular laid heavy emphasis upon road construction. By the 1920s there was regular truck service between Ayaviri and Yauri, and primitive but serviceable roads criss-crossed the southern highlands. By 1926 the department of Puno boasted 1,633 kilometers of roads (Romero, 1928:472–483, 536–537).

By the early years of the twentieth century the highland fairs at which wool was traded had become largely a thing of the past. The market at Vilques had all but disappeared. Some wool was sold at weekly markets in the villages of Yauri, Pichigua, Accocunca, Tocroyoc, and elsewhere, mostly by small peasants and members of Indian communities, but most of the wool was sent directly to the railway stations at Ayaviri, Santa Rosa, Chuquibambilla, and Sicuani (Romero, 1928:317, 499–500; Orlove, 1976:7). According to a contemporary observer, the fairs were overcome and replaced by the expansion of transport facilities: the railroad, the steamship line, and particularly the road system (Romero, 1928:499). Foreign firms, rather than sending representatives to local fairs, established branch houses in provincial capitals. By 1915 several foreign firms, primarily Italian and British, had established wholesale houses in Puno, Juliaca, Sicuani, and Cuzco, and a branch of the Bank of Peru and London had been established in Puno (Romero, 1928:499). These new centers permitted the construction of an alliance between the foreign exporters and those groups within the hacendado elite that could gain control of political offices in the regional capitals. Repressive mechanisms were also elaborated, primarily through the foundation of the Guardia Civil, or rural police, established in 1922 (Orlove, 1976:8).

With the transformation of patterns of communication and the new advantages offered by participation in the political system, the local provincial elite had new leverage. Between 1876 and 1915 the number of haciendas in the southern highlands grew dramatically. In Puno the number of haciendas grew from 237 in 1876 to 373 in 1915. In Azángaro the number rose from 184 in 1876 to 611 in 1915. In the department of Puno as a whole there were 705 haciendas in 1876 and 3,219 in 1915 (Romero, 1928: 426). Unless existing estates underwent an extreme process of fragmentation during the last decades of the nineteenth century, these figures suggest considerable concentration of landholding. Data are not currently available on the distribution of landholding in the 1920s, but a comparison of data on the region of Puno in 1958 with the material presented earlier on the southern highlands in the mid-nineteenth century shows an extreme concentration of landholding from the earlier period. In 1958, 79.4 percent of the population of the department of Puno was involved in agriculture. Of that total only about .8 percent were classified as hacendados, and only 1.5 percent of the persons engaged in agriculture held sufficient land to maintain themselves without outside labor. Of those engaged in agriculture, 23.8 percent were either agricultural workers or peons resident on estates, while 74.7 percent of that population were *minifundistas*, people who owned tiny plots too small to maintain themselves by that means alone (Dew, 1969:63). The picture was undoubtedly not so extreme in the 1920s, but I suggest that the process had gotten underway by that time.

The concentration of land that took place in the last years of the nineteenth century was not accompanied by any significant change in the volume of wool exports. Llama and alpaca wool exports rose steadily throughout the period between 1840 and 1920, while sheep wool exports remained relatively stable. The landowners used political factors to appropriate a growing share of the income produced by the wool trade. Through their control of provincial political offices, a small group of landowners used the road-building program to connect their estates to the major regional centers, isolating district capitals and traditional villages (Orlove, 1976:9). Through their alliance with the Guardia Civil, they appropriated land by jailing peasants or community members for nonpayment of fake debts or by falsifying records of land sales. The concentration of land did not lead to increased production; it led to the concentration of that same income in fewer hands.

Now what does this process mean for the evaluation of class structures and alliances? The rise of the great estate and its control of commercialization meant the gradual constriction and elimination of the middle groups: the trader, the smaller landholder, and so on. The process is never absolutely complete, but the direction of change is clear. And it is also clear that groups that were being squeezed—at least the village peasantry—resisted the process. The pattern of revolts in the southern highlands is only beginning to be studied, but just a selected list of risings indicates the extent of the conflict. The first great rising was in 1866, in Huancané, and another followed the next year in Chucuito. Between 1880 and 1905 there were at least four risings; between 1910 and 1925 there were eighteen more recorded (Piel, 1967:380). The immediate cause of risings was usually a new and onerous exaction, such as a labor levy or the imposition of a head tax. But the revolts were also a response to the pressures squeezing the small landholders and lower groups of the provincial towns. The process of land concentration affected the entire structure of rural society. Smaller landowners and village members were reduced to the status of landless or semilandless laborers. The holdings of corporate villages were squeezed as the haciendas appropriated their lands. The provincial small towns and the petty commercial and service groups linked to the earlier patterns of wool commercialization and export were also affected. The concentration of land in the southern highlands meant not only the elimination of smaller landholders but also the decline of the local town as markets became a matter of direct transactions between the larger hacendados and foreign export houses.

The process described above constitutes the second major transformation of the southern highlands, which was at its most intense during the period from about 1910 to 1940. During this period a regional elite that based its power primarily upon its access to commercial and repressive forces outside the region consolidated its holdings at the expense of not only the Indian villagers but also of the local village and small town elite groups, whose wealth and power were built upon a monopoly of local agricultural and mercantile activities combined. The new provincial elite was linked to the merchant groups of larger provincial and regional centers such as Cuzco and Sicuani, and to the political authorities. Through these contacts the new elite obtained market access as well as the ability to call upon the Guardia Civil to support their bids for land appropriation and commercial monopolies.

In our evaluations of the local revolts in the southern highlands during the period from 1880 to the 1920s, then, we must look not only at the reaction of a long-oppressed peasantry against the hacendado elite. In these rebellions there were undoubtedly many among the rebels at the margin of existence. But there were others who were not only relatively well-to-do but familiar with the laws, political structures, and customs of the larger society. They included members of the village elite, owners of considerable land with aspirations to take over or maintain a share in petty commerce. They included members of urban society. And increasingly, in the larger urban centers of the highlands such as Puno and Cuzco, alliances were formed with intellectuals and local politicians who began to articulate and press demands for land reform. Such demands accompanied the process of land concentration and permitted politicians to build a position for themselves on the basis of championing not a group that was yet to emerge, but one that still existed and was being pushed to the wall.

The control of the local hacendados, on the other hand, depended essentially upon the support of the political forces in Lima. Again, their control was political, not economic. The modernization of their estates was difficult and largely incomplete. It required investment in fencing materials, breeding animals, and other equipment necessary to upgrade their herds and increase the production of wool per animal. And even those few who had or could borrow the necessary cash found it difficult to carry out the other actions that were part of that process of modernization: the expulsion of members of communities from frontier lands, the elimination of much of the resident population from the estates, the exclusion of the grazing animals owned by the shepherds who cared for hacienda herds. The efforts of the hacendados to transform the existing relations of production brought immediate protest, which was crushed only through the hacendado's access to the brute force of the national government.

Under these circumstances the power of the great estate, while real and brutal, was essentially fragile. It depended not upon any real economic advantage in terms of either technology or scale but rather upon the total support of the national government in Lima. The hacendado was not wrong in viewing as a threat any new action, any change—whether it was the establishment of a school or the election of a local political official—that was not the result of his dictation. Only with a total monopoly of power could the hacendado retain control and maintain his excessive share of the wealth produced in the region. And according to currently available data, the provincial landowning elite achieved that total control in the southern highlands only for a relatively short period of time—in historical terms, at any rate—during the first half of the twentieth century. Since its power was dependent not upon its own efforts but upon outside support, the hacendados tended to see any challenge, no matter how limited it appeared, as a threat to the entire structure. And they were essentially right. Their wealth depended upon their monopoly of political power, and that in turn depended upon the willingness of the forces in Lima to provide them with the support of the civil guard and, when necessary, the army. Without that alliance they could not long survive.

Notes

1. See, for example, Archivo Nacional del Perú, Sección Histórica, Derecho Indígena, Cuadernos 438 and 491; Archivo Nacional del Perú, Sección Histórica, Tierras de Comunidades, Legajo 2, Cuaderno 16; Legajo 5, Cuadernos 42 and 44.

2. Benjamin Orlove, personal communication.

CHAPTER 5

Colonos on Hacienda Picotani

Laura Maltby

The power structure of the Peruvian hacienda system has been the subject of a great deal of writing. The purpose of much of this has been to show the oppression suffered by the hacienda workers, who are known as colonos. Leading Peruvianists have formulated the "baseless triangle" model to explain traditional rural society (Cotler, 1969). This model presents rural society as fragmented into a number of units, each of which constitutes a closed system with one dominant figure and numerous subordinates completely dependent on him. These dependents have relations neither among themselves nor with members of society at large. All communication between the dependents and the outside world is filtered through the dominant figure. In the case of the hacienda, the hacendado (hacienda owner) is the dominant figure who exerts complete control over his dependents, the colonos. Other authority figures with whom the colonos come into contact, such as local government officials, lawyers, and priests, act in conjunction with the hacendado in his domination of the colonos.

It is undeniably true that the hacienda system is based on inequality and that there are haciendas which form closed social systems, controlled by the hacendado. There, in exchange for working on the hacienda fields as many days as the hacendado considers necessary and performing a multitude of other services required by the hacienda, the colonos receive small plots of the poorest land, no wages, and frequent beatings. The colonos are not free to leave the hacienda nor even to dispose of the meager products of their parcels of land as they choose. The hacendado effectively dominates every aspect of the colonos' lives.

However, within the hacienda system, there are significant variations in the duties which the colonos are required to perform and in the benefits which they receive in return. The baseless triangle model is constructed with data taken from the agricultural haciendas. Peruvian haciendas can be grouped into three broad categories: agricultural, pastoral, and mixed. The nature of the economic activities of the pastoral hacienda vary significantly from those of the agricultural hacienda, with the mixed falling between the two extremes. On the agricultural haciendas there is relatively intensive use of land. The colonos are required to perform agricultural labor on specific plots of land over extended periods of time. In return for their services they are given a plot of land for their own use. The colonos live concentrated in villagelike settlements called *caserios*. In contrast, on a livestock hacienda, land use is extensive rather than intensive. The main duty of the colonos is to watch over the grazing animals. Additional tasks are generally limited to two relatively brief periods a year, one for the shearing and another for the slaughter of the hacienda animals. The colonos gather together in the *caserio* at these times and spend the rest of the year scattered throughout the hacienda lands. The physical distance between the colonos' huts (*cabañas*) makes communication among the colonos extremely difficult and severely limits opportunities for mutual aid. However, it also makes effective control of the colonos by the hacendado difficult and complete domination next to impossible. Thus, while the colonos of an agricultural hacienda are concentrated and fixed in space, the colonos of a pastoral hacienda are scattered and mobile. A close look at one livestock hacienda will show the severe limitations which this implies for the baseless triangle model with its characterization of the colonos as a completely powerless group.

Picotani was one of the largest haciendas in the department of Puno.[1] The origins of Picotani are unclear. Most of the haciendas in this region were granted in the colonial era, and the existence of a colonial chapel at Picotani indicates that it fits this pattern. It was not until late in the nineteenth century that these haciendas began to be exploited as economic enterprises. At this time three smaller properties, Picotani, Toma, and Cambría, were incorporated into one economic unit. In 1932 the hacienda was incorporated as the Sociedad Ganadera Picotani, Sociedad Anónima.[2] This, however, signified no fundamental changes in operation or organization of the hacienda. Picotani remained a hacienda until 1969, when the owning family voluntarily turned it over to the Agrarian Reform. It was then reorganized as a SAIS cooperative (Sociedad Agrícola de Interés Social) and currently retains this form.

Located in the province of Azángaro, district of Muñani, the hacienda Picotani extended over fifty-four thousand hectares of the mountainous region, or *cordillera*, which separates the flat lands of the Lake Titicaca basin from the tropical rain forest, or *selva*, to the north. Land at this altitude (4,400 to 5,000 meters above sea level) offers very limited possibilities for economic exploitation because of the extremely harsh climate and the irregular topography. It is completely unsuitable for agriculture. Not even the potato, the staple crop in most of the Peruvian highlands, will grow (La Barre, 1948). Eighty percent of Picotani's lands were classified as third-class pasturage and the remaining twenty percent as wasteland (Compañía Nacional de Recaudación, 1924). Picotani was then, of necessity, dedicated strictly to the raising of sheep and native cameloids, principally alpacas.

The case of Picotani clearly shows the problems the hacendados must have had in controlling their work forces. Although the hacienda covered fifty-four thousand hectares, in the mid-1920s, the maximum number of families employed as colonos was eighty. The earlier property divisions of Picotani, Toma, and Cambría continued as semiindependent administrative units, which alleviated the difficulties of controlling such a dispersed population. The administrator, the highest-ranking employee who spent all his time on the hacienda, was responsible for the operation of the whole unit. However, he spent most of his time in the main offices, located in the *caserio* of Picotani. (In the late 1940s the offices were moved to Cambría, located at a lower altitude where the climate is less severe). His direct subordinates, the *mayordomos*, one for Toma and one for Cambría, were largely responsible for those two sections of the hacienda. The *mayordomos*, like the administrator, were hired by the hacienda representative in Arequipa and sent to Picotani. Communication among the three *caserios* was difficult enough, as it was more than twenty kilometers from Picotani to either of the other administrative centers. Only in the late 1940s was a telephone system installed to facilitate communication among the *caserios* as part of a larger attempt to modernize the hacienda.

However, even within the three subdivisions, supervision of the work was not easy. Each *caserio* had generally three *rodeantes* or overseers, chosen from among the ranks of the colonos. Since these men travelled on horseback over a limited but still large area, supervising and occasionally helping with the work, their contact with the *caserio*, as well as with individual colonos, was sporadic.

The problem of control existed on a higher level as well. Following the pattern of large haciendas in the sierra, Picotani was owned by an absentee landlord. The owning family, again not untypically, had interests in a wide variety of economic enterprises, of which Picotani was not the most important. Thus visits to the hacienda by some member of the family were brief and usually took place only once a year. The main responsibility for the administration of the hacienda was delegated to the *representante*, the direct representative of the owner. However, the representative had his office in Arequipa, over three hundred kilometers from Picotani. Although correspondence between the representative and the administrator, his direct subordinate on the hacienda, was quite regular, the difficulty of effective control or supervision of the actual workings of the hacienda is obvious.

Within this strict hierarchy, it was the colonos who formed the backbone of the hacienda's labor force. The primary task of each colono was the pasturing of his *cargo*, the sheep, llamas, or alpacas assigned to his care by the administrator. He was also required to perform certain duties on the hacienda, such as the annual shearing and slaughter of the animals belonging to Picotani. Theoretically, each colono was required to put in only forty days a year in these tasks. Although the administrator almost certainly did not feel bound by this limit, in fact the number of days spent in the service of the hacienda did not significantly exceed this number, as there were relatively few tasks to be performed.

There were additional services required of the colono, such as *pongueaje* and *alquila*. *Pongueaje* was personal service in the house of the administrator. There was only one *pongo* at a time at Picotani, so that the task was not particularly burdensome when shared among the various families of colonos. *Alquila* was the transport of the products of the hacienda to Pucará, the nearest railroad station, and of foodstuffs and other necessities of the hacienda from Pucará to Picotani. This trip was made once a year by each able-bodied man. The actual carrying was done by llamas, the colono merely being in charge of the llama train. Nevertheless, this obligation was seen as a real hardship by the colonos because of the long duration of the trip, eight days each way.

These were the only major responsibilities of Picotani's colonos. On an agricultural or mixed hacienda, the colonos would have been required to perform agricultural labor. On such haciendas not only would the total demand for manpower be higher, but the seasonality of the demand made it more burdensome. Planting and harvesting of crops must be performed at a precise time, so that the colonos are required to work in the hacienda fields at the very time when their own fields need attention. Timing is less vital for activities such as the shearing or slaughter of animals. Thus, the economic nature of the livestock hacienda limits the potential for exploitation of the colonos.

The colonos of Picotani received remuneration of various kinds in return for their services. The most important of these was the right to graze their own livestock on hacienda land. The amount of livestock owned by the colonos was startlingly high. Very rare was the colono without sheep, llamas, and in lesser quantity, alpacas of his own. In 1929 the forty-nine colonos owned a total of 11,648 sheep (one family alone owned 2,203) and 7,741 llamas and alpacas (the largest flock numbering 652). By 1943 the number of alpacas and llamas in the possession of the hacienda's fifty-nine colonos had almost doubled, now numbering 14,722, while the number of sheep had declined only slightly to 9,971. The colonos also owned a much smaller number of horses, cows, and burros. The hacienda placed no restrictions on the number of animals which the colonos were entitled to have in their possession, despite frequent complaints of overgrazing.

These animals provided not only food and clothing for their owners but also existed as a potential source of considerable quantities of wool to be sold in the markets or to merchants in neighboring towns. A major market for wool was Crucero, one of the nearest towns and once capital of the province of Carabaya. Unfortunately, almost nothing is known about the marketing of wool or of meat products, which were possibly sold. The marketing was clearly not conducted through the hacienda, as there is no mention of it in the hacienda papers.[3] The colonos had, therefore, a sizable potential income completely independent of the hacienda. If, as some writers have suggested, they did not shear their own flocks regularly, it may have been that they had no regular need for a cash income or that they preferred to leave the wool on the animals when market prices were low.

A second benefit received by the colonos was a monthly salary, which remained relatively constant over the years. The average salary rose between 1909 and 1924 from four to almost seven *soles* a month. The average salary reached a peak of 9.40 *soles* in 1927, then sank to just above six *soles* in 1933, where it remained for more than a decade. In 1945 salaries were more than tripled across the board. However, this was the direct result of a decision to raise the price that the colonos paid for their monthly food allotments, called *avíos*. The prices they paid for potatoes, corn, barley, and sugar, which the hacienda made available to them, had remained constant since 1924, despite the constantly rising cost of these products. The decision was made to give the colonos their *avíos* at cost, which had approximately tripled, meaning that the increases in salary were necessary to keep their income on the same level as it had been previously. There was a second significant increase in wages in 1948, which brought the average salary up to thirty-seven *soles*. This was accompanied by only a slight increase in the price of *avíos*, and thus constituted a real increase in income.

A formula for determining salaries, laid down by the administrator in 1925, stated that the hacienda paid twenty *centavos* a day for the grazing of ordinary sheep and forty *centavos* for the grazing of the finer animals. A second principle stated that the colonos were paid two *centavos* a month for each sheep in their flocks. However, neither of these guidelines was ever followed. The colonos were not all paid the same wage, but those receiving higher wages were responsible neither for the finer sheep nor for larger flocks. There seems to have been no economic basis for the wage differential. It does, however, reflect the fact that even within the lowest segment of hacienda society all were not treated equally.

A further benefit to the colonos were the aforementioned *avíos*. This monthly food allotment was of particular importance in an area of severely limited agricultural productivity. The *avíos*, generally imported from the city of Cuzco, were resold to the colonos at the purchase price or below it, making no adjustment for transportation costs. Other benefits included free food during the time the colonos were performing such duties as shearing or serving as *pongos*, and a hut to live in. The hacienda also provided free medical care for all of its employees. There were several outbreaks of typhus in the area, and each time either a doctor or a *sanitario*, a health worker, was sent to the hacienda from Puno, Juliaca, Arequipa, or even Cuzco. Further, when necessary, employees, including the colonos, were taken to hospitals in Juliaca or Arequipa.

One additional responsibility which the hacienda was much less effective in fulfilling was its duty, in the words of one colono, "*de proteger a los colonos.*"[4] The hacienda could not seem to prevent the theft of the colonos' livestock, harassment of the *alquilas*, or the arrest of colonos as well as higher-placed employees by bands sent into the hacienda by the local authorities. But if the hacienda could not keep these abuses from occurring, the administration did accept responsibility for righting the wrong, occasionally taking matters into its own hands or, more frequently, choosing to deal through established legal channels.

The hacienda also gave the colonos a legal umbrella while they were away from the hacienda. Indians from the neighboring communities, without a hacendado to protect them, lacked this protection. In 1930, for example, a band of twenty-eight strange Indians passed by Picotani. They purported to have been sent by their hacendado from Azángaro to Huacchani, but as they had no papers to back up their statements, they were detained overnight in Picotani until their story could be confirmed. If they had not been hacienda Indians, they would almost certainly have been turned over to the local authorities. *Colonos* who suffered abuses always had recourse to their hacendado, whereas *comuneros* could only go to local authorities who might or might not pay them heed.

There are a number of factors which are assumed to have bound colonos to the haciendas. Most important was the lack of viable alternatives. However, it has been shown that the colonos of Picotani had an independent source of sustenance in their large herds. Debts to the hacienda have been presented as being restricting factors on the mobility of the colonos, but this was not the case in Picotani. Almost none of the colonos there were in debt, both because they had independent access to money and because the hacienda had little opportunity to become the creditor of its colonos. Picotani supplied neither seeds nor landworking tools. Since primary foodstuffs were distributed through the *avíos*, there was no hacienda store. Furthermore, the sale of alcohol, a prime source of credit in other haciendas, was strictly forbidden in Picotani after 1924, although it was common practice under an earlier owner.[5] The only debts incurred by the colonos were for *fallas*—missing livestock— but the hacienda was generally reimbursed immediately for these losses, either with sheep belonging to the colono or in cash.

Without legal obstacles to mobility and with relative financial independence from the hacienda, the colonos could, and frequently did, leave Picotani. It was a fairly common practice to go from one hacienda to another in search of the best working conditions. The turnover in colonos was quite significant. New names constantly appear on the payroll and the old names disappear, sometimes permanently and sometimes only temporarily. Hacendados did try in some cases to prevent their colonos from moving to another hacienda by refusing to accept the return of the flocks in the colonos' care. However, a colono would often leave despite this restriction, taking the flock along with him to his new place of work. It was then the responsibility of the new employer to persuade the former employer to accept the return of the flock. Meanwhile, the colono would be pasturing three flocks, those of the two hacendados as well as his own.[6]

The mobility enjoyed by the colonos threatened to eliminate the hacienda's entire labor force. The administrators were quite conscious of this possibility, as they complained almost constantly of a labor shortage. The strongly feared possibility that the colonos would desert the hacienda en masse kept the administration from acting without regard for the colonos. Any proposed changes in work procedures were carefully considered in order to determine the probable reaction of the colonos. One change in the organization of the hacienda which had been regarded as essential years before it was put into effect was the separation of the colonos' flocks from the flocks belonging to the hacienda. The castration of the colonos' rams was another proposed alternative. As early as 1930, a visiting agrarian engineer hired as a consultant by Picotani signalled the absolute necessity for designating separate grazing areas for the colonos' sheep, as any attempt to improve the quality of the hacienda sheep was futile as long as the sheep belonging to the colonos, usually of rather degenerate stock, grazed side by side with those belonging to the hacienda. Such an experiment was put into effect with one family of colonos in order to determine what the general reaction would be. Within a month the project was abandoned, as various colonos were threatening to leave the hacienda if the practice were made general. Their objection may have been grounded on the fact that watching animals in two separate grazing areas required additional manpower.

The matter was not brought up again until 1937, when permission was requested to castrate the sheep of the colonos and to designate a special flock of rams selected for breeding purposes which would be available to the colonos upon request. Permission was denied on the grounds that it was incorrect to deal with the colonos in such an arbitrary fashion. Not until 1943 was the castration actually carried out. Even then the administrator was careful to explain to the colonos that the measure was in their best interest. Such was the case, however, only as long as the colonos remained on the hacienda. The castration imposed new limitations on the colonos' mobility by making them dependent on the hacienda's stud rams.

There were other examples of actions taken to appease the colonos. In 1936 a gratuity was granted to the *alquilas* who transported the wool, in addition to their wage. One of the factors taken into consideration in the decision to buy the first truck for the hacienda was the discontent caused by the *alquila*, although several years later *alquilas* were still transporting considerable quantities of wool. The decision was also made to give an ounce of coca for each day's shearing in order to keep the colonos content and to provide an incentive to do a better job.

Relations between the colonos and the administration were not, however, free from conflict. The primary sources of discontent among the colonos were the *alquila* and disputed *fallas*. Aside from the burdensome nature of the *alquila* and the length of time it demanded, the colonos also suffered frequent harassment along the road either at the hands of hacendados whose lands they had to cross or of other Indians. Disputes frequently arose over *fallas* when the hacienda confiscated sheep belonging to the colono as payment for fallas which the latter denied. Such complaints were reported to the absentee hacendado or his representative either by the administrator or by the colono himself through letters obviously written by intermediaries.

At one point, in the years between 1925 and 1928, the situation within the hacienda reached a crisis. Frequent complaints of abuse by the hacienda employees began to be made almost immediately after a German took over the position of administrator. A number of colonos wrote letters to the hacendado complaining about the conduct of the *mayordomos*, who treated them, according to one letter written by a colono, with "kicks and sticks and punches," and of the *rodeantes* who sexually abused the colonos' wives, expropriated their livestock without reason, and made threats on their lives. At first the only complaint against the administrator was that he did not speak Quechua and that therefore the colonos could not make him understand their grievances. But later the administrator himself began to be singled out as the major cause of the colonos' discontent.

A letter signed by a number of colonos on September 28, 1927, stated that they had been subjected to abuse by the administrator and other hacienda employees for some time. The administrator was requiring additional labor, beating the colonos with sticks, making unjust charges of *fallas*, and burdening them with much larger flocks than was customary. Their letter received immediate response from a relative of the hacendado who was visiting Picotani, as the colonos had declared themselves ready to take extreme measures if necessary. The following letter was written to the administrator, warning him of the critical nature of the situation.

> You must know, as I believe you will have heard talk there, what Indian uprisings are. In these, the colonos of a hacienda, with the help of those of neighboring haciendas, commit enormous offenses and crimes. Very close to there [Picotani] in a neighboring hacienda, it was a very few years ago that the Indians, upset with the abuses of the *patrón*, rose up and attacked the *caserío* and, dedicating themselves to pillage, assassinated the owner. This is an occurrence which is repeated constantly in the *sierra*, and is owed exclusively to the abuse of the Indians who, as is natural, have rights and are part of humanity.
>
> Treating these helpless creatures with sticks is the worst method which one can use. The Indians are vengeful and their vengeance always takes a cowardly form.
>
> In Picotani the matter is more serious since the colonos formerly enjoyed consideration and good treatment, and if this has disappeared, the annoyance of the victims and their desire for vengeance will have to be greater. It is not out of the question that in the moment least expected an uprising will occur, and that you will be the first victim.
>
> I know that one of the colonos had bought a rifle and that you took it from him. This is the best evidence that you have that the colonos are plotting against you and for that reason it is necessary, from the moment you receive this letter, that you find the way to change those radical, extreme measures of continual punishments for prudent measures which defend the interests of the hacienda and at the same time are not abusive of the Indians.
>
> (A new *mayordomo*, a former employee of Picotani, is being sent to help you out.)
>
> One of the principal points with which you must concern yourself is to obtain more colonos in order to make the distribution of huts in the customary

proportion, so that each one can care for and be responsible for the livestock in his care without having an excess of work.

The administrator, in his reply to the above letter, did not deny hitting the colonos. Instead, he defended his behavior on the grounds that such treatment was necessary in order to get the colonos to obey his orders. Neither could he deny that the colonos had larger flocks than before. The number of sheep had been increased significantly, and many colonos had left the hacienda. As a result, the size of the average flock had risen from 504 in 1925 to 806 in 1926, and to 1013 in 1927. This would have represented a burdensome increase in the duties of the remaining colonos.

The situation came to a head in 1928, when it was discovered that the colonos were plotting to attack the *caserío*. The colonos and the hacendado alike agreed on the necessity of firing the administrator. The increase in the number of sheep concerned both parties, the colonos because of the increase in their work load, and the hacendado because it was impossible for the colonos to take proper care of such large flocks. The result was a large number of diseased animals, an increased mortality rate, and a decrease in the quality of the wool and meat being produced. The discontent of the colonos resulted in the exodus of approximately half of the total number, with the others threatening to follow them if the administrator were not fired.

The administrator was fired, the number of colonos augmented, and the size of the flocks drastically reduced. In seven months' time, the average flock was down to 861, and by 1930 it was back to a customary level of 697. From this time on, the size of the flocks never sank below 663, but never again was their such a drastic fluctuation. This incident, in sum, illustrates not only the benevolent attitude taken by the hacienda owners toward the workers but also a very real mechanism internal to the livestock hacienda whereby colonos could and did leave the hacienda when severely mistreated. Aside from this near confrontation, relations between administration and colonos were unmarred by violence. Despite various uprisings in the area in 1924 and again in 1929–30, life at Picotani remained calm.

Such was the state of relations within the hacienda. Just as the hacendado or administrator was not the omnipotent figure within the hacienda as he is generally portrayed, neither did he dominate the colonos' relations with the world outside Picotani. Contacts with the outer world were necessary if the colonos were to eat more than meat. The haciendas did import basic foodstuffs for the workers, but there were other vital needs which Picotani either did not fulfill or which the colonos felt could be better taken care of elsewhere. As mentioned previously, the colonos had commercial dealings in Crucero and other neighboring towns in order to sell the wool and meat from their flocks. They also made occasional visits to Putina, Cuyocuyo, or Crucero to attend mass, for although the hacendado generally tried to contract a priest to spend a few days each year in Picotani to preside over the fiesta, at times the priests failed to arrive. These contacts in nearby towns would have been important in terms of the colonos' mobility, for it must have been during such visits that they learned of employment opportunities on other haciendas.

The colonos' contacts extended even farther afield than these small towns. They travelled to Pucará and later to Juliaca as *alquilas*. Although on hacienda business, they were not under supervision during these trips. Several of the colonos even took it upon themselves to travel as far as Arequipa in order to meet with the hacienda representative or lawyer. The colonos' dealings with the outside world, while limited, did take place free from domination from the hacienda.

Education was not an important link to the world outside of Picotani. The first hacienda school was not opened until 1946, at which point there was already a school in the neighboring Indian community of Chijos. In 1944, upon the insistence of the authorities of Muñani, the administrator of Picotani agreed to enroll the children of its colonos in the Chijos school, although ridiculing the idea as completely unfeasible owing to the long distances the children would have to walk. Two years later Picotani opened its own school, providing it with a teacher, furniture, and supplies, despite its claim that it was not legally required to do so.[7] However, even within the hacienda, the distances were too great for the children to walk every day. Because of the enormous size of Picotani and the scattered settlement pattern, the majority of the students lived anywhere from five to fifteen kilometers from the school. The irregular terrain made these distances even more difficult to traverse. The first year attendance was limited to fifteen pupils, and the following year the school failed to function a single day.[8]

It would seem that the duties required of the colonos were not unreasonable in terms of the benefits which they enjoyed as the result of their status on the hacienda. The administrators frequently complained about the "spoiled" colonos, who they felt had little work to do. One administrator reported that the colonos "lack discipline and do not report regularly to work.... In order to get them to work, it is necessary to send the *rodeantes* to bring them by the hand. In addition, they do not fulfill the orders given them, arguing that it is not customary to work. Here they are in error, thinking that because they are shepherds of the *cordillera* and have no fields they are not obligated to work, having become accustomed to doing as they please."

Obviously the life of the colono was not as rosy as the administrator would have had outsiders—or even the hacendado himself—believe. Yet it would appear that his situation was significantly better than that of the colono on the baseless triangle model agricultural hacienda. This is partly a result of the personal character of the hacendado of Picotani, who took his paternalistic role seriously. Actions such as providing the colonos with *avíos* below cost may have been quite unusual. But more fundamental is the basic difference between the agricultural and the pastoral hacienda. In the latter, the demand for manpower is much lower and the problems of control much more pronounced, thus decreasing the attraction of and the possibilities for exploitation.

It is frequently maintained that the colono enjoyed a more secure position than the members of the Indian communities (Dew, 1969; Saénz, 1933). While this might seem to be true in the case of Picotani, there is evidence that it was nonetheless less desirable to be a colono. Despite an almost constant labor shortage, there was no great influx of *comuneros* into the hacienda. The main source of new colonos was other haciendas. Colonos from distant haciendas were preferred, as the farther away from the hacienda, the less likelihood there was of legal disputes with the former employers.

Even though the *comuneros* did not flock to the haciendas for employment, it was impossible for the Indian communities to isolate themselves completely from the hacienda system. There were two major complaints which forced them to deal with neighboring haciendas. The first source of conflict was disputes over land ownership. Disputes between Picotani and the communities of Chuquini and Chijos concerning the ownership of a number of pieces of land raged on and off from 1928 until 1949. The conflicts all involved land which Picotani had acquired in the first decade of the century. There are numerous references to Indian properties being bought by Picotani between 1908 and 1911, but by 1924 the hacienda had apparently finished its process of expansion.

The other major cause of disputes between the hacienda and the communities was *daños*, the pasturing of livestock belonging to the Indians on land belonging to the hacienda. When *comuneros'* sheep were found grazing on land claimed by Picotani, the animals were taken into custody until payment for the *daño* was agreed upon. Since, as the hacienda employees themselves admitted, Picotani's boundaries were unclear, there was room for dispute over the ownership of the land on which the animals were grazing. There are recorded complaints by the communities concerning unjust charges for *daños* throughout the years, but they never exist in abundance. Nor was there any period during which complaints were more common than in any other period. The usual form of protest was to write to the hacendado or his representative. Large scale abuse would probably have incited stronger forms of protest. One incident, the burning of a barn, was attributed to a dispute over *daños*. It was, however, an individual act, receiving no wider support.

The absence of serious conflicts between Picotani and the neighboring communities could, then, have been the result of lack of abuses on the part of the hacienda. This is undoubtedly true to a certain extent. However, a second factor of perhaps greater importance is the sparsity of the population in the area. The opportunities for conflict were thus much fewer than in areas where the haciendas were surrounded by overpopulated communities and where the competition for land was much more crucial.

The hacienda had to deal not only with neighboring communities but with the local governmental authorities as well. In the case of Picotani, the hacendado and the authorities were not, as is generally portrayed, merely two sides of the same coin, dedicated to the promotion of the same interests. The administrators of Picotani were sharp critics of local authorities, particularly those of Muñani, the district capital, with whom they had most frequent contact. The whole town was, in the words of one administrator, "a nest of thieves, and we suspect that the *gobernador* [the executive head of the district] generally is the ringleader...[and] protector of the rest of the band. We encounter all classes of obstacles when we ask him to do justice, in the cases of robbery, etc."

Such conflicts were not limited to the authorities of Muñani. A more serious problem arose in 1943 with the judge in Azángaro, the provincial capital. Several employees of Picotani, including one of the *mayordomos*, were arrested in connection with a suspected homicide. According to one member of the owner's family, the judge had an unfounded hatred of the hacienda and was planning on causing Picotani as much harm as he could: "If we let this go by, the hacienda will become the laughing stock of all the lesser authorities of Azángaro and the whole area. I believe that the moment has come for us to do everything possible to assert ourselves.... For some time, the people of Picotani have been known as people without guts." In order to remedy the situation, he suggested making appeals to Lima, where the influence of the family was apparently greater. Nonetheless, four months later there were still three colonos in jail, and the hacienda had to make a second attempt to free them, this time working through their commercial agent in Azángaro, who was a friend of the judges and lawyers in that town.

The relationship between the hacienda and government authorities is further illustrated by a case brought against Picotani by the members of the community of Chuquini concerning the return of several parcels of land. These had been purchased by the hacienda early in the century, but the conditions of their purchase had been a source of dispute for decades. In 1947 the case was brought before the Dirección de Asuntos Indígenas (Bureau of Indian Affairs), a branch of the central government. There were apparently real grounds for argument, as some of the land was resold to Chuquini in 1917 with the boundaries unspecified in the bill of sale. The hacienda owners privately admitted ignorance of the exact boundaries of their land, but they began to use their influence to have the case decided in Picotani's favor. On a local level, the Dirección de Asuntos Indígenas in Ayaviri decided in favor of Chuquini. But the case ultimately had to be decided in Lima, where the hacendado exercised his greatest influence. In 1948 the Ministerio de Justicia y Trabajo (Ministry of Justice and Labor) issued a resolution stating that the land in question belonged to Picotani. Beyond this, no appeal was possible.

It seems, then, that at least in the case of Picotani, the stereotype of the hacendado as absolute ruler of the local area, based on his own position and reinforced by the collaboration of local authorities, did not hold true. The local officials could and frequently did oppose the hacendado, causing him considerable inconvenience. The hacendado's influence in Lima, which kept this opposition from seriously threatening Picotani's interests, was far greater than that enjoyed by the average hacienda owner. Local opposition could have been extremely prejudicial to the interests of less prominent hacendados.

Neither the system of personal relations within the hacienda Picotani nor that between the different groups on the hacienda and the outside world seems to have fit the baseless triangle model. The hacendado was not the uncontested ruler of both the hacienda and the surrounding area, strictly controlling the few contacts which the colonos might have had with outsiders. Although the hacendado or his administrator was clearly the principal authority, the power of either over the colonos was not absolute since they had the genuine option of leaving the hacienda. This freedom was made possible by the large numbers of livestock in their possession, a source of income completely independent of the hacienda. Furthermore, they had a number of alternatives once they left the hacienda, as there were opportunities for employment on other haciendas. Similarly, the colonos had dealings with the outside world, primarily with commercial agents, but also with lawyers, priests, and other professionals, which were not dominated by the hacendado. Neither was the hacendado the undisputed ruler of the local area, as the authorities often acted to the detriment of Ficotani's interests.

None of these factors, however, seriously challenged the superior position of the hacienda. Nevertheless, it is important to recognize the significant differences between the hacienda of the baseless triangle model and a pastoral hacienda such as Picotani. Conditions on the two were necessarily quite different because of their different economic functions. Although the hacienda may have been the most powerful institution, it was not able to completely dominate all other elements of traditional rural society.

Notes

1.   The information on which this chapter is based was taken primarily from papers of the hacienda Picotani, which are now located in the Archivo del Fuero Agrario in Lima. This archive contains papers from many of the haciendas which have been affected by the Agrarian Reform. It is thus an invaluable source of information on the Peruvian hacienda. This study of Picotani is one of the first to use this new resource.

The papers from Picotani are very complete for the years 1924–49 and include a few scattered documents dating farther back in the twentieth century. The papers consist of regular correspondence between the administrator or *mayordomo* and the hacienda representative in Arequipa. This correspondence was normally carried out on a weekly basis and covered a wide variety of topics—all aspects of hacienda activity, relations with neighboring haciendas and Indian communities, and anything else which touched upon the interests of Picotani. There are also folders of correspondence with the commercial agents of the hacienda, located in Azángaro, Pucará, and Juliaca. The final category of correspondence is labeled "General" and includes information concerning commercial, legal, and personal matters.

In addition to the correspondence, there exist detailed records of the economic side of the enterprise. Information concerning the number of sheep, the production of the hacienda, bookkeeping ledgers, and the like are among the types of records to be found.

Additional information was gathered during a week-long stay at Picotani in March 1973 from conversations with the employees who had worked for Picotani when it was still a hacienda (there is one employee who has worked at Picotani for thirty years). A brief interview with a member of the former owning family in Arequipa in May of the same year helped to complete the picture of the hacienda.

2.   Often these *sociedades anónimas* were formed to prevent division of a hacienda at the owner's death. The heirs all preferred to own shares of the larger and more efficient operation and did not want to divide it up. However, the hacienda continued to be run as a family enterprise. Benjamin Orlove, personal correspondence, March 17, 1975.

3.   To this day, the members of the cooperative sell the wool from their own flocks in the towns rather than to the cooperative, although the latter has offered to buy it at the price paid by the town merchants.

4.   To protect the colonos. From a 1927 letter from a colono to the hacendado.

5.   In 1939 one of the *mayordomos* began the sale of alcohol to the Indian colonos at relatively high prices. A relative of the owner reported this on his annual visit, suggesting instead that two bottles of alcohol be provided at cost as part of the *avíos*, in an attempt to prevent abuses and displeasure among the colonos. However, the *representante* answered that, although he realized that the colonos would procure alcohol elsewhere if they could not buy it on the hacienda, its sale by employees of Picotani would remain strictly prohibited.

6.   The papers from 1924–49 note five cases of colonos coming to work at Picotani still in possession of their former cargos, which involved the hacienda in disputes serious enough to require the intervention of local authorities.

7.   The Educational Reform Law of 1941 stated that any hacienda that had a *caserío* with thirty or more school-age children was obligated to provide a school. Although there were clearly more than thirty children in Picotani, they lived scattered throughout the hacienda lands rather than in a *caserío*.

8.   The problem has been resolved, not entirely satisfactorily, in the past two years by the opening of a boarding school for the children of the cooperative members.

CHAPTER 6

Landlords and Officials: The Sources of Domination in Surimana and Quehue

Benjamin S. Orlove

Introduction

Many studies of the Andean countryside treat peasant communities and haciendas as the fundamental units of agrarian society. As earlier chapters in this volume document, investigators in a number of different disciplines, including anthropology, history, sociology, and political science, have adopted this view and a set of implicit assumptions that follow from it. Both haciendas and communities are seen as clearly bounded in both spatial and social terms. They are composed of groups with specific sets of members who have exclusive rights in clearly demarcated extensions of land. Much of the literature on the Andes would lead one to believe that every parcel of land belonged to a particular community or to a particular hacienda, and that every peasant was a member of a specific community or a peon on a specific hacienda. In this view, group membership determines access to land for peasants.

One corollary of this emphasis on haciendas and communities is the belief that community members and hacienda peons are fundamentally different in terms of economic and social relations. What distinguishes them from each other is the nature of land tenure: *comuneros* reside on their own land, and peons live on the lands of the hacendado. The basis of elite domination is landed wealth: the elite are powerful because they are hacendados, and they are hacendados because they own land. Their relative monopoly of land permits them to exercise their influence over *comuneros*, as well as over hacienda peons, although in a different fashion.

This chapter[1] challenges two of these assumptions; it shows similarities as well as differences between *comuneros* and peons in their relations to elites, and it emphasizes bases of elite power other than land holding. The earlier views are disputed for two reasons: they view haciendas and communities, rather than households, as the bases of rural society, thus oversimplifying a complex set of relations between peasants and elites, and they state that local power rests only on the control of local resources. The links of local elites to wider systems, particularly national administrative agencies, are often as important a source of their power as their land ownership; these two sources may be shown to be mutually reinforcing.

This chapter compares two villages, Surimana and Quehue, and their surrounding rural areas. These small regions[2] are located in the province of Canas, department of Cuzco, in the southern Peruvian highlands. The contrast is a useful one. Since the two regions resemble one another in a number of ways, the differences between them can be isolated and examined with relative ease. There are several important similarities between them. They are located close to each other in the same sort of environment. They share a common set of ties to certain political authorities and to market systems. Each region has the same general structure: each is composed of a village and peasant population which is dependent on it. The population is composed of two social classes, the elites resident in the villages and the peasantry located almost exclusively in the countryside. This chapter will not consider in detail the effects of the 1969 Agrarian Reform since it was applied to the area in 1974, after the principal period of field work.

The chief difference between the two regions is that the village of Surimana has remained in the official status of annex (*anexo*) but Quehue became a district (*distrito*). These statuses are at the bottom of the set of administrative units which compose Peru. With the single exception of the port city of Callao, the territory of Peru is divided into a three-level nested hierarchy of departments (*departamentos*), provinces (*provincias*), and districts. This administrative structure is highly centralized, and most positions are held by appointed rather than elected officials. For each department, province, and district, there is a town, in virtually every case the largest, which is designated the capital. It usually bears the same name as the administrative unit that it heads. It is only on the subdistrict level that there is any variation at all. Larger hamlets within rural districts are usually labeled annexes although they are sometimes called lots (*pagos*) and chapels (*capillas*).

The change in the status of Quehue with regard to this administrative hierarchy was due to an interaction of local and extralocal forces: the initiative of the village elite in conjunction with a general tendency in the sierra to create new administrative units by dividing old ones. The shift in official status has led to marked differences in the two regions in the relations between elites and peasants; the former retain more wealth and power in Quehue than they do in Surimana. A model of agrarian society which took communities and haciendas as the basic units would not explain this difference, but a view that built up from peasant households would have greater success. A simple dichotomy between *comunero* and peon would be insufficient to account for the diversity of elite-peasant relations.

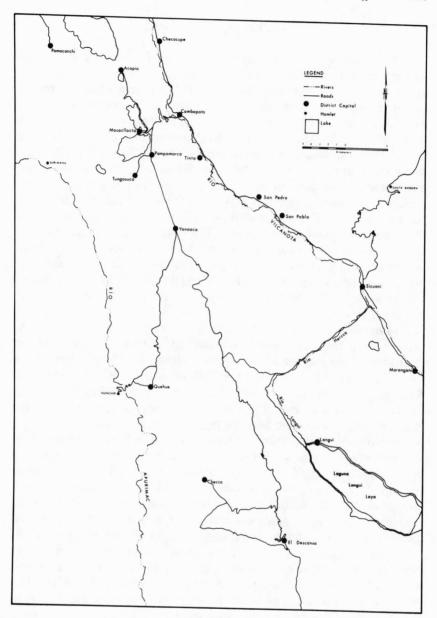

Map 3

The Ecological Context

A brief overview of the environmental setting of the two regions provides information useful to a discussion of economic activities and class relations in the two regions. The villages of Surimana and Quehue are located approximately twenty-eight kilometers apart in similar environments (see map 3). They lie at 3,586 and 3,676 meters above sea level on the eastern side of the valley of the Río Apurimac. The rough mountain topography leads to considerable variation in elevation, exposure to sunlight, soil fertility, and surface moisture in relatively small areas. These numerous micro-environments, each with a different agricultural potential, can be grouped into two principal environmental zones in both regions (Vargas Calderón, 1967). The puna consists of rolling grasslands from 3,700 meters to above 4,500 meters dominated by perennial bunch grasses. The valley (*quebrada*) runs from the bottom of the deeply incised river canyon to the puna. Its soils are more fertile, and the lower altitude and more sheltered situation moderate the rigors of the highland climate. Frosts are less frequent and less severe. In both regions the villages are located in the upper reaches of the *quebrada*. Most of the peasants live in the puna.

No two regions can be entirely identical, but the differences between these two are small and may be easily summarized. Surimana's location further downstream gives it access to lands at lower elevations. The Río Apurimac is about 3,550 meters above sea level at Quehue and only 3,250 meters at Surimana. There are also differences in geological formations. The soils in Quehue lie over a deposit of porous volcanic rock so that moisture is not retained quite as well there as in the lands around Surimana.

The two regions have similar patterns of production. Extensive pastoralism is practiced in the puna grasslands. Cattle and sheep are the most common herd animals, although llamas and alpacas are also raised. In the lower sections of the puna, cultivation of tubers (potato, *oca*, *olluco*, *añu*) and grains (barley, *quinua*, *cañihua*) is practiced with a long fallow period. The more rapid processes of decomposition and soil formation at lower altitudes, and the use of dung and ash as fertilizer, reduce the need for fallow in the *quebrada*. It is not practiced at all in the favored lower portions close to the river. Valley crops also include wheat and broad beans. *Capulí* trees are grown for their fruits, and lettuce, onions, and cabbage are garden crops. Surimana's slightly lower location permits maize, kidney beans, and a domesticated lupine called *tarhui* to be raised; apple trees also grow there. In the lower puna and in some parts of the *quebrada* certain agricultural lands are divided into *laymi* or sections. Most households in a given area own plots in each section. In successive years each section passes through the same sequence of crops and fallow; the different plots that are planted in a given year would therefore be adjacent to one another. The use of *laymi* leads to each household's holdings being scattered rather than contiguous.

The particular topography of the Río Apurimac canyon affects local trade patterns. As in many parts of the sierra, rivers hinder rather than facilitate travel. For much of its course the canyon is deep and narrow, but it can be crossed at both Surimana and Quehue. Surimana lies at the point on the Río Apurimac where it comes closest to the valley of the Río Vilcanota, a trade route of great importance in linking the highlands with the coast. Quehue contains the site of one of the famous Andean suspension bridges. The rope bridge at Queshuachaca, over thirty meters long, is likely to be the longest such bridge that is still being maintained in the entire Andes, despite Gade's assertion to the contrary (1972:93–99). These locations at points where the Río Apurimac could be crossed have favored trade between the villages and other provinces, particularly when goods were carried by donkey and llama caravans on pack trails. They became more isolated with the advent of motor vehicle roads.

A Brief Economic and Political History

Surimana and Quehue are similar both in terms of their environment and (as shall soon be discussed) their histories during the nineteenth century. However, the position of the elites in the two regions is different. Those in Surimana lost control of their lands and no longer can compel the peasants to provide them with cheap or unpaid labor. The Quehue elite, though no longer the unchallenged masters that they once were, have retained more of their land and can still control peasant labor with a fair degree of success. (Anecdotal information collected from informants in 1974, 1976, and 1979, suggests that they were able to retain a good portion of their lands and influence over the peasants even after the Agrarian Reform.) Since the two regions are not different in other ways, this current variation in elite position can be explained by their different administrative status. This section will examine in more detail the history of the two regions and the mechanisms by which the Quehue elite used the status of their village to continue their domination of the peasantry.

Quehue and Surimana both had the status of annex since the colonial period (Aparicio Vega, 1971:9). For several centuries they have been small villages in the classic highland pattern of a number of houses clustered around a central square on which a church is located. Small, partially endogamous groups of elite families reside in the villages (Morner, 1978). Like some other hacendados in neighboring provinces, they appear to have acquired land by obtaining title to the church estates which they began to rent around the time of independence. Through the nineteenth century these elites owned land in the valley and maintained herds in the puna. Some of the elite land was held as haciendas with resident peon families. It is important to stress that these predominantly stock-raising haciendas were smaller than the comparable ones in many other parts of the sierra. Ccochayhua in Quehue was by far the largest at two thousand hectares, and the median size was as low as one hundred hectares. The peons cultivated fields in exchange for usufruct rights on other plots and herded animals in exchange for grazing rights. Other freehold peasants worked these haciendas at times of seasonal peaks of labor demand. However, the land tenure and labor patterns were more complex than the simple hacienda-community dichotomy, sketched in the previous sentences, would suggest. There was a variety of types of relations between elite and peasant households. In some cases elite land was worked not as haciendas but in *mink'a* or payment in kind (see p. 41) or by nonresident sharecroppers or renters. These arrangements were particularly common in the case of the numerous small fields held by members of the elites in the *laymis*. Some herders in the puna pastures were given annual wages in cash or kind, but they grazed the animals of the elites on the same lands that the other peasants used; these pastures were not clearly assigned either to haciendas or to communities.

The elites received other services from the peasants. Through *faenas* or unpaid communal work teams, peasants constructed public and private buildings in the villages and maintained the streets and water systems. Groups of peasant households provided domestic servants (*pongos*) on a rotational basis. On occasion they made gifts and offered tribute to the elite. The elites were able to exercise such control because of the lack of other economic activities; the peasants had few other employment opportunities. The elites also held local appointive offices, particularly as justice of the peace (*juez de paz*) and lieutenant governor (*teniente gobernador*). Other representatives of the national government had little influence in the area.

Peasant households owned plots of agricultural land in the *laymi* and, less frequently, in the richer portions of the valley which were continuously cultivated. Grazing rights on pasture and fallow fields were open to all, although the elite tended to monopolize the best lands. The peasants appear to have worked their lands and tended their herds primarily through the use of *ayni* (pp. 35–36) and *mink'a*. Local areas tended to be endogamous for peasants as well as elites, although the strictly endogamous communities reported for other parts of the Andes were not found. Adult male peasants could pass through the lower ranks of a hierarchically arranged series of civil and religious posts in the villages. These posts required the sponsorship of a variety of celebrations of patron-saint festivals. The higher positions in these civil-religious hierarchies were restricted to the village elites. The set of posts and the *laymi* were both single systems for each region; there were no communities with their own *laymi* or patron-saint festivals.

The political and economic domination of the elite began to lessen during the 1920s, and weakened further during the 1940s and after. There were several reasons for this decline. Economic opportunities for peasants outside the region increased with the expansion of export production and the growth of cities. Improved transportation networks facilitated out-migration, which ended the elite's local monopoly on employment. The growth of the local marketing system, with new annual fairs appearing in the 1940s and weekly marketplaces in the 1960s, allowed the peasants a closer set of purchasers for their goods; they were provided with yet another economic alternative. These changes permitted peasant households to control a larger portion of the lands in the two regions, as will be discussed in greater detail.

The political monopoly of the elite was also undermined as government agencies established direct links with peasant groups for the first time. The village elites began to lose their roles as sole intermediaries. The biggest change came with the provision in the 1920 constitution that established the official legal recognition of *comunidades indigenas* (Indian communities), which became *comunidades campesinas* (peasant communities) in 1969. Government resolutions in 1925 created an official registry of communities and established simpler bureaucratic procedures for their recognition. The appearance of this legislation coincided with attempts by the elites to carve better-defined haciendas out of the puna pastures. Thus peasants and elites both sought to limit the other's access to land.

In halting manner, the government began to provide certain services to the peasantry. Ministry employees and government personnel, such as school-teachers, policemen, and agricultural extension agents, played an increasingly important political role on the regional and local level. National social control agencies were also strengthened, and government agencies began to regulate the conscription of peasant labor, especially for road construction. These functions had previously been entirely in the hands of the local elites.

The elites were unable to retain their previous domination of the peasants. The peasants built chapels in the hamlets and held patron-saint festivals there, apart from the rituals in the villages. This shift was significant, since it meant that the peasant households began to organize *faena* labor for their own ends. In making arrangements for the masses to be celebrated with the festivals, they entered into direct contact with priests, rather than relying on the village elites as intermediaries. The festivals also provided an ideological support to the growing identity of the communities (Favre, 1977). The construction of schoolhouses in the 1960s had similar consequences. The communities gained official recognition, thus strengthening their claims to land. The establishment of chapels and schoolhouses predated the official recognition, except in two communities in Quehue, which received such recognition quite early. The communities in Quehue that have this official title are Chaupibanda (1929), Huinchiri (1938), and Ccollana Quehue (1966). The communities in Suri-mana all were awarded this status in a period of eighteen months: Rosasani, Huaylluta-Surimana, and Pampahuasi in 1966, Toccoccori and Ccochapata in 1967 (SINAMOS, 1974). In general, the communities were located at higher elevations than the villages and sought to control the puna grasslands; several of them also retained agricultural lands in the *quebrada*. The large *laymi* systems in Surimana and Quehue split into a number of smaller ones, and the elites retained little land outside the particular *laymi* system closest to the village, apart from the haciendas which they were able to consolidate at this time. The titles formalized a process of increasing peasant control of land.

The elites also found peasant labor difficult to obtain. They could no longer continue the relatively labor-intensive agriculture on the valley lands.

Abandoned fields and apple orchards in Surimana attest to this process. In Quehue one small hacendado has blocked a spring that used to irrigate his fields since he cannot get workers during planting and harvest season. The elites had partial success in retaining shepherds to care for their animals since this activity requires much lower labor inputs than agriculture. For this reason they shifted from working large *laymi* plots to emphasizing their pastoral haciendas.

This general decline of local elites occurred in both villages although it was more pronounced in Surimana. There is a difference in their history, though. Sometime between 1912 and 1917, Quehue became a district, but Surimana never did. Quehue's change in status reflects a general tendency in the southern highlands. Between 1876 and 1976, sixteen new districts were created in the five southern provinces (Canas, Canchis, Espinar, Chumbivilcas, and Acomayo) of the department of Cuzco, raising the total from twenty-three to thirty-nine. The reasons for Quehue's new position, then, lie in the political structure of the highlands. There were general pressures for the creation of new administrative units, which permitted the multiplication of local political offices and the granting of patronage. During this period, government revenues were increasing. Even the poor areas in the remote interior began to receive larger funds, and the money slowly trickled into new areas.

The formation of new districts also gave local groups greater power on the regional and national levels since representation in certain departmental councils and national congresses was based on the number of administrative units. The creation of districts was paralleled on higher levels by the creation of new provinces and departments. Such splits often took place when the oligarchic electoral parties were in power.

The Quehue elite took advantage of this possibility of *distritalización*. They organized a committee which restored the old church in 1909, giving the village a more presentable urban air. The members of that committee were the grandfathers of the current elite. They appear to have petitioned formally for the higher status on several occasions. The efforts of the Surimana elite in this direction were sporadic. In any case they would have encountered more resistance, due to the peculiarities of local history. Quehue was an annex of Checca, an old and rather large district which had not previously been divided. Surimana had earlier been attached to the district of Pampamarca, which had also had two other annexes, Tungasuca and Mosocllacta. These two both separated from Pampamarca to become districts of their own. Rather than remaining as a part of Pampamarca, Surimana became an annex of Tungasuca, which, as a small new district, was unlikely to give up any of its territory. Checca, by contrast, could more easily afford to lose Quehue. See Table 6–1 for the demographic consequences of this difference.

The inactivity and isolation of Surimana are also responsible for its retention of annex status; it is the only annex dating from colonial times in the provinces of Canas and Canchis that has not become a district.[3] In general,

Table 6-1
Population of Quehue and Surimana

	1876	1940	1961	1972
Quehue	94	98	112	129
Surimana	170	152	135	—[a]

SOURCE: National Population Censuses

[a]The 1972 census does not provide population figures below the district level, as earlier censuses do. My impression is that the population of the village when I visited it in 1973 was between 80 and 140.

there was little local opposition to annexes becoming districts, as the cases of Layo in the province of Canas and Pitumarca in the neighboring province of Canchis show. Protest arose only when new commercial towns that had grown up on roads wanted to become districts. El Descanso in the province of Canas and Tocroyoc in the adjacent province of Espinar met considerable resistance for this reason before their final successes.[4] The village elites appear to have felt more threatened by the emergence of new commercial interests in their midst than by the increased autonomy of the traditional annexes.

Surimana remained an annex. It no longer had important central functions in its region. It lost virtually all control over the peasant groups in the puna. They became linked more directly to the district capital of Tungasuca as they established their own chapels and schools. Their official recognition as communities completed this process.

As a mere annex, Surimana receives a small portion of the provincial and departmental allowances for public works.[5] Trucks and other motor vehicles cannot reach it. It has difficulty placing any project for itself on the proposed budgets which are sent to Cuzco and Lima. The local justice of the peace and the lieutenant governor get little outside support. The district officials in Tungasuca do not pay attention to their complaints about peasants who refuse to fulfill sharecropping obligations, nor can they insist on receiving faena labor from the independent communities.

The village elite does not receive the appointive positions that are established in districts. A few schoolteachers in the communities aside, there are no permanent government employees with whom the elites can form links. The official declaration of the community status of the peasant groups that used to depend on the village has weakened the elite further. The remnants of the elite families in Surimana no longer have access to the lands that are now part of these communities, except for a few small haciendas that they have established in the punas. They hold relatively little land; puna haciendas form 20 to 30 percent of the land in the Surimana region, well below the provincial average of 37 percent (Peifeder 1971). Some of these haciendas are owned by residents of Tungasuca. The village elite do not retain as large a share of the production of their lands as most other hacendados in the province do. They are no longer able to establish favorable labor agreements with peasants. Large work parties are now infrequent and forced unpaid labor has disappeared entirely; these practices, though inefficient, were cheap. Instead, the elite has shifted to rental and sharecropping, which leaves them with a smaller share of the products than *mink'a* and peonage arrangements did. In *mink'a*, the owner retains 70 to 85 percent of the harvest and the workers receive 15 to 30 percent. Peonage is similarly favorable to the owner since peons typically receive plots smaller than the ones that they cultivate. Under sharecropping arrangements, each party receives 50 percent, although the worker is often able to contrive to retain slightly more. In rental, the workers keep the entire harvest but give the owner 10 to 15 percent of its value, in effect retaining 85 to 90 percent. These arrangements thus establish different balances between the elites and the peasant households. With their land base reduced, the elite have gradually changed in their consumption patterns, and the old elite families have accustomed themselves to wearing sandals instead of shoes and to eating more potatoes and less bread. Their houses have deteriorated as both unpaid peasant labor and ready cash to hire workers become increasingly scarce. The consequences of this shift have been a dramatic social leveling. Visiting government officials cannot distinguish between the descendants of the former village elite and the *comuneros*, and classify both as mere Indians or "*indigenas*" (Instituto Indigenista Peruano, 1968:18). Both groups engage in agricultural work on their lands, and most former differences in level of consumption have been erased.

The elevation to district status has permitted the Quehue elite to avoid the fate of Surimana. New appointed officers were accorded to the village, most importantly a governor (*gobernador*). Several offices of ministries and government agencies were established.

The positions of power in Quehue are shared between the village-elite families and the government employees, who tend to come from outside.[6] The former hold appointive office; they remain in their positions for a number of years at a time. The latter hold ministry positions and tend to be transferred to other places after a few years. They view villages such as Quehue as undesirable posts and obtain transfers after establishing a few years' seniority and informal connections in zonal and regional offices.

The two groups are closely linked. The employees who come from outside find life in the village primitive and dull. They visit the elite families to drink and converse, and the more intellectually inclined members of both groups play chess. The employees remain more distant from the peasants and do not frequently engage in informal social interaction with them.

The teachers provide the basis of the link between the local elite and the employees. The daughter of the justice of the peace, who owns a small hacienda, is the only local person to return to Quehue permanently after receiving a professional education.[7] She is a teacher and is married to the

Table 6-2

Government Employees in Quehue and Surimana (1973)

Government Agency	Office/Official	Number of Officials	
		Quehue	Surimana
Ministerio de Educación	nucleo escolar/director	1	0
	escuela/profesor	12	7
Ministerio de Agricultura	sector agrario/sectorista[a]	1	0
Ministerio de Salúd y Bienestar Público	puesto sanitario/ sanitario[b]	1	0
Ministerio del Interior Guardia Civil	puesto/guardia civil[c]	2	1

SOURCE: interviews

[a]Agrarian sector; rural extension agent.

[b]Health and Public Welfare Ministry; clinic, clinician.

[c]National Police; police station; policeman.

director of the *nucleo escolar* (school district), the son of a hacendado in the adjacent province of Espinar. The policemen take their meals at her house. She and her husband are *compadres* of one of the policemen. They are also close friends of the *sanitario* and the *sectorista*.

This social interaction provides a context for informal cooperation between the employees and the village elite in economic and political matters. The director of the *nucleo escolar* helped the *sectorista* to organize peasants from the communities in the district into collective work projects for maintaining the road and enlarging public buildings. Without external support, it is unlikely that the elites would be able to have such *faena* labor performed. The governor and the justice of the peace also supervise these activities. The opportunities for graft, though limited, are not neglected. The policemen and the justice of the peace cooperate in tracking down thieves, and they coordinate their efforts in resolving disputes among peasants.

These links are of mutual benefit. The employees gain the pleasure of acceptable companionship in this remote village. They also find their work considerably smoothed by the cooperation of the village elites, who continue to wield influence over the peasants through *compadrazgo* and other relations. The police in particular give solid backing to the economic power of the village elite and permit them to continue to obtain peasant labor. The employees also provide a certain amount of business to the elite storekeepers. Although a dozen civil servants at low pay scales could hardly maintain three stores even if the stores were quite small, their frequent purchases of foodstuffs, beer, and alcohol are quite welcome.

The village elite in Quehue has been able to maintain its economic position somewhat better than its counterpart in Surimana. The extent of the haciendas in Quehue is difficult to determine, but a comparison of several sources[8] with informants' accounts suggests that about 40 percent of the land is contained in haciendas. The elite continue to work the land with a few permanent peons.

More importantly, the official recognition of communities, even though it came early in some cases, did not end the access of the Quehue elite to those lands, as it did in Surimana. Several of them maintain herds of sheep and cattle on community pasture. They hire community members as shepherds, paying them small salaries. The permanent peons on the haciendas also retain community membership and have the right to work lands and graze animals there. Some elite members rent parts of their haciendas to community members, frequently on the condition that they join the large work groups. The peonage and rental arrangements bear a strong similarity: hacendados let peasants use part of their lands in exchange for labor.

The village elite is able to use its position to obtain labor. Though not as common as in earlier decades, large work parties are still prevalent at peak labor periods, such as during the potato harvest and sheep shearing. Peasants who bring complaints and disputes to the justice of the peace often find that he requires several days' unpaid labor before he considers their cases. The police will support a local hacendado who insists that a peasant, whether a peon or a community member, work for him to pay off an alleged debt. One common pretext is the accusation that the peasant's animal strayed onto hacienda land and grazed there. Such fines could not be collected in Surimana.

The older practices such as peonage, though not as common as they are elsewhere, link individual peasant households with members of the Quehue elite and sustain their relative wealth. The elite obtain some domestic servants and workers through adoption of peasant children who perform routine tasks in the household and fields. The use of *pongos*, though disappearing, has not entirely passed. Elite households still have one or more servants, and they continue to exercise traditional control over their servants' lives. An eight-year-old girl from the punas above Quehue was taken from her parents and put to work without pay as a domestic servant in Sicuani for nearly a year in the house of a relative of the justice of the peace. He and the justice of the peace are *concuñados*; their wives are sisters. The *concuñado* is a *compadre* of the *juez de tierras* (land court judge), who is in charge of land disputes for the southern part of the department of Cuzco. In other words, the justice of the peace provided a gift (the labor of a young girl) to a kinsman in town in return for an expected favor (the influence of the kinsman on his behalf in an important suit); his internal domination of peasant households and his external articulation to a major town are interrelated.

The status of Quehue as a district permitted the building of a road which linked it with the interprovincial road running several kilometers to the east. Road-building funds are limited; they are administered by the zonal office of the Transport and Communications Ministry (Ministerio de Transportes y

Comunicaciones) in the town of Sicuani. Quehue tends to neglect roads which do not link it with other important centers. The road has allowed the further growth of the village. A market takes place every Sunday. The accessibility of the village to trucks has permitted the opening of stores by local elite members.[9] A soccer league composed of teams from the communities in the district also meets on Sundays after the market ends. Quehue's annual patron-saint festivities, with horse races, bullfights, bands of musicians, and formidable quantities of alcohol, are in sharp contrast to Surimana's subdued and uneventful celebration. In these ways the more active economic life in Quehue associated with its district status offers benefits to the peasants as well as to the elites.

In summary, village elites in both Surimana and Quehue no longer retain the monopoly of local level power that they had seventy-five years ago. They have lost part of their control over land and labor. A series of economic and political changes in Peru weakened their position, while national policies favored the peasants more than before. The Quehue elite have been able to maintain part of their former domination and wealth because the village gained district status. This change provided them with additional sources of power. The comparable elite in Surimana, a mere annex, have declined more completely. Without their wealth, land, and influence, they have now become Indians and are on the same level as the peasants.

Conclusion

The hacendado elites in both Surimana and Quehue have lost much of the power which they enjoyed at the beginning of this century. This weakening is due in large part to the opening of alternative economic and political opportunities for the peasants. The decline has been less severe in Quehue. However, the difference between the two lies not only in the fact that the hacendados in Quehue control about 40 percent of the land, whereas their counterparts in Surimana have less than 30 percent. It is connected also with labor practices, such as the ability of the Quehue elite to obtain permanent and seasonal workers for their lands and herds, to demand *faena* labor, and to continue to procure domestic servants. The Quehue elite also have better access to community pastures.

The difference lies in the official status of the two villages. The elite in Quehue were able to gain additional positions for themselves and to establish relations of mutual support with government employees. These ties offer some advantages to the peasants, who benefit from the better transportation facilities and the market, and who have had better access to government agencies for a longer period. These ties, however, have also allowed the elite to retain greater influence in the area. Without such support, they would have been likely to follow the downward path of the Surimana elite.

Land ownership is only a partial basis of elite domination; the elite must also have links to the national government and its representatives (Mariátegui,

1928:198–203). The rural elite is not identical to a group of hacendados. The political aspects of relations between elites and peasants in this area are only partially separable from the economic aspects. The internal organization of these regions, especially the elite-peasant relations, can be analyzed only in conjunction with their external articulation. This organization is so complex that a tripartite division of agrarian society into hacendados, *comuneros*, and peons is of relatively little analytical use. A comparison of Quehue and Surimana supports these points. The differences between the two regions can be understood by examining the local households and the complex shifts of their ties to landlords and officials, rather than by rigidly classifying the local populations on the basis of a set of previously established categories.

Notes

1. Research for this chapter was carried out from May 1972 to October 1973 with the generous support of the Foreign Area Fellowship Program. Briefer trips to Peru were sponsored by the Institute of Ecology of the University of California at Davis in 1974; by the Wenner-Gren Foundation for Anthropological Research and a Summer Faculty Fellowship from Davis in 1976, and by the National Science Foundation in 1979. I am grateful to Arnold Bauer, Sebastián Bocaverde, Daniel Chirot, Mario Dávila, Miriam Wells, and the contributors to the volume for their helpful comments and criticisms, although I remain responsible for any errors.

2. The regions are defined by the villages that are their centers. The villages have administrative authority over certain activities and thus focus social networks. They provide some of the links which articulate local populations with wider systems.

3. Santa Bárbara in Canchis became an *anexo* of San Pedro in early Republican times and has not achieved *distrito* status.

4. For the case of El Descanso, see Alencastre 1965. The case of Tocroyoc is documented frequently in the copies of the correspondence between the *subprefecto* of Espinar and officials in Cuzco in the decade of the 1920s; these records are stored in the archive of the *subprefectura* in Yauri.

5. Since Surimana was the birthplace of Túpac Amaru, the village had received some additional support. The military government saw him as an important forerunner of independence and of the goals which they proclaimed. A road was built to Surimana in 1971, but it washed out soon after and has not been fully repaired. The government also restored the village church and paved the main square. The difficult economic conditions which the regime began to face in the mid-1970s and the strong association of Túpac Amaru with the early radical days of the revolutionary government make it unlikely that more funds will follow.

6. In some other areas many sons and daughters of local elite families return as school-teachers. This pattern of migration is not so common in Quehue. The elite does educate its children outside the village, though; they attend high school in Sicuani and Cuzco, and some continue to attend university.

7.   She engages in what is conspicuous consumption for Quehue. She feeds her cat pieces of bread. Most local cats forage for themselves or content themselves with potato peels and other scraps. Bread itself is scarce, and many peasants go weeks without eating any. A piece of bread is an acceptable gift from one friend to another in peasant circles. The elite families lend each other bread if they have run out when visitors arrive. On one occasion I saw an old peasant woman kiss the piece of bread that a hacendado had given her. Feeding a cat bread in Quehue is like feeding a dog a fine cut of steak in North America or Europe.

8.   See Alencastre, 1967:39; Ministerio de Agricultura, 1973a.

9.   Village elite members own two of the three stores. I do not know who owns the third one.

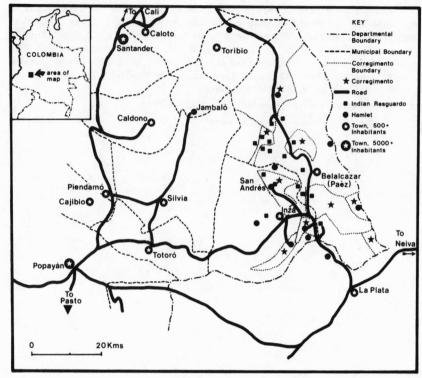

Map 4

CHAPTER 7

The Structure and Regional Articulation of Dispersed Rural Settlements in Colombia[1]

Sutti Ortiz

In the introduction to this book, Orlove and Custred correctly criticize anthropologists for emphasizing community and hacienda studies while neglecting the examination of less neatly structured population aggregates. Such a biased sample has led to highly simplified descriptions of power imbalances within rural sectors and of forms of integration to higher level centers; these descriptions are pertinent only to areas where the stereotypic hacienda and corporate community predominate. Furthermore, the simplistic Frankian-type models based on such descriptions have misled theorists into thinking about integration as consisting of simple static sets of links rather than of multifarious processes. They also have encouraged us to look exclusively for exogeneous factors as determinants of the imbalances in linkages. Yet we must recognize that the Frankian-type analysis has helped us to recognize more vividly regional imbalances and the consequences of such imbalances. Higher level political powers, for example, do extract local resources in the form of tax, tribute, and votes; landlords whose interests are aligned with national rather than regional concerns do fail to return to rural areas the benefits they have gained from the exploitation of local land and labour resources. Exploitation is a consequence of an alliance of interests between landlords and capitalist marketeers. The rural settler, in this sense, is a pawn of national interest, but he is not the passive object implied by most static dependency models. A large proportion of rural settlers either control most (though perhaps not all) means and tools of production or are only partially dependent on a landlord. The choice of mode of production made by rural settlers is not entirely constrained. Their choice of modes and means of production, in turn, engender integrating links as relevant as those brought about by the demands of external agents. Rural residents are both pawns and actors; hence the complex and often contradictory nature of the integrating process.

In this essay I first want to describe the structure of a marginal rural area of Colombia which, though unique in some historical and demographic aspects, is not unique in terms of marginality; about one-third of Colombia's rural settlers live in marginal areas. I secondly want to examine the nature of the multifarious integrating links. Long (1975) has suggested that the best way of examining structural dependency is probably to move from structural models to ego-oriented models; only then, he argues, can we fully explore the dynamics of dependency imbalances.[2] I shall do so by focusing on the individual as a transactor (that is, a stereotypic transactor) and look at the determinants of the transactions. In this way the nature and dynamics of the balances and imbalances will become apparent. This approach has the advantage of allowing for the incorporation of historical changes. The use of the term *transaction* evokes the contribution made by Barth in his writings (Barth, 1966), though I trace my roots to Firth's interest in choice. Yet this essay is not, strictly speaking, an application of decision or transactional analysis; the differences will become apparent in the text.

Marginal regions are integrated into national life most obviously through political institutions. National agencies extract tax in order to discharge administrative responsibilities. In turn they offer services and redistribute national revenues. The balance between the flow and counterflow of money-labor services depends on the conflict of interests and imbalances in power between national and regional polity. Historical events shaping the organization and fiscal structure of the polity may contribute to such imbalances. In Colombia national government is highly centralized and leaves little room for autonomous action on the part of the municipality. Furthermore, the fiscal structure is such that marginal regions have minimal independent cash resources to initiate projects. Such projects have to be initiated by development agencies which respond only to national directives.[3] Moreover, since local residents only elect a fraction of the administrators, the power of their vote is highly circumscribed. Understandably, few people bother to vote in rural areas, and those who do have only an ephemeral relationship with local politicians. Traders, middlemen, landlords, and credit agencies are of more importance to rural settlers. They must establish an ongoing relation with at least a middleman, and it is through this relationship that they may be able to manipulate other agencies or gain information about neighboring regions or higher level centers.[4]

In Colombia the integration of marginal rural areas is more effectively achieved through the links engendered in the process of production and commodity exchange than through the links that stem from the administrative process. It is for this reason that I concentrate on the first, only briefly reviewing the second. When other areas of Colombia are examined in detail, looking closely at the variety and nature of links that producers or political actors forge with individuals or agencies external to the region, we will be able to have a clear comprehension of the imbalance between metropolis and various types of rural areas. This is very much in line with suggestions by Hunt and Nash (1967) for Mesoamerica.

The *Vereda* of San Andrés

In the eastern part of the department of Cauca, mountain ranges face each other, leaving no room for valleys or plateaus. This region is known as Tierradentro. In 1961 it could be approached from the southern town of La Plata via a road that branches from the Neiva-Popayán commercial thoroughfare, meanders around the steep slopes, and eventually reaches the municipality of Inzá, where the *vereda*[5] of San Andrés is located. In the last five years the major Tierradentro settlements have been connected more directly to a second road that cuts across the mountains and reaches Inzá before linking with the Neiva-Popayán thoroughfare. The new road puts an end to the isolation that has characterized Tierrandentro until now. After all, only twenty years ago no roads penetrated into this area; goods instead had to be brought on mule from Popayán across high mountain passes, a slow and expensive form of transport.

Steeply sloped and eroded mountains, only occasionally separated by narrow valleys and soft plains, make up the topography of the region. Only at higher altitudes (around three thousand meters) do the mountains slope more gently and retain some of the virgin forest. The higher altitude plains are adequate for cattle grazing; the softer, higher slopes yield good crops of potatoes and wheat. Because of transport and processing costs, wheat, potatoes, and cattle are no longer sources of cash for the small farmer of the *vereda* of San Andrés. Only wealthier ranchers can profit from cattle breeding in the higher slopes and lower valleys. Whereas higher slopes yield more bountiful harvests, the crops grown on lower slopes are less costly to market. Furthermore, coffee and sugar cane, two major cash crops, can only be grown at lower altitudes. These mountains and valleys were, until quite recently, populated by Indians and a small minority of white settlers. Although more immigrants have moved into this area, it still remains sparsely populated, like much of Colombia, and until 1970 it was quite isolated from important centers. An historical account of immigration will best describe the nature of the population of the *vereda* of San Andrés, as well as the process of its social and political integration to the rest of the nation.

History of the Vereda of San Andrés

Spaniards made several attempts to cross the mountainous area of Tierradentro during the sixteenth century in order to ensure safe passage from Popayán to Bogotá. They finally succeeded during the following century, after exterminating one of the many independent Indian tribes and decimating others. The native population withdrew further into the mountains and the Spaniards decided not to further colonize the area. Later in the century, however, the territory was parceled out into three *encomiendas* and the resident population was used as a labor force in haciendas and mines far away. At about the same time the crown granted land *in corpus* to Indian families, who had rights of residence over a mountain or slope; this is the origin of present day Indian *resguardo* of San Andrés.

Although it is probable that some Spaniards settled in what is now the *vereda* of San Andrés as far back as the eighteenth century, it is unlikely that the native population had to cope with an influx of alien settlers until 1873, when the town of Inzá was founded. In fact, it was not until 1807 that a church was built in the San Andrés hamlet and regular pastoral visits were made. Fifteen years after Inzá became a town, San Andrés was still mostly settled by Indians with only a few alien residents.

Indians did not react favorably to the growth of Inzá and the appearance of more whites in their territory. Opposition to the newcomers precipitated a rebellion led by Quintin Lame, who organized the Indians from the *resguardo* to the north of San Andrés and marched south to Inzá, where they were defeated in 1916. Resistance to white settlers continued in the San Andrés area until 1940, but it was limited to a prohibition against renting reservation land or houses to outsiders and to expressions of violence against those who settled in areas surrounding the *resguardo*. Exceptions were of course made and close ties were sometimes forged with the newcomers, who either stayed for a few years or chose the San Andrés area as their permanent residence. Some of the white settlers recognized and cared for the children they fathered, most of whom have now been accepted as members of the white community of San Andrés.

In time, the Inzá settlement grew and the town became a municipality, that is, a political subdivision of a department with administrative responsibilities over surrounding countryside, which in this case encompassed a number of *resguardos*. Although never attaining a large size (the 1954 census indicates a population of 497 inhabitants), it was big enough to attract farmers to settle in its territory. When Quintin Lame attacked Inzá in 1916, 2,850 white farmers and traders were residing outside the town but within the municipal district. At first the Indians were able to contain the intruders to areas around and between *resguardo* boundaries. But by 1938 more immigrants had come into the area and it became difficult to prevent the 8,717 rural residents from encroaching on *resguardo* property. In the 1920s farmers in search of land began to pressure municipal authorities to confiscate lands from the San Andrés *resguardo*. Colombians were at that time particularly interested in developing coffee plantations, and San Andrés had lower land suitable for coffee trees. By 1926 the municipality confiscated approximately six hectares of land and declared it an area of settlement, offering the land in lots to any buyer regardless of ancestry. New settlers with limited capital took advantage of the offer and converted the land immediately into small coffee plantations. Some of the settlers became traders as well and managed to make a fair income. With the influx of newcomers who built their houses around the old church and on the path leading to the church, the character of the region changed from an entirely Indian area to a peasant area with an Indian majority. This demographic development, which differentiated San Andrés from other areas within the municipality, was given recognition in the adoption of the term *vereda*. The boundaries of the new *vereda* were to encompass the original

Indian settlement with a population between two hundred and three hundred families,[6] the lands taken away from the *resguardo* by the municipality and the area occupied by a small group of settlers (thirty-seven families) who had built their houses at the lower end of the San Andrés creek.

Some of the settlers who acquired land in what is now the *vereda* of San Andrés were not totally alien to the area or to the *resguardo* Indians. The sons of at least six of the pioneering families who founded Inzá had, for some time, cultivated land between Inzá and the San Andrés *resguardo*. Some of these farmers were more successful than others and expanded their plantations, to the concern of the Indians. Others managed small subsistence farms just big enough to support a wife (perhaps of Indian descent) and children. These poorer farmers often established close links with the Indian community, but the bonds were not often sustained in subsequent generations. In some rare cases where the links remained close, the white farmers were allowed to farm *resguardo* land as *agregados*[7] and to participate in the fiesta cycle.

It was the ambitious sons of the poor first settlers who, together with the numerous sons of the more successful settlers, began slowly to encroach on the *resguardo* area and finally to take advantage of the lands that the Inzá municipality had made available for them in San Andrés. By 1930 seven of them had settled around the San Andrés church or on the path to the hamlet. Shortly afterwards they were joined by two other poor farmers from farther south and by an Ecuadorian ambulant trader. Meanwhile immigrants with some capital were able to buy holdings outside the *resguardo* or just within its boundaries. These holdings have been sold in turn to others, who have consolidated them into larger units owned now by three different landlords.

Most of the new immigrants were rejected by the Indian residents. In turn, the settlers took every possible occasion to demonstrate that they regarded *resguardo* Indians with disdain and as fair game for improper transactions. The social wall that *resguardo* residents had built to protect their interest was then matched by an equivalent status-protecting device erected by the new settlers. No longer did the non-Indian settlers of the *vereda* (i.e., whites) marry or forge multiple symmetrical ties of reciprocity with Indians. Some ten Indian families, on the other hand, opted to disregard the obvious social difference between the two communities and managed to gain the respect and acceptance of whites and *resguardo* residents alike. Loyalties and marriage ties with earlier white settlers and *resguardo* Indians account for their anomalous social status.

The death and destruction that swept through Colombia during *La Violencia*[8] in the forties and fifties disrupted the life of many families. Many of them fled to San Andrés as this small area remained almost untouched by the bitter political controversies and uprisings that rocked even the neighboring municipality of Belalcazar. When peace was reestablished some returned to their original homelands, while others remained and married in San Andrés. This was how the *vereda* of San Andrés was settled by whites, who comprised in 1961 a total of thirty-seven households.

Although white residents of the *vereda* neither shared a common background nor had attained equal levels of economic and educational achievement, they have, since 1940, been able to maintain their separateness from the Indian community and to acquire a sense of identification with their locality. The people of San Andrés asked departmental and municipal authorities to upgrade their administrative status from *vereda* to *corregimiento* in 1961. In other words, as a *corregimiento*, it was recognized as a subunit of the municipality and assigned a *corregidor*, or administrator, capable of handling internal affairs and of insuring the upkeep of roads, bridges, and other property used by the community. The request was granted and a *corregidor* was appointed and remained in office for about half a year.

Since the time that San Andrés became a *corregimiento* in 1961 the *vereda* has not changed demographically or politically. No new migrants have flocked into the area, and normal vegetative growth has not, in so short a time, affected the demographic balance between Indians and whites.

Another set of newcomers, however, has upset the tranquility of the place and have probably introduced new frictions and new hopes. In 1965 the Institute of Anthropology opened an inn to lodge visitors and researchers; in 1972 a small hotel opened its doors. But the four thousand annual tourists pay only a fleeting visit to the archaeological sites and help enrich only some of the local traders. Otherwise the economic impact of tourism is minimal.

More important for the local economy has been the completion of a direct road linking Belalcazar-San Andrés to Popayán. Now daily buses and trucks from Belalcazar can go to Popayán via Inzá-San Andrés.

The new road has not only eased the transport of crops, merchandise and people, but has probably helped to bring San Andrés in closer contact with the most politicized western municipalities and with the Guambiano Indian reservation. Independent organizations like ANUC (National Association of Peasants) and CRIC (Regional Cooperation of Indians from Cauca) are very active in the municipalities to the west of Inzá as well as in the northeast of Belalcazar, encouraging Indians to demand more services and the return of usurped land. They have had some success. Some Indian communities have taken over the lands that the church once held within their reservation territory, and Indians have backed CRIC's ultimatum to central government to immediately ratify the boundaries and titles of the various *resguardos*.

The heat of the threats made by the San Andrés Indians may be dispelled by the proposed action of INCORA (Agrarian Reform and Colonization Institute) to purchase and return to the reservation some of the land now owned by white settlers. It is also thanks to the efforts of an INCORA agent that the title to the original land grants has been retrieved from the archives and returned to the San Andrés *cabildo*. This agency has now opened an office at Inzá and hopes to be able to offer technical advice, organizational services, and low-interest loans to Indian and non-Indian farmers alike. INCORA has been in operation since 1961 as a semiautonomous entity dependent on the Department of Agriculture. It has been mostly concerned with clarifying titles over land, redistributing large extensions of land, and offering technical assistance. INCORA, however, lacks sufficient legal powers and adequate cadastral surveys to enact multiple land reform projects. Limited financial resources and personnel not only slow projected land reform efforts but also curtail INCORA's attempts to organize cooperatives, extend credit, and provide other agricultural services. It is only in the past seven years that the efforts of INCORA have begun to be known and used in San Andrés.

Another semiautonomous entity within the Department of Agriculture that has had perhaps a smaller but longer influence in San Andrés is the Agrarian Bank (*Caja de Crédito Agrario*). By 1961 San Andrés Indians already knew of the existence of this institution and on occasion travelled to La Plata to purchase tools from its cooperative store. A smaller agency of the Agrarian Bank was located at Belalcazar where Indians and whites alike could request low interest loans. Some did avail themselves of the latter services, but on the whole the efforts of the Agrarian Bank were directed to rather small commercial farmers.

Formal Local Political Structure and Linkages to National Order

As a *corregimiento*, San Andrés is politically dependent on the municipality of Inzá.[9] The *corregidor* is appointed by the mayor and paid a salary that even by local standards could not sustain a family. Only occasionally is a local resident or recent newcomer willing to assume the responsibility of the office of *corregidor*, which offers no privileges to compensate the low payment received (*corregidores* have little prestige and very limited authority). In fact, if the duties are conscientiously handled, a considerable amount of work is involved. While I was in residence, the *corregidor* served as a messenger for the mayor and local white residents. He felt himself to be above the Indian community and did not bother to represent their needs to authorities at Inzá. Indeed, he only managed to preside over Indian affairs when the Indian community insisted on his intervention in litigations; he then passed quick verdicts based on his notion of what was proper, while avoiding time-consuming investigations and negotiations. While the litigating Indians were aware of the superficiality of the *corregidor's* judgments, they welcomed them because they could use them as powerful arguments when publicly confronting their opponents. Thus, the office of *corregidor*, even when filled,[10] cannot bring political unity to the *vereda* of San Andrés nor effectively integrate the neighborhood with municipal government. The sense of political impotence that local residents have is partly due to poor linkage to government agencies, but it is also due to the ineffectiveness of the administrative bodies to which they are linked. As in other municipalities of Colombia, the mayor and council of Inzá are responsible for collecting taxes, as well as for providing and organizing local public services. Such enormous responsibility is not matched by a realistic administrative budget (the Inzá budget for 1961 was 6,300 U.S. dollars). On the one hand, low property taxes, high delinquency rates, and low contributions from the central government are responsible for the limited independent financial resources available to municipalities. On the other hand, the cost of administering a population spread over inaccessible mountain slopes is very high. Although it is possible that administrative effectiveness could be upgraded with higher budgets or more imaginative budgetary allocations, Davis (1970) has suggested that drastic reforms must be implemented to adapt the present administrative system to local conditions. Mayors, for example, not only lack financial resources but are also often ignorant of local conditions and needs. They are appointed by governors of departments, and in the poorer marginal municipalities they are often outsiders brought in to perform an impossible task. Not surprisingly, there is in Inzá a constant dissatisfaction with the appointed mayors, which contributes to factional conflict. Mayors can be demoted by the governor who often acts under the advice or information of prominent residents in the municipal township. During a period of one year, three mayors came to Inzá. Needless to say, the only residents of the *vereda* of San Andrés who bothered to forge personal links with the mayor were the traders who sold at the Inzá market square and were in need of his favors (his help in collecting debts and willingness to set low market tax rates).

Surrounded as they are by ineffective and apathetic municipal and *corregimiento* administrators, local residents seldom bother to organize projects which lie beyond their resources. The people of San Andrés do not believe that money for a project will be made available when requested. They know from experience that only if they are able to gain the patronage of a political boss can they hope to have priority over scarce government resources. In principle, the functions of political patrons could have been filled by the personnel of the Community Action Programs (Department of Community Development and Integration of the Ministry of Government). The Department of Community Development operates by sending representatives to rural areas to meet with local residents, and help them implement rural improvement projects. In recent years this department has initiated some projects in the municipality of Inzá (e.g., a radio program) and has maintained a group of traveling experts. The services of a communal action promoter, an agricultural expert, a nurse, a carpenter, and a mason are available to the various Tierradentro communities. In the last couple of years the communal action promoter has organized three meetings in San Andrés. The meetings were attended only by the white residents and did not inspire the local population to organize and carry out any development projects. The failure can probably be accounted for by the infrequency of visits to the *vereda* by any of the experts. But a more poignant reason for the failure is that in Indian areas the programs are organized in coordination with the Division of Indian Affairs, an administrative linkage that in effect conveys the message to the white residents that they are regarded as part of the Indian community. It must be remembered that whites take a great pride in differentiating themselves from Indians.

The Indian Resguardo

The *resguardo* is an Indian landholding corporation created by the Spanish crown. The original members of the corporation were all the Indian families who lived on the granted land. Rights of membership were thus initially contingent on residence; subsequently they were contingent on descent from the original settlers and residence.[11] All present-day Indian families who are members of the *resguardo* have a right to use a share of the land belonging to the corporation in exchange for their help in the upkeep of the communal property and their support in defending the boundaries of the *resguardo*. Although wealth differentiation[12] and competition for resources have strained bonds and brought disunity, there is no question that the Indian community is an operative social unit.

A council of household heads (the *cabildo*) assembles occasionally to discuss administrative problems (upkeep of church, school, roads, and bridges) and legal problems (disputes over boundaries or seizure of property). The council is convened by officers who must implement the decisions passed in each session. Thirty years ago the *cabildo* was a powerful political institution with recourse to legal sanctions, but while I was in San Andrés in 1961, the *cabildo* rarely met and its officers had no authority and little influence. Furthermore, because of their geographic isolation they had little access to the help and guidance that the newly created Division of Indian Affairs (Department of Agriculture) could extend to them. Perhaps thanks to the activities of ANUC and CRIC the San Andrés *cabildo* has regained some local influence.

Social-Economic Links and Cleavages Within the Vereda *and the Rest of the Country*

Although members of the Indian *resguardo* control the forces and most of the means of production (though they may have to lease some extra land), they must transform land and labor into commodities for the national market in order to acquire other important tools of production (e.g., machetes, fertilizers, and the like). Eroding land resources and high prices of imported commodities make it imperative for them to limit purchases. Reliance on subsistence farming to supply their own needs and cash cropping to obtain needed tools still remains the most useful and most commonly employed strategy. On occasion a farmer fails to produce enough to feed his family; instead of purchasing the staples at local stores, he will approach a close friend or kinsmen and either buy at reduced prices with deferred payment or exchange the needed food for labor or eventual repayment in kind. The Indian farmer is very aware of the importance of maintaining a small group of friends, neighbors, or kin who will be ready to help him when he is in need (Ortiz, 1973). In other words, their choice of strategy has forced them to maintain symmetrical links with other Indians and in some cases with poor white neighbors.[13]

An Indian who is particularly short of land must also turn to a landlord who will offer him a small allotment in exchange for fixed labor payment. Poverty often forces a poor Indian farmer to establish other asymmetrical relations with traders or wealthy Indian farmers whereby he will receive cash or goods on credit in exchange for the assurance that he will be willing to work as a laborer.

Consanguinity and wealth by themselves do not determine patterns of interaction; distance and travelling time also determine with whom an Indian family is likely to forge symmetrical or asymmetrical links. Most exchanges occur between kinsmen who live or have lived near each other. For example, those Indians who live east or north of the hamlet of San Andrés attend the weekly market, buy from San Andrés stores, and meet kinsmen who live in the same section of the *resguardo*. Those who live to the west of San Andrés have closer relations with Inzá traders, who make more attractive patrons. Despite the clustering of interpersonal links along topographically defined areas, Indians share enough interests in and obligations toward the *resguardo* to be identified as a bounded social subunit or closed corporate community.[14]

In many ways the white population forms an equally bounded subunit. The opposition and discrimination that all new white settlers faced when they moved into San Andrés forced them together in order to plan defensive strategies. At first they were not allowed to attend mass in the Indian church or to bury their dead in the cemetery, and they were jeered and threatened in their houses. Although four of the first ten settlers had married local women of Indian descent and thus had established links with some of the Indian families, they were marked as intruders and regarded with apprehension. They could count on the support of their affines but not necessarily on the support of other Indian families. Some of the animosity has been resolved through diplomacy or brutal counterthreats, but the distrust remains and has been extended to later arrivals as well as to the descendants of all settlers. The distrust is warranted; migrants came to the area guided not by altruism, but by profit motives. They wanted higher incomes and greater prestige. Those in need of land or wishing to expand their holdings could buy cheaply or even confiscate *resguardo* land suitable for coffee growing or cattle breeding. Those whites who intended to become traders, yet lacked the capital to compete with the successful traders in more densely populated areas or towns, could always make a quick profit by selling high and buying cheaply from Indians. No great fortunes were made, but there is no question that the economic exchanges between whites and Indians benefited the former more than the latter. Indians are well aware of their disadvantage and of their need to stick together and to avoid too many commitments to white settlers, from which they may not be able to extricate themselves. They prefer to be free to sell to the highest bidder and buy from the cheaper stores: at the same time, need for credit and for services forces them to sell to a particular patron or white client at a lower price than they would have gotten on the open market square. Poverty and uncertainty force Indians to turn to small traders and landlords who make a living by extending credit and lending capital assets at a high hidden interest.[15]

Some of the traders are only marginally better off than Indians and they face as much uncertainty as the Indian farmers. Clever and lucky traders can keep one step ahead by making outrageous profits from Indians who owe them money or coffee beans, while selling to other potential clients and debtors at more reasonable prices. Their success and solvency depend on their being able to maintain a monopoly on market information; they must also make the Indians believe that they have greater economic power and technical knowledge, as well as swifter access to political power, than any member of the Indian community could ever achieve. It is easy for the white settlers to monopolize price information on industrial products as very few outside traders venture into the area; furthermore, it is too costly and time-consuming for Indians to travel to other commercial centers. But it is harder to misguide Indians on the price of coffee, except at the beginning and end of coffee harvest, when sharp fluctuations are known to occur within a short period of time.

Ultimately, traders who buy coffee for resale depend for their success on their ability to create a belief about their power that extends beyond their actual resources. Aloofness from Indians is to their advantage; thus they profit from the initial reticence of Indians and their exclusion from community affairs. Traders do not want to tear down the wall that separates the two communities. On the contrary, for social and economic reasons they want to stress the differences.[16]

A style of life that relies on purchased imported goods and foods serves to symbolize basic economic distinctions between Indians and whites. The former are subsistence producers who also sell cash crops; the latter are totally involved in production for the cash market. The *fiesta* celebrating the patron saint illustrates the wish for separation by the two population sectors. The white residents nominate a committee to collect required funds and to allocate responsibility for decorations. It is a more sumptuous occasion than the subsequent Indian *fiesta*, but it lacks the private parties that characterize the latter. Although Indians are expected to attend and help finance white celebrations, they are not assigned responsible tasks nor are they allowed to hold the images during the procession. By the same token, whites are not allowed to organize Indian *fiestas*, and are not invited to their private parties. The celebration of *fiestas* illustrates how the boundary-maintenance ritual draws the white settlers together, engendering some sense of community activity. A closer examination of rituals and participation reflects as well the cleavages within the white population: only the traders-entrepreneurs are members of the all-male committee and groups of siblings work together to outdo the other displays that decorate the plaza. Most of the wealthy landlords only contribute with small sums of money; they are not so concerned with boundary rituals and are not closely linked to San Andrés traders.

Boundary-maintaining rituals thus tended to draw together only the population of white traders and entrepreneurs who live around the church and on the pathway to the hamlet. The smaller farmer and the wealthier landlord remain a bit aloof from these activities. If the population and wealth of the *vereda* grows, it is likely that San Andrés will assert its separate identity and gain some financial independence. Under the circumstances, it is likely that the administrative elite will emerge from amongst the sector of traders-entrepreneurs and will not cater to the needs of the small full-time farmer.

Although traders[17] are keen to maintain social distance from Indians, they are also interested in attracting a constant clientele of buyers of merchandise and sellers of coffee. It is possible to be assured of a clientele in spite of high prices by offering small services and credit. In other words, friendship and reciprocal exchanges are used by traders to ensure their commercial success. Such a strategy at the same time blurs the social distance that traders like to keep and has to be balanced against the boundary-building strategy used to increase power and revenue. The extent to which each trader uses one strategy more than the other depends on his cash assets, the time available to collect overdue debts, and the availability of opportunities other than trading for capital investment. In San Andrés one of the traders is known to be willing to extend credit and friendship to a large number of Indians in order to increase and ensure the number of customers, while others prefer to bolster an image of power even at the risk of diminishing their clientele. Traders who have land for farming and are able to exploit other opportunities choose the second strategy.

The need for traders to use competitive techniques to attract a large clientele can lead to tensions within the trading community. Hence, when opportunity allows it, traders prefer to honor mutual social and kinship obligations and avoid rivalry. In 1961, for example, one trader was able to branch out into a new noncompetitive field: preparation of planks for a local builder. Another trader chose to produce high-quality brown sugar cakes (*panela*) for local consumption. Yet another, in cooperation with a traveling entrepreneur, processed *cabuya*[18] leaves to obtain fibers for bag making. The expansion potential of such noncompetitive side activities is limited, but road improvement has encouraged tourism in the area, and eventually other equally profitable ventures may be available to the same small group of resident trader-entrepreneurs. Thus competition and estrangement was, and probably still is, kept in check. Communal bonds between them are probably still strong enough to serve as a platform for joint action.

The need to search for other opportunities has encouraged traders to establish meaningful commercial links with wealthy middlemen or entrepreneurs in other towns. Not all of the traders have the resources to travel and search for such contacts. Three of the San Andrés traders instead have to content themselves with buying small amounts of merchandise from wealthier local middlemen or traveling salesmen. For these three poorer traders it is of utmost importance to have local market information, local credit, and the cooperation of Inzá authorities. They spend a great deal of time, as well as money, on drinks to ensure a stable relation with wealthier traders in Inzá and San Andrés, and with members of the political elite of Inzá. The plight and dependence of these poorer traders affects the nature of the links they forge;

they cannot hope to be an equal in exchanges with other middlemen or to have the ultimate bargaining word. Furthermore, although patrons enjoy the support and small services provided by the small trader-client, they do not require his votes to stay in office nor his support to gain power. Thus patrons are unlikely to help a trader-client if the request means a sacrifice of power or time.

Five other traders have diversified their source of cash so as to be able to equalize their income throughout the year. Most of their stock was, at least until 1961, purchased in Popayán and Neiva from producers, as well as from middlemen selling wholesale and retail. Although these traders can afford frequent trips to stock their stores, they are nevertheless short of capital, and they have to become clients of a well-stocked wholesaler. The Neiva or Popayán patron of the San Andrés trader, in turn, is assured a distributor for his own stock without having to assume administrative responsibility for salesmen. Some of the patrons are wealthy enough to have access to departmental bureaucracy and are willing on occasion to help the San Andrés trader with needed documents or municipal complaints. The balance and permanence of this relationship depend on the number of petty traders in search of patrons and on the commercial potential of the region where the petty trader comes from. The San Andrés petty trader is not a prized client to the Neiva or Popayán patron.

Two other traders from San Andrés have enough capital in cash, cattle, and land to be able to afford their own trucks. In this way they are free to sell when it suits them and to make sure that their produce reaches the market place before those of other traders. Furthermore, ownership of a truck opens to them the doors of the vast world of truck owning wholesalers who reside in other towns. These wholesalers buy at the large industrial centers and resell from their own truck at large regional markets more cheaply than middlemen in Popayán or Neiva. San Andrés truckers not only profit from a cheaper source of supplies but also from their clientship to these powerful trucker wholesalers. Municipal mayors are interested in attracting the wholesalers as they contribute with a large municipal market tax. In order to attract them the mayors are willing to extend favors and services to the local clients of the wholesalers. One such favor is the granting of a license to carry passengers within the municipality.

In summary, although traders help link San Andrés to other centers, such links are seldom politically useful. Only occasionally can a middle-income trader attract the attention of departmental administrators to local complaints or regional needs. Links with Inzá are equally useless as the San Andrés client has little leverage to demand the attention of the Inzá patron and to request the use of influence on behalf of the *vereda*.

Whereas commercial activities force traders to search for capital and credit, agricultural activities force farmers to search for two other scarce means and tools of production: land and labor. In this area of Colombia, farming is not capital-intensive; only a few seeds and tools have to be purchased every year. Fertilizers and sprays are rarely used and no machinery has to be rented. As long as a farmer grows enough food for his family he can keep his land productive with minimal cash resources. Only at harvest time is he likely to need coffee pickers if he has one or more hectares planted with this crop. The farmer is then faced with a double problem: how to attract some of the few Indians who are able and willing to work as coffee pickers,[19] and how to acquire the money to pay their wages. Wealthy farmers and landlords can easily surmount this difficulty because either they have enough cash to entice the poorer and hungrier Indians with an advance on their wages, or they have enough tenants owing them labor rent to have to hire only a minimal crew of coffee pickers. The smaller farmers growing one to two hectares of coffee are the ones to feel the financial squeeze: unless they are able to obtain a small loan, they cannot afford to pay wages until they have sold some of their coffee. In an attempt to attract a crew of coffee pickers willing to work without an advance in wages and willing perhaps even to wait a week for a payment, small farmers forego status differences and befriend a number of Indians, with offers of help and protection in the hope that the Indians will feel obliged to reciprocate with a promise to work as wage laborers. Small farmers thus favored symmetrical relations with Indians that could be used as starting points for farming partnerships. For example, a small farmer who is short of capital resources offers an Indian partner sugar cane cuttings in exchange for the use of the Indian's land and labor. At harvest time the Indian delivers the crop and the white farmer processes it and markets it. When the crop is sold, the Indian receives either a share or a fixed payment. In this way, small farmers can avoid the heavy initial capital outlay yet expand their agricultural activities. Alternatively, they can obtain a loan from the Agrarian Bank (*Caja Agraria*), but in 1961 this was a slow and cumbersome process as no agencies were located within the municipality. Since the opening of an INCORA agency at Inzá, low interest loans are probably more easily available to Indian and small white farmers (see page 134), rendering partnerships less necessary. Of course, some small farmers are also traders and consequently can make use of other strategies to attract labor and capital. In the first place, they can entice Indians to buy on credit just before the harvest time and then demand that the debt be cancelled with labor. In the second place, it is easier for them to accumulate cash and to obtain small short-term loans.

Landlords with about ten to twenty tenants are wealthy enough to have ready cash for wage payments or are able to acquire government loans. In contrast, their tenants are totally dependent on them. Tenants are usually Indians who either have not been able to acquire enough land or who have lost their land to encroaching landlords. In exchange for a small piece of land on which they can plant some coffee trees and enough food crops to feed their families, tenants have to work three days a month for the landlord as cattle hands, farmers, coffee pickers, or *trapiche*[20] workers. Often they are asked to spend more than three days on the property of the landlord, in which case they receive a payment commensurate with prevailing wage rates. Those tenants who have managed to harvest more food than they can consume are often pressured to sell cheaply to the landlords, who use the food as provision to feed laborers. Although tenants are oppressed and dependent,[21] they are not entirely helpless in expressing dissatisfaction or asserting their rights. Most often they express dissatisfaction by slackening their pace at work, yet it is not uncommon for a tenant to take more vigorous action and to appeal to departmental labor offices for help. The ultimate illegal threat a landlord uses is eviction, the unspoken but real counterthreat tenants use is invasion. In San Andrés the asymmetrical and potentially exploitative relation between landlords and tenants has not yet reached a violent point. In fact, many landlords are tolerant and protective of their tenants.

Regardless of how ruthlessly some of the local landlords treat their tenants, their behavior does not conform to the stereotypical image of the hacendado. None of them has jural powers over his tenants or the right to evict them. Even those landlords who have up to forty hectares of land and ten to twenty tenants, live on their property, supervise field tasks, and assume full responsibility for marketing the crops or animals. They spend their time and energy administering the farms rather than in political activities; in fact, they are rarely seen at Inzá or San Andrés except during festive occasions. Each one of them remains aloof from all others and from influential residents, to the annoyance of Inzá politicians. More often than not they sell their crops and animals for cash directly to important middlemen in Neiva or Popayán who are interested only in bulk buying. They acquire capital resources through equally impersonal channels: banks and government credit institutions. In fact, none of them seems to have, or is in need of, powerful political contacts.

The landlords' power rests simply on ownership of land, a prized and scarce commodity, which allows them to tie tenants (i.e., workers) to their farms. However, the asymmetry in this exchange (little land for considerable labor at wages below subsistence) is not fixed; the balance can alter with changes in the landlord/tenant ratio or with changes in economic conditions. If requests for tenancy arrangements by poor farmers increase, so will the power of the landlord: the undercurrent of opposition between the interests of landlord and tenant will come to the fore. A new set of explosive problems may develop.

It is also possible that farming profits will slacken. A landlord will then not be able to keep his tenants busy for more than three days a month[22] (tenants depend on extra income from wage labor on landlord farms). He will likely lose power over them and may have to accede to larger land allotments in order to retain them, thus losing capital resources in order not to jeopardize the future availability of labor. In San Andrés, when faced with a temporary slump in agricultural prices, landlords are more likely to allow tenancy arrangements to lapse in order to protect their capital resources, gambling on a future increase in the supply of labor when, and if, real prices increase again. They have also turned to cattle breeding, which requires less labor.

Some traders and other residents rely on entrepreneurial activities for some or all of their cash income. I have mentioned that some farmers enter into contractual agreement with Indians to supply them with sugar cane that entrepreneurs then use to produce brown sugar cakes (*panela*) for sale at the Inzá market. I observed another resident who entered into a partnership with an ambulant entrepreneur who owned a fiber-extracting machine and who needed a local resident who could approach Indians and convince them to sell them leaves from *cabuya* plants growing in their property. Yet another resident had started a small lumber business using trees growing in the *resguardo*. All of these entrepreneurs have to be able to convey trust to Indians when enlisting their cooperation in contractual agreement or when convincing them to sell a product, of yet undetermined market value, at the entrepreneur's bidding price. At the same time, the entrepreneur has to manage to retain sufficient power in the exchange to be able to sanction a contract that favors his interest (small-scale enterprises succeed only when marginal profits are high). Thus, like traders, entrepreneurs have to maintain a fine balance between trust and power while forging asymmetrical relations with Indian partners.

Summary and Conclusion

The rural neighborhoods or remote municipalities in Colombia are poorly articulated to formal national political agencies. The poverty and administrative inadequacy of municipal governments impede administration of rural domains, particularly when such domains are territorially extensive[23] and most of their population resides in scattered farms. Furthermore, as a large number of hamlets or *veredas* lack any municipal representatives, the burden of administration rests on the underpaid and underprepared personnel residing in the municipal town center. Thus rural neighborhoods are neglected and depend for national articulation on the links that residents forge with outside agents in the course of their productive activities. One exception to this general rule occurs when national agencies, such as development institutes or political pressure groups, send their own representatives to rural areas, as has been the case in San Andrés in the 1970s.

In the 1960s and early 1970s, however, the main avenues of communication by which San Andrés residents could manipulate municipal authorities were the links engendered through commodity exchange. This is not a particularly useful channel of communication as these linkages are asymmetrical and place San Andrés in a subordinate position with respect to its own municipal authorities. Only the poorer traders and some of the Indians are likely to have forged and sustained ties with power-holders at Inzá. Furthermore, the transactions that forge the ties are more likely to increase than to redress the social imbalance that separates the transactors. Poor traders and Indians can only offer the Inzá politician-trader their vote and small amounts of cash in payment for merchandise. Neither of these benefits is a scarce resource to Inzá power-holders; hence their ascendancy is unlikely to be challenged and they remain free to set the terms of further exchanges. Inzá power holders, it is true, are often quite helpful to their clients. The point I want to make is that they do not have to help them for fear of losing them.

More balanced articulating links with outsiders are those established by landlords with outside buyers. However, as the transactions are impersonal and involve goods rather than means of production, they do not help forge effective links. More useful articulating links are established by wealthier traders with middlemen who reside either at the capital of the department (Popayán) or at the capital of the neighboring department (Neiva). Both centers are of importance. Popayán is an administrative higher-level center for San Andrés, and Neiva is where some important government agencies (e.g., a Federal Highway Department) are located. Those middlemen in Popayán and Neiva who themselves have been able to develop symmetrical relations with government agencies can offer the San Andrés trader some fringe services and thus may be in a better position to attract him. The fringe service does not ensure that the San Andrés trader will choose to buy and sell from the middlemen who offer it. After all, when choosing a source of supply or a buyer for coffee beans, the San Andrés trader is looking for someone who can offer good price, variety of goods, and credit; his main concern at that moment is with cash rewards and not with the potential need for a political favor in the future.

In order to evaluate how useful such articulating relationships are, one must determine whether the favors granted by the middleman in his role as broker are likely to serve only the needs of his San Andrés clients, or if, through the client, they are likely to serve the needs of other *vereda* residents. It is at this point that one must recall that resources are not equally available to all residents and, consequently, that interests conflict and status differences prevail.

Some residents lack resources to become independent producers and, as the reward for wage labor is not high enough to cover subsistence needs,[24] they are forced to become tenants. Wage labor is only profitable when the laborer has enough land to grow most of the food his family needs; without land he is destitute. It is evident that tenants are too helpless to demand anything beyond minor fringe benefits (e.g., a personal loan, health care, the purchase of tools from cheaper stores in Popayán or Neiva when the landlord goes there, protection). It is also evident that requests are granted only when the cost to the landlord is low or when a high price is set on securing the cooperation of his tenant. If the tenant insists on a request that the landlord considers outrageous or counter to his own interest, the landlord will find it more expedient to terminate the contract at the first possible opportunity. It is also obvious that landlords are not likely to serve as brokers on issues where there is a conflict of interests or on issues that will enhance the unity and power of the tenants. Furthermore, by insisting on purchasing coffee or any surplus food, landlords effectively block potential links between tenants and middlemen.

The links that small white farmers have established with middlemen and municipal authorities are also unlikely to profit Indian farmers, and vice versa. Poor white farmers may indeed want to forge friendship ties with Indians, but at the same time they are competing with them for land and are willing to use any opportunity at hand to gain a greater share of this resource. It is rare for white farmers to be in a position to incorporate new holdings, for Indians have a greater chance, through their *cabildo*, to organize a defense and gain representation than do a handful of poor and disorganized white farmers. The white farmers must fear the presence of CRIC even more than they fear the trading elite, and they are thus unlikely to represent the needs of the poor land-hungry Indian farmers.

Trader-farmers are in the unenviable position of having to foster an image of power while having to derive their power from municipal officers, wealthy local competitors, or patrons residing elsewhere. It is only because isolation and social barriers hinder communication that they can manage to convey power with a minimal resource base. Traders, in fact, depend for their success on the internal differentiation of the neighborhoods into Indian and white, as well as on their ability to block access to agencies. Kinship ties and loyalties amongst traders have made this task possible for the moment. Thus the articulating links that this population sector forges with outside agents is not likely to be made available to the rest of the population. Traders and wealthy farmers will use these contacts only for their own benefit. While one should not minimize the fact that there are many circumstances under which traders (more so than landlords) are likely to share with small farmers the same concern for increased productivity, cost-lowering agricultural techniques, and better transport, one should not forget that they are equally interested in maintaining the dependence of the Indian sector. Thus, while white traders would profit from INCORA's presence, they must regard the efforts of this agency with suspicion and are likely to block some initiatives.

San Andrés is thus linked to the municipal authority at Inzá through the minor and infrequent efforts of the mayor, or through the more arduous but ineffectual efforts of the *corregidor* in San Andrés, or through the personal channels forged by the San Andrés traders. None of these links can be effectively used in the present-day to demand scarce welfare or development resources from the municipality. Without outside intervention, it is unlikely that a change will occur in the relationship between San Andrés and Inzá. The attitude of municipal authorities, however, may change if the wealth and power of the San Andrés trading community increases. Municipal authorities may then fear frequent complaints and appeals to departmental authorities for intervention. The success of such missions, as well as of other articulating functions, will depend on the effectiveness of the personal links that the wealthier traders are able to forge with power-holders at the departmental centers. A change in the market or the utility of some prospects may affect the buying and selling strategies of the traders. It may even discourage them from maintaining very active stores or trading activities. If coffee prices remain low and the circulation of cash decreases, traders may choose to expand cattle breeding enterprises. If such changes in strategy occur, it is likely that the patron-client ties they had once forged with Popayán residents will decrease in effectiveness. Endogenous economic changes, even when such changes may bring greater wealth to a sector of the population, may make it more difficult for the neighborhood of San Andrés to demand services from municipal and central governments than it is at present.

In summary, the integration of a marginal area like San Andrés is complex and multifarious. The most effective links are those engendered through the exchange of means of production and commodities. Kinship links are important, but often self-interest supersedes them. Political links between a party boss and his following are relevant only for active politicians or administrators at the municipal township; rural residents in poor and marginal municipalities are most often outsiders to local politics. It is also clear that each type of trader or producer is able to make use of different types of integrating channels. The community as a whole is not jointly integrated to a particular higher-level center. Each segment integrates itself to one or more centers, sometimes in a dependent position and other times as an equal partner. In other words, it is unrealistic to conceptualize national integration as a nest of boxes, each under the power of a higher-order box. On the contrary, some of the higher-level centers are not able to exact resources from their domains. In fact, a higher-level center may find itself in competition with another center of equal hierarchical position for the political and economic resources of a given domain.

Notes

1.   In my description of the neighborhood of San Andrés, I stress the low density of population, the smallness of the population aggregates, the cost of traveling to larger centers, the unimportance of political activities, and the minimal resources that are available to residents through municipal authorities, because all of these factors are important conditions for the analytical procedure used, as well as the argument presented in this essay. The main concern of the San Andrés resident is to forge ties that are helpful or necessary to his business and farming endeavors. In other areas where politicians, voters, and administrators are useful resources not to be neglected, the scope of the analysis should be wider and political transactions should also be examined.

I have chosen to focus mostly on economic factors and on the strategies that may explain existing and continuing transactions in order to isolate the process of formation of articulating dyadic ties. Like Barth, I am focusing on transaction in order to isolate social process (Barth, 1966). The approach differs from his in that I do not justify the continuation of a transaction by assuming that the value of the expected gain is necessarily greater than or equal to the value lost. In other words, I do not assume the partners in the transaction to be competitive game players. A farmer may exchange his labor as rent for land not because he values three days a month of labor less than the acre he is allowed to cultivate, but because he needs the land for subsistence.

Furthermore, he is landless because others with greater financial resources and influence were able to purchase or confiscate land. Willingness to pay inflated rents can only be explained as a consequence of past decisions that have affected the subsequent availability of opportunities. In other words, the maintenance of the tenant-landlord relationship does not have to be explained in terms of the value of the goods and services exchanged at the moment, but in terms of the financial freedom to choose an alternative course of action. The relationship has to be explained historically as a consequence of an earlier strategy.

Articulation is a process that may or may not be channeled through formal institutions, as endless studies on the political significance of kinship ties have demonstrated. The present study makes it clear that ties other than kinship must also be examined and that it is not enough to focus on relationships associated with individuals who, because they hold either power or authority, have been said to have the role of brokers. Brokers perform articulating functions, but they are not *the articulating process*. This confusion is similar to Weber's confusion of entrepreneurial function with the entrepreneur. Let us hope that we can shed this legacy by moving away from ideal types and focusing more on process. As we focus on the latter, we should not forget that process must be studied historically whenever possible.

2.   My approach also follows Wolf's (1956) suggestion that anthropologists focus on group interrelations and power balances in order to piece together national studies. I diverge from Wolf's approach in that I do not assume the region to constitute a group, and I do not isolate a set of brokers as articulators of the groups to higher national centers. Instead, I assume that every resident does perform a brokerage function and that articulation is a more complex process.

3.   Occasionally, central government agencies open regional headquarters in rural areas or send representatives to peasant areas. At the appropriate points, I describe the activities of the various central government agencies that have recently been active in the area I have studied.

4.   There is little movement of resident traders between rural *veredas* of remote municipalities. Markets in this area are not organized to accommodate the trading needs of local petty traders but of middlemen who reside at higher-level commercial centers. At least until 1961, markets were held on the same day at Inzá and in neighboring municipalities (Ortiz, 1967); this is not necessarily the case in other rural areas (Symanski, 1971). In the past two years, new roads have been completed and marketing patterns may have changed accordingly.

5.   The term *vereda* has been used in Colombia since colonial times to refer to rural neighborhoods, whether or not they are territorially defined political units. Every mountain slope, valley, or nook has a place name, and those that cluster together around a pathway, route, or postal delivery center are closely grouped together under the term *vereda*. In some instances, such as Saucio (Fals Borda, 1955) and San Andrés, the *veredas* become recognized units of administration within a municipal territory, but the term may also be used to refer to areas of settlement that lack communal identity and are not administratively defined. *Resguardos* are small landholding corporations with membership limited to descendants of original settlers. Politically the *resguardos* are dependent on the administrative authorities of the municipality where the *resguardo* is located. The municipality, which has a town of at least five hundred inhabitants as its center, is, in turn, dependent on the departmental authorities.

6.   There are no reliable recent population figures for the area of San Andrés. In 1954 Bernal Villa carefully surveyed the area and gave a figure of 216 families. The initial tabulation for 1974 of the Census Bureau indicates 206 Indian families (1,055 inhabitants) and 36 non-Indian families (109 inhabitants). Although the latter figure seems accurate, the number of Indian families listed seems too low, which makes me suspect that the census taker has probably not been able to locate many of the houses that lie hidden under coffee or plantain trees in hard-to-reach slopes. Non-Indian houses are much more accessible and hence easier to survey.

7.   *Agregado* is an individual who requests temporary membership in the *resguardo* in order to be able to farm land loaned or rented to him by an Indian friend or client. The white farmer must make a formal request to the *cabildo* if the land is located within the *resguardo*. *Agregado* privileges are only temporary. Sometimes such temporary permits extend themselves for so many years that the *agregado* becomes a de facto member of the *resguardo*. Furthermore, on occasion

illegal land transactions with whites have been rationalized by making the white farmer an *agregado*. Once the *cabildo* (*resguardo* council) has accepted the petitioner as an *agregado*, the latter must contribute his labor to the upkeep of community property.

8.   When liberal politicians faced persecution by conservative forces, they met the threat with counterattacks. Soon this confrontation degenerated into senseless killings of anyone who belonged to an opposing camp, whether rich or poor. Rural areas suffered most during this period, particularly when well-organized bands conquered and settled a territory which, for all practical purposes, remained closed to any outsider. The area surrounding San Andrés suffered considerably from such organized militant bands. An Indian settlement ten hours by horse from San Andrés was attacked, and devastating confrontations occurred in Belalcazar. During this period there were also countless uprisings by workers and by peasants, and quasi-military republics emerged in some rural areas, including one in the area just north of Belalcazar. During much of this period the people of San Andrés, fearing attacks, spent most of their nights in the bush away from their houses.

9.   Colombia has a highly centralized form of government. The country is divided into departments, with governors appointed by the president of the republic. While it is true that elected departmental assemblies legislate on departmental affairs, governors have a strong veto power. Departments, in turn, are subdivided into municipal territories headed by mayors who are appointed by governors. Residents of a municipality, however, have the right to elect a municipal council, but their choice is limited by the fact that the equal representation of conservatives and liberals has been mandated since 1958 until recently. This body is responsible for local administrative decisions and for the appointment of minor local officials. Some municipalities, with extensive territories and important settlements within their boundaries, may parcel out for administrative purposes some sections of their domain as political subunits, or *corregimientos*. These have their own administrator, who has limited authority that is totally derived from the municipal mayor. Not all of the municipal territory is subdivided into *corregimientos*.

10.   No *corregidor* has been appointed in the last few years. Instead, a *comisario* (who, when I was in residence, was an Indian) with very limited policing functions serves as the messenger for the municipal mayor.

11.   Regulations governing Indian *resguardos* apply nationally. However, because they are not enforced with the same speed and zeal in all areas, and because the regulations themselves have changed in the course of time, some areas have been more deeply affected than others by short-lived national policies. For example, in 1821 a law was passed urging the subdivision of the *resguardo* and the granting of individual titles to Indian farmers who resided therein. In some areas *resguardos* were promptly surveyed and subdivided. In other areas the law was never enacted and *resguardos* were able to survive until 1858, when the earlier directive was repealed. At present, a *resguardo* can only be divided when two-thirds of the families who have rights of membership so request it. Most of the Paez *resguardos* have remained untouched by the earlier directive, and so far only one *resguardo* has requested subdivision (an underpopulated *resguardo* near San Andrés).

12.   Most of the land tilled by an Indian family is a share of the land that was previously farmed by the husband's father; for quite some time, the *cabildo* has failed to redistribute land to ensure equality of holdings. The obvious consequence is that those who descend from populous families have smaller farms than those who are only sons. Furthermore, in practice, all sons do not inherit equal shares (see Ortiz, 1973), and the land does not depreciate at the same rate throughout the *resguardo*. Wealth does not depend only on the size and the fertility of the soil available to the farmer, but also on its suitability for planting with the more profitable cash crops. It is thus not surprising to find a wide range of variation both in the amounts of land held by Indians and in the wealth of families.

13.   See Ortiz (1973) for a detailed description of the socioeconomic differentiation within the reservation and the exchanges of goods and services that link socioeconomic groups to each other.

14.   I here use Wolf's (1956) definition of closed corporate communities but without its behavioral and ideological attributes. See Keating (1973) for a critical evaluation of the concept of

closed corporate communities.

15.   The information received is contradictory and, as complete records are not available, I am not able yet to confirm the exact number of loans that have been granted to Indians. One source mentions that twenty-seven families have received loans, while another questions such a high number. I have only been able to confirm that three Indian families had requested and had been granted loans: none of these loans amounted to more than $600 (U.S. dollars).

16.   This analysis is based on the data gathered during 1960–61. It is probable that the quality of some transactions and the linkages have changed as new opportunities and political events have affected the area. It is impossible for me, for example, to determine at the moment to what extent the movement and contact of traders or Indians has been affected by the new road, or to what extent population growth has affected the balance in the landlord-tenant relation. Detailed information is as of yet not available. The value of this analysis is, however, not hampered by the fact that it is based on dated information. In the first place, this analysis is here presented as an illustration of an approach; in the second place, it can be used as an historical account. In fact, the analysis is formulated in such a way as to encourage rather than discourage the incorporation of changes in transaction or directions in the flow and recent political upheavals.

17.   In 1961, there were ten white heads of households who were active in trading activities. According to the 1974 census, the trading population remains stable.

18.   *Cabuya*, a common American agave; the fibers are used to make ropes and carrying-bags.

19.   Despite the fact that the *resguardo* is overpopulated, the supply of wage laborers is limited. The reason for this apparent contradiction is that most wage laborers have also at least a small subsistence farm and must plant, weed, and harvest at the time when others request their services. When I was in residence in San Andrés, I knew of seventy-two male Indians over the age of fifteen who were in need of cash and had to work for at least three to four months during the coffee harvest seasons. Others had enough land to be able to attend first to their own agricultural needs, only working a few days each week during harvest season. Altogether, I estimated a labor pool of 390 man-days during harvesting season, just barely enough to satisfy the needs of contractors. If the 1974 census is to be trusted, the number of individuals who work consistently during most of the harvest season has decreased. For the tabulations indicate only sixty-nine wage earners over the age of eight. I am inclined to distrust the accuracy of this information.

20.   *Trapiches* in Colombia are sugar mills powered by animals. The sap extracted is either used to make a mildly fermented drink or to produce cakes of brown noncentrifuged sugar (*panela*, one of the most common staples in rural Colombia). In San Andrés the *trapiches* are very small operations and the word has been extended to cover equally small operations with two-cylinder motor-powered mills.

21.   It would be inaccurate to describe the landlord-tenant relationship simply as a contradictory or noncompatible relation. The landlord and tenant offer each other resources the other lacks and requires. The conflict does not lie in the initial exchange but in the imbalance of power that may otherwise exist that allows the landlord to monopolize land and to force the tenant not only to become dependent on him for land, but also to proceed with exchanges that run counter to the tenant's farming interests. In other words, the relationship becomes conflicting and contradictory if there are power imbalances between the two parties and if such power is used to enforce other peripheral exchanges.

22.   When coffee prices fall, plantations are weeded and harvested with less care in order to reduce the cost of upkeep.

23.   Some municipalities have to administer only about two hundred square kilometers, while others have to administer four thousand square kilometers. Furthermore, in many of the territorially small municipalities the population is highly concentrated in the municipal township, while in other more extensive municipalities the population is scattered. Inzá has to administer 624 square kilometers and 96 percent of its population resides either on farms or in tiny hamlets.

24.   The average daily wage rate in San Andrés in 1961 was $3 (Colombian pesos) and the maximum was $5. If wage earners had to survive only on their income, they would have had to

earn at least $15 a day. According to the 1973 census, 81 percent of the population of San Andrés earns between $5 and $15 and the expected wage is $10 for Indians and $20 for whites. At the moment, the minimum wage rate for Colombia is $40. There has always been a disparity in wages between San Andrés and other areas, but the disparity seems to have increased. While in 1961 wages in other highland areas were 17 percent higher than in San Andrés, in 1974 they were 63 percent higher.

CHAPTER 8

The Political Role of Mestizo Schoolteachers in Indian Communities

George Primov

The most notable consequence of the Peruvian *Indigenismo* movement of the early twentieth century was the development of the concept of officially recognized *comunidades de indigenas*. However, the *Indigenismo* movement was also responsible for other innovations which, although less salient, were nevertheless equally important. One of these other results was the expansion of the educational system into the rural areas. The beginning of the wide-scale establishment of rural schoolhouses probably can be dated to the early 1940s and the process is still very much in force today. Despite the many social differences among Indian communities, one remarkably persistent current feature is the green schoolhouse with its noble motto proclaiming *"El pueblo lo hizo."*[1] Although sometimes the schoolhouse is not green or does not have the plaque, schoolhouses are found in a very great number of Indian communities. Schoolhouses mean schoolteachers and, in the Andes, school-teacher means mestizo.[2] Yet the implications of this very simple observation have not been recognized in the social science literature.

Community studies and ethnographies have generally regarded mestizo school personnel as quite extraneous and peripheral to the community and have therefore relegated them to minor importance or have abstained from dealing with them altogether. For many years the intellectual party line of Andean scholars has been to view the Indian community as the direct descendant of the pre-Incaic *ayllu* and to consider it a pristine reserve of a primordial egalitarian ethos which binds its members in bonds of extreme *Gemeinschaft*, where every peasant has the dubious privilege of being equally downtrodden and primitive.

Recently this view has come under attack, and the Andean noble savage is, it seems, turning out to be amazingly human, possessing both selfishness and greed. We are now learning that Indian communities can be significantly dissimilar and that they are marked by strong structures of inequality (Webster, 1974). From within and without, the Indian community is subject to strains and stresses which dispel the previous notions of social discontinuity across community boundaries. In short, the Indian community is not solely for Indians, by Indians, and of Indians. There is also good reason to suspect that it has never been so in the past.

The political boundaries of the Indian community have never coincided with ethnic boundaries. Mestizo power and influence have never stopped at the gates of the Indian community. Interethnic ties of *compadrazgo* and client-patron relationships have always allowed mestizo interests to penetrate the community from without. However, mestizo influence has also operated from within the community. The institutional agent for this endogenous source of mestizo influence has been the rural schoolteacher.[3] It may be argued that the political functions of rural schoolteachers far surpass in importance their pedagogical functions.

In this paper I will describe some of the noneducational functions of rural schoolteachers. I will show how these activities are institutionalized in the role of the rural schoolteacher and how these activities are an important element in the decision-making process of the community as a whole. Most of the material is based on ethnographic work done in the Indian community of Tocra (district of Colquepata, province of Paucartambo, department of Cuzco) during 1972 and 1973.

Tocra was officially recognized as a *comunidad de indigenas* in 1942. In 1943 formal education was introduced in the community with the arrival of a thirteen-year-old mestiza who had completed primary school and had been hired by the Ministry of Education as a rural teacher. This woman remained in Tocra for the next fifteen years as the only teacher in the community. It is difficult to assess the educational impact that she had on her students, but the political and social results of her activities in the community are still evident today. Under her direction and guidance, the community engaged in a series of self-help projects, such as building a schoolhouse. She traveled with the community president to Lima in order to obtain donations of books for the school. This venture in public relations was rewarded not only with books but also by exposure in the newspapers and by a highly publicized meeting with the President of the Republic. Her activities in the community were not defined by her role as a teacher, but rather were the result of diffuse and informal personal relations within the community.

At the time of our research, Tocra had four resident schoolteachers. Each teacher was assigned to the community for approximately two years before being reassigned to another post, usually a more urban one. As had been the case two or three decades earlier, the pedagogical achievements of the present schoolteachers have been mediocre at best. However, the political importance of schoolteachers has become more institutionalized and more specific. Although schoolteachers neither lead nor are involved in most community activities, they are involved in the formal decision-making through which most important community decisions are made.

The current pattern of schoolteacher influence on the community's decision-making structure must be understood in the context of the more general relations between Indian communities and the dominant mestizo society. The community dwellers stand in a position of double subordination to the mestizo society. As Indians,[4] they are culturally subordinate to the Spanish-speaking mestizos. As peasants, they are economically subordinate to the urban national society. This state of double subordination is fully understood by the Indian peasant; his strategies for coping with it, which to outsiders smack of traditionalism and ignorance, are quite rational responses to his marginal situation. However, the Indian peasant is not only aware of his compound subordination; he is also aware of the causal relationship between cultural and economic inferiority. To the Tocra villager, the key to mestizo political and economic superiority is education and, more specifically, monopolistic knowledge of Spanish.

From the perspective of the villagers, the mestizo schoolteacher now is a potential ally that can be utilized to attack the basic causes of their subordination. Schoolteachers mean education, and education is inexorably tied to the ability to be fluent and literate in Spanish. Thus the schoolteacher is perceived as an emissary whose task it is to make available in the community the knowledge which has been a monopoly of mestizos and which has served as an instrument of ethnic domination. However, the schoolteacher is simultaneously a mestizo and thus a member of the dominant group. He is therefore perceived as a double-edged blessing. He may be potentially beneficial, but he may also be potentially harmful or costly. This ambivalence characterizes the receptivity of the community to the proposals, suggestions, and directives issued by the local schoolteacher. It also explains the attempts to compartmentalize the affairs of the community in such a manner that schoolteachers have strong influence in certain matters and none in others.

The reason for this ambivalence is found in an examination of the present role of rural schoolteachers. In the *sierra* the schoolteacher is not merely an educator but also a civil servant. The Velasco government increasingly transformed civil servants into agents for "social mobilization." This meant that rural schoolteachers became official representatives of the central government. Today the rural schoolteacher is empowered by law to perform tasks unrelated to his educational activities. Whereas in the past the influence of the rural schoolteacher stemmed principally from his membership in the dominant mestizo group, at present his power is increasingly based on his role as a political agent. Although in the short run mestizo status and political authority are mutually reinforcing, in the long run these two roles are incompatible. The advantages of mestizo status are based on the inequalities which education and "social mobilization" purport to combat. The *maestro concientizado* is not only one who creates a literate peasantry but also, and more importantly, one who creates a political constituency for the central regime. In this function, the schoolteacher was meant to complement the political task of the ubiquitous *promotores* from SINAMOS.

With this general background, we can now examine more closely the influences of mestizo schoolteachers in the community of Tocra. By comparing briefly the first schoolteacher with the present ones we can show changes in the nature of the relationships between the schoolteachers and the community. By describing the present situation we can show the wide spectrum of functions which rural schoolteachers perform today.

Perhaps the most notable fact about the first schoolteacher was that she began teaching at age thirteen after only having completed six years of schooling. Clearly, her role as a teacher was legitimatized by her mestizo status. To teach Indians, it was sufficient to be a mestizo. It seems to have been the case that the arrival of this teacher was perceived by the community not in occupational terms but rather in ethnic terms. The same ethnic membership that provided her with the knowledge that she would supposedly transmit to the children also made her a powerful and highly valued asset for the community as a whole. Through her membership in the mestizo group, through the knowledge and skills which this membership implied, and through her personal contacts within the mestizo group, the community could avail itself of previously unavailable contacts and resources in its dealings with the mestizo society. In short, the schoolteacher was perceived, and turned out to be, a lobbyist representing community interests within her own ethnic group.

The establishment of a patron-client relationship between the schoolteacher and the community apparently served to reinforce the ethnic identities on both sides. Thus the relationship became a microcosm of mestizo-Indian relations in general. The difference between having mestizo patrons or *compadres* in Colquepata (the neighboring district capital) and within the community itself was perhaps purely subjective. It is undoubtedly easier to trust a mestizo who lives in the community than one who lives elsewhere. At any rate, fifteen years of close contact did not decrease the social distance between the teacher and the community,[5] although it did much to alter the relationship between the community and the outside world.

Perhaps her most pervasive effect was the expansion of the social horizons of the community. A great number of the elderly had never been outside the district boundaries, whereas most of the generation raised after the arrival of the schoolteacher had been to Cuzco at least once. However, the most important result of her presence was the instigation of successful community strategies for coping with mestizo institutions. Local recognition as an official Indian community enmeshed Tocra, like all other similar communities, in institutional linkages with mestizo legal and political structures. The realization that benefits could be obtained from such linkages led to an increasing expertise in dealing with the various agencies and ministries. In this process, the schoolteacher had a central role. Although she failed to educate the children of Tocra, she succeeded in training a generation of skillful community leaders adept at dealing with mestizo bureaucracies.

If it is still permissible today to speak of manifest and latent consequences, then one might suggest that the presence of mestizo schoolteachers in Tocra thirty years ago had formal education as an intended consequence, and political representation and education as an unintended consequence. The first failed conspicuously, while the second proved significant. Although her pupils failed to learn Spanish or gain any formal education, they did learn how to cope with mestizo authorities and how to maximize their benefits from interactions with them. In the long run, the activation of personal and ethnic resources by the schoolteacher proved much more significant than her formal educational activities.

The present situation in Tocra is much different. There are now four schoolteachers. Their functions in the community and their relationships to it have become more restricted and more formalized. Today's villagers make a clear distinction between the role of "teacher" and the status of "mestizo." The predominant orientation towards the school personnel is occupational rather than ethnic. Consequently, the relations between the teachers and the community are increasingly characterized by a bureaucratic orientation. This is not to say that ethnicity has ceased to be of importance; rather, ethnic membership has ceased being a sufficient condition for structuring all relations between the two groups.

The contemporary rural schoolteacher is a nexus between the national political structures and the community political structures. The imposition of a government-decreed political hierarchy within the community, the *Juntas de Vigilancia y de Administración*, was predicated on the ability of school-teachers to maintain and control the workings of these committees. If the case of Tocra is typical, then it may be assumed that these committees would soon be abandoned in most communities if it were not for the local schoolteachers, who routinely channel many community affairs through these political bodies.[6]

The schoolteachers who are at present assigned to Tocra, as well as those assigned to most other similar communities, are recent graduates who have little teaching experience or training. On the average they stay for a period of two years. Most of them view their stay in Tocra as something of a necessary exile that has to be endured before earning a more "civilized" teaching assignment elsewhere. They all view themselves as vastly different from the villagers and regard their work in the community as a civilizing mission. None of the teachers had established *compadrazgo* ties with local villagers or had assumed any *cargos*. In fact, I never observed a teacher outside of the school compound except during the daily outing to the soccer field. Similarly, Indian adults were almost never observed inside the compound except when there was a meeting of the community. All community meetings were conducted in the schoolhouse.

The institutionalization of the political functions of rural schoolteachers is part of the general process of the politicization of the community as a whole.

The increasing assistance bestowed on some communities by such agencies as SINAMOS has increased the dependence of such communities on these agencies. As some communities found SINAMOS an increasingly versatile and receptive patron, their relations to the mestizo society became increasingly channeled through the government agencies. The government has partially succeeded in structurally integrating Indian communities into a supportive political constituency. One mechanism for this structural integration has been the abolishment of the traditional *varayoc* structure and the imposition of the bi-committee structure. Needless to add, this new structure is totally alien to the community's patterns of self-government and therefore has required outside help for its implementation. The obvious choice: the local schoolteacher.

Tocra has perhaps benefited more than many other Indian communities from government help. Perhaps the fact that its community president met and was aided by the president of the country helped to strengthen a positive orientation to and reliance on government agencies. In this, the village has been rather successful. It has obtained materials to build a schoolhouse and now is obtaining similar help and technical assistance in building a second school building. SINAMOS also built a concrete bridge that allows the community-built road to join Tocra with Colquepata, thus making it possible for motor vehicles to reach Tocra for the first time.[7] SINAMOS also provided tractors and dynamite to open another road that will soon link Tocra to Pisac and thus make Cuzco easily accessible to the villagers. In addition, SINAMOS promised other types of aid. Finally, with the help of the office of Agrarian Reform, the village finally won a land dispute initiated thirty years ago against a neighboring hacienda. For all these reasons, the village became kindly disposed toward the central government and is perhaps one of a few communities where the local *promotor* from SINAMOS was respected and trusted.

As a consequence, Tocra villagers have made an earnest effort to obey the government's decree and implement the *juntas*. The use of schoolteachers as advisors has resulted in their incorporation into the presiding body of the community. From merely advising and chastising the community, schoolteachers now command and direct it, always with the proper charade of deference toward the Indian authorities of the communities. The following is an extreme example of the cynicism and influence of the schoolteachers. At a village assembly, a schoolteacher was charged with keeping the minutes of the meeting. While a certain matter was being volubly and lengthily discussed by the peasants, he proceeded to record the point as settled and then proceeded to write a summary of the discussion of the next point in the agenda.

Many informal and formal factors have aided in this expansion of the power of schoolteachers. The very fact that community assemblies are now exclusively held in the schoolhouse means that they take place in a mestizo, or at least nontraditional, setting. The schoolteacher is master of the school compound and all who enter it. Thus his claim to authority within the compound is not challenged. In fact, it would not be an exaggeration to state that the paternalistic attitude which characterizes teacher-student relations is similar to the attitudes displayed by the teachers toward the community assembly. In many ways the latter are treated as children.

A second factor aiding schoolteacher dominance is the illiteracy of the village authorities. Only two or three villagers can decipher written Spanish or write it phonetically. Therefore the documents directed to the community or issued by it are read and written by the schoolteachers. The reliance of the community on the schoolteachers to interpret all *decretos* and phrase all *solicitudes* converts the latter into informational gatekeepers who can monitor communications with the outside. Obviously there are other channels of communication between the community and the various agencies. But at the level of official communication between the community authorities and outside authorities, much of this linkage is monitored by the schoolteachers. In addition to writing communications, schoolteachers may also be asked to help in recordkeeping. They thus have access to whatever few community records there are. However, there were attempts by the local authorities to handle some of their own records, such as attendance at *faenas*, outstanding fines, communal land assignments, and other similar records. In Tocra it is not clear whether schoolteachers have routine access to these records.

The need to meet with visiting mestizo government officials also strengthens schoolteacher participation in community affairs. Although most government personnel are bilingual, and thus can communicate directly with the villagers, the participation of schoolteachers is mandatory. Furthermore, welcoming ceremonies are invariably held in the school compound. At such ceremonies the schoolteacher, rather than the president of the *Junta de Administración*, acts as the official host. The latter is always in attendance but is routinely ignored by both sides. It needs to be mentioned, however, that schoolteachers do not function as official hosts on all occasions. Whenever SINAMOS bureaucrats or technicians came to the village, it was the local *promotor* who assumed the role of a host. In both cases, however, the local authorities did not attempt to assert their leadership but rather allowed either schoolteachers or *promotores* to act as their spokesmen.

The last, and most important, informal source of teacher influence is what may be termed "civic expertise." The schoolteacher is asked for advice because of his familiarity with mestizo customs and institutions. He knows the ropes of mestizo society and can therefore counsel the community on how things are done or should be done if the community is to be successful in its dealings with the outside. His role as a civic expert is not limited to giving advice. Sometimes a teacher may initiate a proposal and may try to convince the community of its merit. In such cases the passive resistance of the community may be sufficient to thwart any proposals which it finds unacceptable. Whether giving asked-for advice or promoting his own projects and opinions, the schoolteacher is a resource of tactical knowledge which is respected, feared, and humored.

Perhaps the greatest power of the schoolteachers over the community is the threat of withholding advice. Although much advice is given in a facade of disinterested assistance to the community, it is clear that teachers expect their advice to be implemented. If it is not, they invariably resort to a favorite mestizo tactic of accusing the community of being a bunch of *ingratos*, and telling them to go and try to find someone else who will help them. This is an unspoken but powerful threat and does much to explain community acquiescence to schoolteacher demands.

However, the power of rural schoolteachers is not solely dependent on informal mechanisms. It is also supported by formal powers. The principals of rural schools are charged with administering local elections for the various committee posts. They are formally charged with instructing candidates in the duties of the committees and with making sure that only eligible candidates and voters participate in the election. Eligibility is mostly based on membership in the community. In Tocra such membership is generally unambiguous. However, in a rare case where membership is doubtful, the teacher may assume a juridic function and decide the issue of eligibility. Normally, elections are held in the schoolhouse and the votes are counted by the schoolteachers. This means that schoolteachers have some control over the choice of candidates and over the results of elections. In Tocra there was no reason to suspect that elections were manipulated by the schoolteachers; however, the possibility always exists. Perhaps the best guarantee against the dishonest behavior of the schoolteachers in the administration of elections is the fact that their power is not threatened by these internal elections. Unless they have personal ties with a particular candidate, the outcome of the election is pretty much a matter of indifference to them. Mestizo teachers may, and do, make suggestions for candidates.

Such suggestions probably carry some weight. In Tocra the lack of general and informal communications between teachers and villagers has meant that most of the interaction which does take place occurs between the teachers and the community leadership. The leaders of the community, by and large its wealthier residents, seemed to have closer ties with the teachers, and the latter are probably consulted when new candidates are selected. It is very possible that such consultations take place in order to determine the acceptability to the schoolteachers of potential leaders. Since the effective administration of community "foreign policy" depends largely on assistance from the teachers, it would be unwise, from the community's point of view, to elect leaders unacceptable to the schoolteachers.

Formal power also comes from transitory or periodic tasks entrusted by the government to the rural schoolteachers. In the 1972 population census, rural schoolteachers were widely used as census takers in the communities where they were assigned. Similarly, in the 1973 agro-pastoral census they helped personnel from the Ministry of Agriculture in enumerating their communities. A byproduct of this activity is that many schoolteachers may know much more about the characteristics of the villagers than do the villagers themselves. The school principal of Tocra had been in charge of the population census in that town, and he seemed to know a great deal about the economic and social structure of the community and, more importantly, about the wealth of many individual villagers. Such knowledge can be a powerful and persuasive tool for ensuring compliance and cooperation from the wealthier, and politically dominant, segments of the community.

The sources of the political power of rural schoolteachers range from clearly identifiable formal mechanisms to highly diffuse and informal arrangements. The intensity of and bases for such power undoubtedly vary from community to community, but the conditions that give rise to the power of schoolteachers exist in most communities. The net effect is that the schoolteacher becomes part of the community's power structure. This fact is not lost on the schoolteachers themselves or on the community.

When asked to describe the authority structure of Tocra, the school principal replied that first and foremost (*en primer plano*) came the teachers, then the leaders of the community, then the members of the two *juntas*, and finally the rest of the community. He added that the community leadership constantly asked for his counsel since it lacked the proper education. Finally, and most significantly, he stated that the school personnel acts as a resource for the community leadership.

The villagers, on the other hand, see the situation a bit differently. The attitudes of the villagers toward the teachers are somewhat ambiguous and varied. Generally, the teachers are viewed positively by the community. They are felt to have authority within the village but there is no clear-cut consensus as to their relative authority with respect to the local leaders. The most widespread opinions seem to be that the president of the community and the teachers have equal authority, or that the president has more authority but that he is always helped and advised by the teachers.

Some villagers recognize jurisdictional differences and view the president of the community and the teachers as each having equal authority, though the two areas of jurisdiction are different. In general, the political functions of the teachers are well recognized by the villagers; the villagers, however, do not assign to the teachers the political importance which the teachers assign to themselves. There is also a general tendency to describe the decision-making process as one of agreements between the president and the teachers (and, sometimes, the *alcalde*). This consensus model of the local government seems generally accepted and probably represents a close approximation of reality. The teachers are regarded as beneficial and useful advisors, both because they are felt to have more experience and because they can read and write and thus are better informed. They are thus seen as helping the community with their expertise. Perhaps the most succinct statement on the relative status of the teachers was that expressed by an informant who said that "one must obey the local leaders, but must respect more the teachers."

Perhaps Tocra is an atypical case, but there is no reason to suspect so. Observation in other communities generally tends to confirm the data from

Tocra. In fact, it may be the case that political tutelage by rural schoolteachers is so institutionalized that it is accepted unquestioningly both by participants and social scientists.

It is very easy to overstate the case for schoolteacher power and influence within Indian communities. There are occasions when suggestions by the schoolteachers are ignored or rejected. This is apt to happen when the community is concerned with internal problems which in its view are outside the scope of schoolteacher expertise. In Tocra the schoolteachers' efforts to curb certain "immoral" practices during the annual *fiesta* have been completely futile. The villagers simply feel that this is none of the teachers' concern. The same villagers, however, are quick to adopt suggestions regarding the best manner of obtaining a priest for the same *fiesta*.

Bearing in mind this qualification, we may make some generalizations. Since their arrival, rural schoolteachers have influenced decision-making within the communities. For the most part, this influence has been greatest in the field of community decisions about exogenous matters, that is, school-teachers have acted as "foreign policy" advisors. Initially, their status as mestizos assured their preeminence in such matters. More recently, rural schoolteachers have become part of the community's political structure by virtue of both informal and formal mechanisms. At present their advice is sought not simply because they are mestizos, but also because they possess valuable expertise both as educators and as political agents. They represent the national government and mediate relations with it. Thus all but the most involuted communities must cope with and submit to a certain degree of schoolteacher power and influence. In some communities such influences may be great, as in Tocra, while in others it may be minimal. Whatever its degree, it is a pervasive factor in most Indian communities, and although it is not easily detectable, it must be taken into account if one desires to understand fully the decision-making structures of many Indian communities.

Notes

1.   "Built by the people." This motto, however, dates only from the presidency of Fernando Belaunde Terry.

2.   The one exception to this is the Adventist schoolteachers in the department of Puno. These teachers are of Indian background, and although they speak Spanish, they are not considered mestizos, nor do they consider themselves as such.

3.   For the purposes of this paper, a rural schoolteacher is one who is assigned to teach in an Indian community.

4.   Although it is a prevalent practice to refer to the rural Andean populations as peasants or *campesinos*, this practice disregards the basic ethnic distinctions between this group and the dominant mestizos. The use of the term *peasant* implies that this group is essentially an economic group. Although the Andean Indian population certainly constitutes a peasantry, it is a peasantry which is ethnically different from the dominant sector of its society. Ethnic and economic factors are separate determinants of social stratification; it is my impression that in the Andes, ethnic identity is the more basic and important.

5.   Perhaps an indication of the vast social distance which separated the mestizo schoolteacher from the community is her statement that the most difficult aspect of her long stay in Tocra had been her loneliness, for, as she explained, "there was no one to talk to!"

6.   In fact, the community has been reluctant to abandon the traditional *varayoc* system. It recently petitioned the central government to be allowed to retain the *varayoc* structure for the internal administration of the community, while implementing the *juntas* system for dealing with exogenous problems. Although there are apparently legal provisions for incorporating the *varayoc* into the newer political structure, Tocra has been unsuccessful in having its petition accepted.

7.   Until very recently, Tocra was inaccessible to motor vehicle traffic. Even though the new road has been open for over five years, the only vehicles which use the road are government trucks and tractors. My car was the first private vehicle to reach Tocra and most probably is still the only one to have done so.

CHAPTER 9

Ccapana: The Demise of an Andean Hacienda

Pierre L. van den Berghe

This case study documents the last days of a large hacienda in the province of Quispicanchis, department of Cuzco, while it was in the process of expropriation under the 1969 Law of Agrarian Reform. The study of Ccapana, conducted during several visits between August 1972 and October 1973, was part of a much larger research project concerned with class and ethnic relations in the department of Cuzco.[1]

Introduction

Before launching into a description of Ccapana, I shall briefly react to the conceptual framework suggested by Orlove and Custred in the first two chapters of this volume, if only because the framework within which this study was conducted differed substantially from theirs on a number of points. Orlove and Custred suggest a network approach, using the household as the main unit of analysis. They explicitly reject the validity of any hacienda-community dichotomy; they implicitly grant little importance to ethnic differences within the Andean population, holding more to the unitary than to the dualistic view of Andean culture; and they deny much analytical power to the conventional Indian-mestizo distinction. The research strategy they present traces networks of relationships, primarily economic exchange relations, from the bottom up, starting with individual households. Their strategy makes only occasional references to the formal political and social structure of higher-level units, such as the community, the hacienda, the market town, and so on, as sources of external constraints on the local-level organization. Such a strategy has been applied with considerable success by Orlove in his regional study of the wool trade in southern Peru (Orlove, 1977a). Orlove and Custred argue that since there is such a wide variety of local settlement types even within a small area of the southern Peruvian Andes, any simple dichotomy between hacienda and community hides more than it reveals, and there is thus little gained by

trying to define either term. Though they do not address themselves extensively to the ethnic issue here, they also imply that the Indian-mestizo
distinction is empirically too muddied to be analytically useful.

There is one crucial point in which I am in complete agreement with Orlove
and Custred, namely, the necessity of relating peasant communities to larger
regional and national systems in order to understand anything at all about
them. For this reason, it is artificial and sterile to treat local communities as
isolates. There is, of course, nothing novel in this conclusion, since linkages
with the outside world are the basis for differentiating peasants from "tribals"
(Wolf, 1966). I am also in agreement with Orlove and Custred concerning the
great empirical diversity of local settlements, even in small areas. Clearly, our
differences of approach are not based on different perceptions of reality, but on
divergent analytical emphases, and hence research strategies, dictated in part
by the problems to be solved, and by available time and money to solve them.
My theoretical points of departure have been, on the one hand, Marxian class
analysis (and its neo-Marxian applications to Latin American situations) and,
on the other, the "plural society" approach applied to the study of the
Caribbean and of the colonial societies of Asia and Africa (Furnivall, 1948;
Kuper and Smith, 1969; van den Berghe, 1974c). Colby and van den Berghe
(1969) have applied this approach to the Guatemalan highlands, and other
formulations, though not explicitly associated with the "pluralism school," are
very close to it, notably Balandier's conception of the "colonial situation"
(1955) and Aguirre Beltrán's "region of refuge" model (1957, 1967).

Here is not the place to give an extensive presentation or critique of the
pluralist approach; I merely wish to make explicit my points of divergence
from the strategy employed by Orlove and Custred. Since the central problem
of social scientists concerned with "plural societies" has been the mode of
incorporation of culturally diverse and socially stratified groups into a
common system of relations of power and production, cultural factors have
been of central concern to the pluralists.[2] Of particular interest to these
scholars have been the articulation of different sets of cultural institutions, the
sociolinguistic aspects of multilingualism, and the subjective and objective
indices of ethnic group boundaries. The plural society model has seen
heterogeneous societies as principally held together through a nexus of
political domination and economic exploitation imposed from the top. This
view, in turn, has suggested a research strategy that consists in looking at such
societies from the top down, rather than from the bottom up. The pluralist
approach, while sharing some basic features with Marxian class analysis,
differs from it mainly in its greater emphasis on relations of power as a main
and often prior cause of inequality.

Applied to the case at hand, the present research was conceived as a regional
ethnography of inequality in the department of Cuzco. The basic hypothesis
was that unequal relations of power and of production were the product of a
complex interplay of class and ethnic factors. Although Peru does not
represent as clear-cut a case of a plural society as, say, South Africa, Fiji,

Ethiopia, India, or Trinidad, linguistic and other cultural differences in the population are far greater and far more important as a source of inequality than in a relatively homogeneous class-stratified society such as, say, France or Japan. It is true that Indians and mestizos are not rigid, sharply bounded, consensually defined groups, but, at the same time, ethnic differences cannot be ignored or reduced to class differences. To be sure, ethnic differences greatly overlap with class, but the two issues are qualitatively distinct. The strategy of research was thus to cover, in a few additional intensive case studies of micro-regions, as much of the entire range of ethnic and class situations encountered in the Cuzco region as was feasible. That is, I deliberately chose a regional metropolis and several market towns, communities, and haciendas. Furthermore, I attempted to cover both towns on the main economic axis of the department (the Cuzco-Sicuani road and railway), where ethnic boundaries are ill-defined and fluid and where class relations are more salient, and more peripheral areas (of which Ccapana is an example), where ethnic divisions are relatively clear and unambiguous.

To return to the central issue of this exploration, namely, the validity of the hacienda-community distinction in the analysis of the Andean society, the present study accepted prima facie the validity of the distinction, and, indeed, incorporated the distinction into the design of the study through the selection of cases. The more the study proceeded, the more aware I became of how much variation these two deceptively simple labels covered. Nevertheless, these terms are consensually recognized categories. They are thought by the people involved (both peasants and urbanites, Indians and mestizos) to represent clearly distinct social situations; the two groups are granted different legal statuses, and they are subject to different policies. Whatever the objective content of these two categories, their subjective (or "emic") definition by the people concerned gives them a reality which cannot be denied or simply brushed aside. The recent agrarian reform program is, of course, in the process of abolishing haciendas, but the "cooperatives" with which the government is trying to replace the haciendas remain on the whole as different from the communities as the haciendas had been before. Old distinctions thus reappear in a new guise.

Perhaps the most serious misconception involved in the terms hacienda and community is that the peasants who lived on the hacienda were "captive," while those who lived in the community were "free." In fact, the inhabitants of many *estancias* or haciendas were far freer than those of many communities. Some hacendados had only nominal control over their *colonos*, or lost their control over the years, as we shall see in the case of Ccapana, and as Maltby also documents for Picotani. Conversely, many *comuneros* with insufficient land had to sell their labor to haciendas or were subjected to many labor obligations, economic exactions, and other forms of ritual, political, and economic subservience by the mestizo petty bourgeoisie of the neighboring market town. Freedom, then, for both hacienda and community people, was and still is a relative concept. The safest generalization that can be made is that

Andean peasants have been oppressed and exploited both as peasants in a class-stratified society, and as members of a defeated nation since the Spanish conquest.

The misconception just alluded to has interesting ideological roots in the *Indigenista* movement and in the leftist creed of the urban mestizo intelligentsia. It continues to be cultivated under the current land reform program because it serves the class interests of the bureaucrats in charge of the reform. Under the guise of abolishing *gamonalismo* (the abusive treatment by hacendados) and restoring peasants to the idyllic communalism that was supposedly part of their Inca heritage, the government is transforming haciendas into "cooperatives" that are in fact controlled by government bureaucrats and technicians. In the words of the classic witticism spotted on a wall in the Plaza San Francisco in Cuzco, "Con amos, SIN-AMOS, no progresamos."[3]

The Hacienda Ccapana

The hacienda Ccapana, expropriated in 1973, was still operated by its former owner when I studied it, and constituted perhaps one of the closest approximations of a large hacienda in a more remote part of the department that was still available for study at that time.[4] I shall, therefore, refer to Ccapana as an hacienda in the ethnographic present. It is located on the Rio Mapocho, in the district of Ccahuayo, on a thirteen-kilometer dead-end road that branches off from the Cuzco-Quince Mil-Puerto Maldonado road. Ccapana as a hacienda in the ethnographic present. It is located on the Rio (population 1,100), ninety-two kilometers from Urcos (population 3,100), the capital of Quispicanchis province, and 138 kilometers from the city of Cuzco. The trip to Cuzco takes three to four hours by car, as nearly one hundred kilometers of the way are over a narrow, precipitous mountain road.

The hacienda covers some 20,000 hectares, of which only some 800 to 900 are arable. No more than 100 hectares of valley floor land are flat enough to be irrigable and cultivated by tractor. Marginal, high altitude pasture covers about 10,000 hectares, and the rest is largely unproductive land (steep slopes, glaciers, and other barren areas). The altitude ranges from 3,200 meters in the narrow valley, where the *casa hacienda* and the village of Ccapana proper are located, to 5,000 meters or over at the permanent snow fields. Most of the pasture for sheep and alpacas is around 4,000 meters, and a herd of some 100 head of Brown Swiss cattle is grazed in the valley and partially fed on alfalfa fodder. Alfalfa is grown as one of the main crops in the crop rotation system. Also grown are potatoes, barley, and, sometimes, maize, wheat, and oats.

The population of Ccapana comprises some two hundred fifty families, and twelve hundred inhabitants living in seven *estancias* or subdivisions of the hacienda. Six of these seven population clusters are nucleated villages, and the seventh one, a high-altitude pasture area, has a dispersed settlement pattern. Some of the villages are as much as twenty kilometers away from the *casa hacienda*. The village of Ccapana proper is next to the *casa hacienda*, at the end of the private road maintained by the owners. It includes some seventy nuclear families, totaling about three hundred individuals. In the village are located a chapel, two stores (including one on the *casa hacienda*), and all the main buildings and other structures of the hacienda, that is, the living quarters of the owners, storage houses, the tractor and truck shed, the piggery, the stable for the pure-bred cattle, the pharmacy, the office, servants' rooms, the cemetery, and other facilities. Three kilometers away, there is a two-teacher lower-primary school with some eighty children enrolled, and several of the other villages also have their own lower-primary schools. The owner and his wife, naturalized Peruvians of German origin, live there with their son, his wife, and his children. The hacendados also own a house in Cuzco, but, unlike most large landowners in the region, they spend most of their time on their hacienda and directly administer it, closely supervising all aspects of its operation. Their recent European origin makes them, in several respects, atypical of local hacendados.

According to the owners, Ccapana, which they bought in two stages in 1929 and 1933, never thrived economically. In the words of the hacendado's son, it is a "white elephant" which barely sustained the family in a modest Cuzco upper-class lifestyle, and which, in the last couple of years, was even run at a loss. Profits from the hacienda were insufficient to send the owner's son to college in Canada. His studies in agronomy were financed from other sources. The hacienda's production consists in part of small-scale subsistence agriculture and livestock breeding by the twelve-hundred-odd Indians living on the hacienda; in part of market crops (mostly potatoes, barley for the brewery, alfalfa for fodder, plus some maize, broad beans, wheat, oats, and other minor crops); and in part of marketed animal products (mostly alpaca and sheep wool, but secondarily cheese, meat, and hides). The hacienda also buys and resells some of the surplus production of the Indian *colonos*.

Adjacent to Ccapana were nine other haciendas, including Q'ero, which was purchased by the Belaúnde government thanks to the intervention of a Peruvian anthropologist, and which became a free community in 1964. There was also the huge eighty-thousand hectare sheep ranch of Lauramarca, which was among the first to be expropriated under the current agrarian reform program and which now operates as a cooperative. Lauramarca is wracked by internal conflicts between the members of the cooperative, and it is reputedly in bad financial condition because of corruption and inefficiency on the part of the government technicians who run the cooperative and because of livestock theft and neglect by the Indians. However, Lauramarca was already in financial straits under private absentee ownership, to the point that the owners reputedly welcomed the compensation they received from the state when they were expropriated in 1969.

Even under close and competent management by the owners, as in the case of Ccapana, production on these marginal Andean lands is quite limited. The owners of Ccapana have had to build and maintain a thirteen-kilometer access road that is continually cut off by rock slides or even washed away in stretches of several kilometers by the river during the rainy season. The area available for intensive, high-yield agriculture is limited to some one hundred hectares of valley land. With proper irrigation and chemical fertilizers, yields may be as high as twelve to eighteen metric tons of potatoes per hectare, but only about 1 percent or less of the land area can be used in this fashion. The rest of the agricultural land is on slopes and can be cultivated only with the foot-plow or, at best, with ox teams, and its productivity is far lower.

As for livestock raising, it has long been beset by a wide range of problems: overgrazing, theft, disease, predation, and continual trespassing. As the livestock figures for 1962 in Ccapana show, the *colonos* grazed some 5,000 sheep, 5,000 llamas and alpacas, 560 head of cattle, and 620 horses and donkeys, while the hacendado grazed 1,600 sheep, 1,940 alpacas, 170 head of cattle, and 10 horses. In other words, some three-quarters of the livestock were owned by the Indian *colonos*, and these were raised mostly to meet subsistence needs and as a form of saving, rather than to sell. Wool and small quantities of barley are the main products from which Indians get cash income. Many of them sell their little surplus to the hacendado, who in turn resells it to traders who come to the hacienda to buy produce, or to town merchants. Indian-owned livestock is often raised for quantity, with little concern for quality. Since 1962 the hacendado's share of the livestock has further declined, and trespassing is on the increase.

Ccapana has a long history as a hacienda. The oldest existing deed goes back to 1712, but it may have existed even before that date. When the last owner purchased it in 1929 and 1933, it belonged to two highly prominent Cuzco upper-class families, who were interrelated by blood and marriage. Their members are descendants of *conquistadores*, and have recently included a chief justice of the Supreme Court in Lima and a rector of the University of Cuzco. The last hacendado is the son of a German banker of French Huguenot descent. He came to Peru as a young man, bought Ccapana with capital sent by his father, brought over his German wife, and subsequently became a Peruvian national. Though the family is multilingual (Spanish, German, French, English, and Quechua), Spanish is now the dominant home language, and the son married into the old Cuzco aristocracy. The son went to the University of Toronto, where he took a degree in agronomy, and then returned to Ccapana as his father's administrator. The hacendado's family spends at least 80 percent of its time on the land, driving or riding up and down the valley, supervising the daily round of activities, going to the high-altitude pastures to watch over the shearing of the sheep and alpacas, and even taking part in the manual labor. Their love of the land and of a rugged outdoor life, and their lack of disdain for physical labor, are highly atypical of the Cuzco landowners and, indeed, of mestizo culture in general.

The hacendado and his wife remained Protestants, but the son converted to Catholicism, and the family maintains a close, amicable relationship with several of the Spanish Jesuits who work in the region. The father is in the unusual position of being disqualified by religion from becoming a godfather to his Indian *colonos*, but the son has literally hundreds of Indian *compadres* and *ahijados*, not only in Ccapana, but also in Q'ero, in Ocongate, and in other locations. Through its relative wealth, its high level of education, its marriage ties in the Cuzco aristocracy, and its upper-middle class European origins, the family is completely accepted by the Cuzco elite. At the local level, in Ocongate and in Urcos, the hacendado is clearly the dominant figure as the largest resident landowner. He is deferentially greeted by Indians and mestizos alike, and his movements seldom go unnoticed. Almost anyone in Ocongate, for instance, can tell one when he or his son has last been seen in town, and which way he was going. Mestizos almost invariably address the owner as "Señor Otto," and his Indian *colonos* call him *papáy* (father). His age (around eighty) makes him a patriarchal figure even among other high-status people in the region, such as the Spanish priests and neighboring hacendados; even his daughter-in-law calls him "Señor Otto," and his place at the head of the large communal dinner table symbolizes his uncontested status as lord of the manor. Charming hosts in the genteel European tradition, he and his wife entertain passing mestizo and foreign visitors at Ccapana, such as government officials, priests, town authorities, other hacendados, mountain climbers and anthropologists.

Their life style is simple, however. They live in the old, somewhat dilapidated, adobe buildings of the *casa hacienda*, which have been equipped with cold running water and electricity (furnished by a motor); though comfortable, their living quarters are certainly not sumptuous. Their only major luxury is a two-way radio, as the son is an avid ham operator. Domestic service is provided by three maids, two of them Spanish-speaking.

The Labor Tenancy System

The peonage system in Ccapana, as in a number of other Andean haciendas, was one of "labor tenancy." The *colono*, or peon, furnished 160 days of labor a year to the hacendado in return for the right to pasture his flock on the ranch and to cultivate a plot of arable land, usually about one hectare per family, of which one-fourth was valley land for maize, and the rest potato land higher up. Other services such as *pongo*, or domestic service, were performed in rotation, often by women and children, but the vast bulk of the labor obligation was performed by the male head of household. This system was outlawed in 1964, after several years of peasant agitation largely fomented by student activists at the University of Cuzco and by left-wing lawyers.

Ccapana had its share of peasant unrest in the early 1960s, some of it brought about through the brutality of one of the *mayordomos*. A *colono* who had been expelled for causing trouble was suspected to have avenged himself by setting the stable afire, thereby killing some of the pure-bred cattle.[5] Groups of peasants from some of the villages filed complaints against the hacendado and formulated demands, and, starting in 1960, the relationship between the hacendado and the *colonos* began to evolve rapidly. These events in Ccapana were related to the land occupations by the peons of La Convención, in northern Cuzco, and to the guerilla movement led by Hugo Blanco. Locally, however, attempts to organize the peasants into a Cuzco-based labor union were largely abortive, but the labor rent and other obligations were reduced, and a process was set in motion through which the hacendado renegotiated his contracts with his *colonos*, which resulted in his increasing loss of control over them. Indeed, the owner himself, feeling the winds of change blow, initiated what he termed his own private land reform program, which consisted of selling the more distant, troublesome, and difficult-to-control *estancias* of the hacienda to the *colonos*, who were to pay off their debt through a share-cropping arrangement. Several such sales took place in 1964, 1965, and 1968, and the former *colonos* formed, in effect, free communities under the special legal status of *asociación agropecuaria*. Even though the lands had not been sold, the hacendado gradually lost control over some of the other *estancias*, and he increasingly concentrated his efforts on alpaca grazing in some high-altitude pastures, and on intensive mechanized agriculture in the best valley-floor land.

Labor tenancy was declared illegal, and wage employment of Indians was substituted for it at an official minimum wage (thirty-five *soles* per day, at the time of this study).[6] Low productivity seriously limited the number of wage-earners the hacendado could profitably employ, even at such relatively low wages, and this in turn led to several developments. There was more incentive than before to invest in machinery to save on labor costs. The hacendado brought a medium-size tractor, cultivated only his most productive lands, and reduced to a minimum the number of wage workers. The remaining Indians, the great majority in fact, no longer owed the hacendado any labor services, but neither could they find wage employment. They therefore reverted almost entirely to a subsistence economy, and much of the more marginal land was left in fallow.

At the time of the field work, the hacendado was cultivating some forty hectares of good valley land, and raising some fifteen hundred alpacas and an equal number of sheep for wool, plus some one hundred breed cattle for cheese. The staff consisted of seven employees (three of whom were family members), some twenty-five regular workers, and another twenty to thirty daily-paid casual workers temporarily hired when there was need for more help, as, for instance, during the shearing season for sheep and alpacas. The hacienda had an administrator (the owner's son), a secretary, (the owner's son's wife), a storekeeper, four *mayordomos* (or foremen), a tractor driver, eleven shepherds, and a fluctuating number of unspecialized field hands seldom exceeding ten on any given day. The total monthly payroll varied between fifty thousand and sixty thousand *soles*.

Most of these regular workers were not ordinary Indian peasants but somewhat acculturated Indians, who spoke some Spanish, and who had received some formal education. (Of the twenty-five permanent workers, seventeen were able to sign their names on the monthly payroll.) The positions of *mayordomo* and storekeeper, in particular, are given to more educated Indians, sometimes orphans, or *ahijados*, who may have been raised in the *casa hacienda*. The storekeeper, for instance, was born in Ccapana, but was sent by his parents to Paucartambo to attend school. There he completed primary school. After that, he spent two years in the army, and came out a sergeant. Since 1965, he was employed by the hacendado, first as *mayordomo*, and now as storekeeper.

During the 1960s, and well before the formal expropriation of 1973, most of the two hundred fifty-odd Indian peasant families who lived on Ccapana lands had, de facto or de jure, gained a wide measure of autonomy, the former *estancias* having each become, to a greater or lesser degree, self-governing communities. Their economy was largely one of subsistence, with communally exploited pasture land, and individual family plots of arable land. Some of the villages retained some ties with the hacienda as, for instance, through the sale of their little surplus, or through the annual payment of rent in fulfillment of their sharecropping agreements, but the old hacienda regime of serfdom was effectively destroyed in the early 1960s. The social etiquette of paternalism between the hacendado's family and the former *colonos* continued to prevail. So did the ties of *compadrazgo*, and the genuine feelings of mutual concern, devotion, and respect which, despite the enormous status gap, linked the hacendado with some of his colonos. But the economic and, to a large extent, the political basis of Indian dependence had already been broken.

The old regime was, to be sure, a despotic one. The will of the owner prevailed, and he brooked no opposition so long as he had the power to suppress it effectively. Nevertheless, the system *was* benevolent in the case of Ccapana. The hacendado did not share the attitude of contempt that most mestizos had vis-à-vis Indians. He respected them and cared for them as individuals, within the quasi-feudal framework of *noblesse oblige* and patron-client relationships. There was no pretense of equality in their relations, but neither was there any abject degradation. The *colonos* could maintain their human dignity, as well as some measure of autonomy, in running their own village affairs. Even in mere economic terms, the feudal regime was only moderately exploitative. It created very little surplus, and the abolition of this old system has clearly not resulted in a material improvement in the condition of the peasants. The owners of Ccapana were probably far more humane than most hacendados, but it remains generally true that the theoretical despotism and exploitation of the old hacienda regime was in practice mitigated by a number of factors: customary restrictions on the power of the owner, traditions of peasant autonomy, mutual obligations of *compadrazgo*, geographical isolation, passive resistance on the part of Indians to exactions, incompetence, inefficiency, and many others. That very little surplus production was extracted from the peasants is shown by the substantial absence of a surplus now that the system has been abolished.

I left Ccapana before the central government took over its administration, but SINAMOS agents had already begun their campaign to try to talk the peasants into joining an enormous super-cooperative planned for the whole area. In several of the communities, opposition to central government schemes was beginning to mount. The incompetent, autocratic, and inefficient way in which government technicians were running Lauramarca had become well known in the area; and, naturally, peasant communities which had only recently regained their autonomy from the hacienda were asking for nothing more than to be left in peace. They were obviously suspicious of any plan to incorporate them, along with total strangers, in a vast enterprise directed by mestizo technicians who were, very possibly, incompetent and corrupt to boot.

One community in particular was incensed by the refusal of the government to release to it the title of ownership to its lands. That community, a former *estancia* of Ccapana, had been sold, in due legal form, by the hacendado to the state. The latter, in turn, had promised to give the peasants their title to the land after repayment of their debt to the state. By this time, the peasants had repaid their debt, but the state invented pretexts for not releasing the deed of ownership to the peasants. The present government claims that the sale, under the previous Belaúnde regime, was "irregular," partly to avoid paying compensation to the owner of Ccapana, and partly to force the community into the larger cooperative. These tactics are regarded by the peasants as sheer chicanery, and they view the land reform program with great and growing suspicion. They have just freed themselves through their own efforts, and now their self-proclaimed benefactor, the Revolutionary Government, is trying to reimpose itself as a new oppressor.

Ethnic Relations in the Micro-Region

In the entire area of which Ccapana is a part, the ethnic boundary between Indians and mestizos is relatively clear-cut. Nearly all Indian women, and most of the men, still dress in homespun clothing. Illiteracy rates among Indians still exceed 90 percent for men and probably 98 percent for women. Almost the same percentages of Indians are Quechua monolinguals. Except for the small town of Ocongate, all areas are rural and are almost solidly Indian, with the exception of a few school teachers, hacendados, and, more recently, government technicians, engineers, agronomists, drivers, and the like.

The local market town of Ocongate is divided into two clearly differentiated sections. A peripheral village, some one kilometer away from the center, is clearly Indian, while the center of town is inhabited by mestizos. On the central square is located the parish church, but there is no resident priest. Also on the central square is a Guardia Civil post of eight men under the command of a lieutenant, which serves as a check point on the road to the jungle and the town of Quince Mil. The town hall, a field office of the Ministry of Agriculture, and a dozen shops owned by mestizo merchants fill the rest of the four sides of the Plaza de Armas. There is also a complete primary school, and mestizo houses stretch a couple of hundred yards along the road on both sides of the Plaza.

The town mestizos, aside from the policemen, teachers, and central government employees, are mostly small traders, labor contractors, and small landowners. They monopolize the positions in the municipal government, and they still call on neighboring Indian communities to perform public works on an unpaid basis. This practice is supported by the local SINAMOS and Ministry of Agriculture agents in the name of "social mobilization." Mestizos supposedly take part in these work projects, or *faenas*, but on the major project we witnessed, the reconstruction of a washed-out bridge leading to Ccapana, only Indians were working, under the supervision of a mestizo foreman. Drunken Indians are rounded up on Sunday (the market day, which attracts hundreds of Indians from neighboring communities), left to sober up overnight in the primitive jail, and made to sweep the square on Monday morning in lieu of paying a fine.

On social occasions, mestizos and Indians each tend to associate with their own group. For instance, during fiestas some events are clearly for Indians (e.g., dancing groups), while others are clearly for mestizos (e.g., the amateur bullfights). The spectators at all these events are overwhelmingly Indian, since they constitute 90 percent of the area's population, but the town mestizos tend to cluster in small drinking groups around the town hall, the church steps, or inside stores.

Except for foremen on haciendas, a few small shopkeepers, and itinerant traders, mostly women, who come by truck for the Sunday market, there are few individuals who are not clearly either mestizo or Indian in the area. One of the reasons for this relative stability in the local ethnic situation is that the more successful and enterprising Indians leave the area altogether. These mostly include sons of peasants who cannot find sufficient land, and who drift into the urban subproletariat or sign up to work as agricultural *peones* in the jungle area; girls who become domestic servants in mestizo households; the few Indian children who go beyond the local village school, and complete primary schooling in Ocongate; and the young men who get drafted into the army.

The reasons why the school system is not more effective in teaching Indians to read, write, and speak Spanish were evident to me after my visit to the main school in Ccapana, a lower primary school that goes up to the fourth grade. The building, erected a decade ago at the expense of the hacendado of Ccapana, is spacious, and of good quality by rural standards (glass windows, cement floor, tiled roof). But the teachers are two poorly qualified and miserably paid mestizas, one of whom is the wife of a small hacendado who lives nearby. Some eighty pupils were registered, but I never saw more than about thirty in attendance, drawn mostly from two communities with a total population of five hundred to six hundred people. On several work days during our field work, one or both of the teachers were absent, and even when the school was in session, the children spent much time outdoors, gardening. When I interviewed the teachers, the main theme of their conversation was how hopeless their educational task was in teaching such backward, degenerate children, whose parents were brutalized by coca and alcohol. The teachers spoke Quechua almost exclusively with the children, and made little effort to teach them to speak, read, or write Spanish. A twelve-year-old boy, who was assigned to me as a guide to a nearby community, was supposedly their best fourth-grade pupil, but he understood little Spanish and spoke even less, though he seemed very bright and lively.

Conclusion

To return to the differences in approach mentioned earlier, it is clear that this region could easily have been studied from the bottom up, through a network analysis of economic, social, and political ties between households. Such an approach would have yielded much more precise economic data than I collected, but economics was not the focus of my research. The network approach would also have revealed relationships of kinship, marriage, *compadrazgo*, clientage, *mink'a, ayni*, and other forms of interdependence. The preeminent position of the hacendado would have been clear from his centrality in the network, and thus network analysis would also have revealed the political structure. Finally, network analysis would have given a good picture of the extent to which the micro-region is articulated to the outside world.

The approach suggested by Orlove and Custred, in short, makes no assumptions about the social system to be studied. The social structure emerges empirically through the tracing of networks of interaction from the bottom up. My approach, on the other hand, consisted in accepting prima facie the natives' categories for describing their social universe (community-hacienda, Indians-mestizos, and so on). Accepting, at least provisionally, the validity of these categories also implies provisional acceptance of the native model of the social structure which underlies the categories. The research procedure then becomes basically an empirical test of the validity of that native model, or, in more sophisticated terms, a search for an understanding of the complex interrelation between *emic* and *etic* reality.

My aim was to understand the basic features of class and ethnic relations in the Cuzco region. Being crucially aware of the limitations, for my purposes, of a "community study" approach, I had to undertake a study of considerable scope. Being equally aware of the diversity of situations in different parts of the department, I knew that I had to examine at least a half dozen micro-regions to gain an adequate overview of the entire system. That, in turn, dictated a research strategy that would maximize the amount of information gathered in a minimum amount of time. Provisional acceptance of the emic model was the most parsimonious working hypothesis.

Even provisional acceptance of emic models presents problems, however, especially in a culturally heterogeneous society. One cannot simply assume consensual definitions of the situation. Much of the research thus consists in specifying more clearly what the subjective definitions are, how several definitions compete or clash with each other, and how these definitions relate to the basic objective parameters of the political and economic structure. As a general rule, the dominant group's definition of the situation bears a closer relationship to objective indices, not because the ruling group possesses greater intelligence, but because it has superior resources by which to implement its vision of society. This is one more heuristic reason to start one's analysis from the top down.

Working from the top down also had other obvious advantages, given my aims. To have patiently plotted the interdependent networks of peasant households would have yielded more precise and more quantifiable data, but it would have been much more costly in terms of time and energy. By observing the actions of the priest, the hacendado, the trader, or the teacher, I witnessed far more significant interaction between status unequals than if I had spent weeks waiting for Juan Quispe to get married, to sell his surplus wool to the hacendado, or to send his son to school.[7] Examining, for instance, the effect of education on ethnic relations, I can gather more information far more rapidly by observing the interaction of a teacher and twenty pupils in a classroom than by following children from various households on their way to and from school.

In network terms, the strategy of working from the top down automatically locates one in hubs of ties, and thus saves one a lot of leg work. Clearly, the balance of advantages and disadvantages inherent in one approach or the other varies according to the problems one wants to resolve. The issue is methodological rather than substantive, and the choice is heuristic. I merely wanted to suggest that in social science the most painstaking, expensive, and time-consuming methodology is not necessarily the best.

Notes

1.   I am grateful to the National Institute of Mental Health for its financial support under grant MH19712, but the views expressed here in no way represent those of the United States government. I wish to acknowledge with thanks my debt to the ex-owners of Ccapana for their gracious hospitality, and to the people of Ccapana for their patience in putting up with an inquisitive foreign social scientist. The results of the main study were reported in van den Berghe, ed. (1974b); van den Berghe and Primov (1977); and Primov (1975). For support and intellectual exchange during the study, I am grateful to Gladys Becerra de Valencia, Sean Conlin, Jorge Flores Ochoa, Oscar Nuñez del Prado, Benjamin Orlove, and George Primov.

2.   I should emphasize that I do not mean by *pluralism* the same thing that W. Kornhauser, S.

M. Lipset, N. Glazer, and many other North American sociologists and political scientists in the Tocquevillian tradition have meant. See van den Berghe (1974c) for a treatment of the distinction between these two usages.

3.   Based on a play on words, the motto translates literally as: "With or without masters, we don't progress." SINAMOS is the acronym for Sistema Nacional de Apoyo a la Mobilización Social, the vast government bureaucracy created to implement the reformist policies of the ruling military junta. Split in two words, SIN-AMOS means "without masters."

4.   The family of the former owner was forced to leave Ccapana in 1974, after the field work was completed.

5.   For an account of Ccapana in the early sixties, see Martínez (1963). The account, is however, superficial and inaccurate in many points, being based on a stay of only two or three days on the hacienda.

6.   The official exchange rate at the time of the fieldwork was 43.38 *soles* to the dollar.

7.   I am, of course, crucially aware that this approach entails the hazard of class and ethnic bias. In this particular instance, the possibility of bias was further enhanced by my ignorance of Quechua (and hence my heavy reliance on bilingual research assistants or mestizo interpreters), and by the dominant group membership assigned to me. It may be that, in an attempt to correct for that bias, I have given a pro-Indian account, or at least that I have given vent to my anarchist distaste for all forms of centralized government. Be that as it may, the "peasant oriented" anthropologist is no more immune to bias nor less susceptible to being ascribed the status of a *misti*.

CHAPTER 10

The Position of Rustlers in Regional Society: Social Banditry in the Andes

Benjamin S. Orlove

Introduction

Abigeato, or animal rustling, is a common feature of rural Andean society. In a number of instances the rustlers have considerable economic and political importance. However, the illegal character of their activities makes it difficult for researchers to gain access to them. It also leads many scholars and social scientists to share the jurists' negative evaluation of rustling; these scholars view it as aberrant criminal behavior that should be eliminated, rather than as a phenomenon worthy of examination. In addition, the strong orientation toward community studies in Andean ethnography has hindered studies of *abigeato*, since the rustlers' area of activity and social networks extend beyond the boundaries of such local units.

This chapter explores this little-examined topic. It contains ethnographic description of rustling in the province of Canchis, department of Cuzco, in the southern Peruvian highlands. The discussion emphasizes the activities and social organization of the rustlers, their position within the rural social structure, and the utility of Hobsbawm's model of social banditry (1959, 1969b) in explaining them. This chapter refers to conditions in the early 1970s, before the application of agrarian reform laws to the region.

It is difficult to generalize about rustling within a nation or even within a smaller area such as the southern highlands of Peru. In particular, the ties of the rustlers to other social sectors vary greatly from region to region, corresponding to variations in landholding patterns and power relations. In certain cases, the rustlers are able to oppose hacendados successfully because of the support which they receive from the local peasantry. In other instances, the peasants are the principal victims of the rustlers' thefts. As other writers have commented (Blok, 1972; Singelmann, 1975), banditry must be seen in the context of local patterns of economic and political domination; it is worth stressing the importance of variation in these patterns.

A brief methodological statement is necessary. Obstacles to the traditional anthropological technique of participant observation made other means of data collection necessary. Interviews with rustlers were conducted in a local jail and other settings. In several cases long-term relations were established which continued well after the rustlers' release from jail. Other people who had firsthand experience with *abigeato* were also interviewed, such as owners and herders on haciendas that had been robbed, other local peasants, traders, policemen, and lawyers. Documents, especially local newspapers, were also quite useful.

The Concept of Social Banditry

The notion of social banditry was first developed in the writings of the British historian Eric Hobsbawm, particularly in two books, *Primitive Rebels: Studies in Archaic Forms of Social Protest in the Nineteenth and Twentieth Centuries (1959)* and *Bandits* (1969). His arguments are not fully elaborated; the first chapter of *Primitive Rebels*, rather than offering an explicit definition of social banditry, lists about twenty features which it tends to exhibit. However, several points are clear. Social bandits, he says, "are peasant outlaws whom the lord and state regard as criminals, but who remain within peasant society, and are considered by their people as heroes, as champions, avengers, fighters for justice, perhaps even leaders of liberation, and in any case as men to be admired, helped and supported" (1969b:13). They occur in traditional agrarian societies in which the early stages of capitalist penetration have begun. Hobsbawm stresses the strength of the ties between the bandits and the peasants. The bandits aim their attacks at the oppressors of peasants, particularly landlords and political authorities, and they seek to redress the abuses which the powerful commit against the weak. Their actions thus rest on a notion of social protest, even though in some cases they may ally themselves with landlords and other elites. In the mentality of the peasants, social bandits are honorable men who steal from the rich and give to the poor, and kill only in justified self-defense or revenge. In many cases this myth of the social bandit is an important stirring of class-consciousness since it offers the peasants an image of a society made less oppressive by the actions of members of their own class.

Blok (1972) offers a critique of Hobsbawm's notion of social banditry. Drawing on analytical concepts from social anthropology and from his historical and ethnological research in Italy, he argues that Hobsbawm overemphasized the element of protest in social banditry. He argues that a more precise examination of the social and political role of the bandit is needed and proposes to "focus on the interdependencies between lords, peasants, and bandits" (1972:496). Bandits generally seek to defend their personal interests by the open use of violence. They attempt to attach themselves to powerful protectors and thus often come to oppress peasants and commit violence and terror against them. Blok also argues that banditry permits some peasants to achieve upward mobility at the expense of others; in this fashion it weakens rather than strengthens class solidarity. The image of the heroic brigand in popular consciousness can serve to awaken and maintain a sense of protest, but this image is usually contradicted by the actual behavior of the bandit.

Singelmann (1975) supports Blok's emphasis on social and political "interdependencies," but shows that disagreement between Blok and Hobsbawm is not as great as the former claims: "Both seem to suggest that social banditry contains elements of primitive protest insofar as it usually originates in acts of defiance, often spares the poor, and particularly as it is idealized in popular myths and ballads. At the same time, both authors agree that in its actual functioning banditry may be at least marginally integrated into an oppressive social structure and undermine class solidarity" (1975:60). Singelmann offers a detailed examination of banditry in northeastern Brazil. His concern is to show that banditry is an "adaption to" (1975:60) conditions in the Northeast, rather than a "reaction against" them (1975:60). The position of the *cangaçeiros*, or bandits, was strongly conditioned by the political structure of the area. The dominant figures were the *coronéis*, or landlords. Regional politics consisted of violent factional conflicts among them, their supporters, and their followers. Peasants attempted to establish patron-client relations with these powerful men, creating a series of vertical alliances that undermined horizontal ties of class solidarity. The *cangaçeiros* were independent armed men, frequently ones who had been on the losing side of a fight with *coronéis* or who had been unable to attach themselves to a powerful landlord. Their attacks were often directed against the rich because they were the most attractive targets. However, the *cangaçeiros* often received protection and support from landlords, fighting on their behalf in return. As Singelmann points out, the activities of the *cangaçeiros* were like those of the armed men whom the landlords maintained. The difference was that the landlords, through their control of the police and courts, were able to have the *cangaçeiros* labeled criminals (Moss, 1979; Winther, 1977).

Singelmann shows that the *cangaçeiros* embodied many of the features of social banditry, particularly in their attacks on the rich and powerful, in the tenacity of popular images of the bandits as folk heroes, and in the support which they received from peasants. He also argues that they reflect the limits which Blok described; in seeking powerful protectors, they become part of the political structure which oppresses peasants. He argues, then, that banditry is an adaptation to conditions in the Northeast; the elements of rebellion, of "reaction against," are secondary.

This chapter draws on all three authors. It shares their goal of demonstrating that the bandit is not an outlaw, somehow existing outside the bounds of society, but rather is involved in social, economic, and political relations with a number of other individuals and groups. Hobsbawm's notion of social banditry as an early form of protest is an intriguing one, despite the limitations which Blok presents. For that reason, the relationship between the rise of *abigeato* and the expansion of haciendas in Canchis will be explored. The chapter also utilizes Blok's notion of "interdependencies" and Singelmann's concern to place banditry in a regional and historical context, following the approach outlined by LeGrand (1977). A detailed examination of one province demonstrates the complexities of rustlers in rural society.

The Setting: The Province of Canchis

The province of Canchis in the southeastern part of Cuzco Department contains two distinct ecological zones: a narrow strip of flat agricultural land along the Río Vilcanota, and the rugged uplands, or *alturas*, lying between this river valley and the chains of snowcapped peaks to the northeast. It is rare to see so sharp a contrast between two zones. Agriculture is favored in the valley because of the altitude (3400 to 3700 meters above sea level), the fertility of its alluvial soils, and the availability of water for irrigation; unlike many parts of the highlands, these lands are planted annually rather than going through a fallow cycle of several years. Most of the land in the valley is held by peasant communities recognized by the national government.

The valley has only about 4 percent of the area of the province, but it contains 95 percent of the population; the population density is over four hundred times as high there as in the *alturas*. The provincial capital of Sicuani, all the district capitals, and nearly all the other small villages are located in this zone (see map 3, p. 115). The valley has good transportation facilities; a highway and a railroad link it with Cuzco, the Lake Titicaca basin, Arequipa, and the coast. Several trains pass through daily, and there is heavy bus and truck traffic on the road.

The rugged, mountainous uplands extend from 3700 meters beyond the snowline at 5200 meters to peaks over 6000 meters. Its population is small and dispersed; there is only one village, Santa Bárbara, with a population of around one hundred. The few roads in the *alturas* are in very poor condition. One truck, which makes a round trip from Sicuani to Santa Bárbara and back on Wednesdays, is the only scheduled motor vehicle service. Most traffic moves on narrow trails. Unlike in certain other parts of the Peruvian highlands, the haciendas here are not fenced in, and so free movement is not impeded. Travelers have a traditional right-of-way through hacienda lands.

The *alturas* may be divided into two sections. The lower one, within eight kilometers of the valley, has some sheltered areas where crops can be grown, especially potatoes, barley, *quinua*, and *cañihua*. In contrast to the valley, where herds of animals are rare, this lower section of the *alturas* has many cattle and sheep, as well as some llamas and alpacas. These lands are also held by officially recognized peasant communities.

Agriculture is impossible in the upper section of the *alturas*, but its proximity to the tropical forest assures it plentiful rain and abundant pasture. There are many *bofedales*, or marshy areas, with permanent pasture. These supplement the seasonal grasses which grow in drier sections during the rainy months. The higher section of the uplands is held by haciendas with absentee owners; there are herds of cattle, sheep, llamas, and alpacas. Most haciendas maintain a *caserío*, or central complex of dwellings, storehouses, and corrals, where the administrator and employees, if any, live.

The herders on these haciendas have a dispersed settlement pattern. Each household has two residences: a *cabaña*, or principal house, near the *bofedales* and an *astana*, or temporary shelter, in the rainy-season pastures. The bulk of the hacienda herds are kept in corrals adjacent to these. The herders receive the right to graze their own animals, known as *waqchos*, on hacienda land, in exchange for their labor. They are also given small sums of cash, which are determined through informal bargaining processes (Orlove, 1977c). For instance, herders may be charged *daños* (fines for loss of hacienda animals) and *yerbaje* (fees for pasturing their own animals), which may be compensated for by *propinas* (tips or gifts). Hacienda animals are herded separately from *waqchos* and kept in different corrals at night.

Although haciendas hold title to the land in the upper section of the *alturas*, there is variation in the directness of the control of the hacendados over the peons. Some hacendados have appointed foremen who make daily rounds of inspection of the *cabañas*, counting the animals, informing the peons of obligations to attend work parties, and the like. In other cases, particularly in the most remote portions of the province, the peons live virtually without supervision; their contact with the hacendado is limited to their yearly trip to Sicuani to deliver wool and meat and to the infrequent trips of inspection by the hacendado or his delegate. The latter cases thus resemble the "captive communities" discussed elsewhere in the volume; they have greater autonomy in managing their own affairs, but they must pay rent in kind, an arrangement that resembles an annual tribute.

The difficult topography and the paucity of roads make the upper section of the *alturas* one of the most isolated parts of the department of Cuzco. There is no resident elite or representative of the national government, and the hacendados all live elsewhere. The one police station in Santa Bárbara, the few small shops, and the schoolhouses are located in the lower section, within a few kilometers of the valley.

The large number of animals, the low population density, and the isolation make the uplands a likely area for *abigeato*. In the predominantly agricultural valley, there are fewer animals and more people to watch them. Rustling in Canchis, then, is effectively limited to the uplands.

The Activity of Rustling

In conventional usage and legal terminology, *abigeato* is understood to refer only to the act of theft itself. The theft, however, rarely takes as long as a half-hour, but each instance of rustling is a long process, often lasting over a week, with several different stages in a number of different locations.

Information-gathering

There are long periods, usually several months long, between raids. This time is spent gathering information, both openly and covertly, which is critical to the success of the theft. Rustlers must be familiar with the topography of the area that they cover. There are a number of things they have to know about a place before raiding it: the number, species, and quality of the animals, the location of dwellings and corrals, and the nature of potential resistance. Much of this information is secondhand. Exchanging stories of previous thefts with other rustlers, they come to know which places have weak defenses but valuable animals. Other contacts also provide useful information. For instance, a rustler may talk to a cousin who went to a hacienda to work for several days shearing sheep. He could be told that the owner has gone to Lima for several months, leaving his property in the hands of an administrator who is known to live in Sicuani and to visit the hacienda only infrequently. Similarly, a rustler could overhear two petty merchants talking in the back of a truck and learn of a patron-saint celebration in a small rural chapel which would provide a motive for strangers to visit the area without attracting suspicion. In the buzz of conversation that follows the sale of a large number of animals at a weekly *tablada*, or animal market, he might discover that a certain number of cattle have just been purchased by a hacendado, a bit of information to be stored for the future.

Rustlers also obtain information directly. There are a number of guises that an individual can assume in order to travel through the uplands without eliciting suspicion: someone going between the valley and the *alturas* to barter products of these different ecological zones, a traveling buyer of wool or cattle, a *comunero* or hacienda herder on the way to market in the valley towns, or an individual looking for work in the small mines that dot the area. These activities may be engaged in by the rustlers for their own sake, as well as for the purpose of secretly gathering information. This firsthand information is particularly important in obtaining a knowledge of the geography of the area.

Plans and Preparations

An act of *abigeato* may be considered to begin when one individual makes the decision to stage a raid. He calls on others to accompany him. Drawing on the long process of information-gathering, they select a place to rob, and plan their route, a method of attack, and a way to dispose of the stolen animals. They often make a preliminary trip to the area, using any of the above-mentioned guises, for further reconnaissance, and to contact other individuals to assist them.

The immediate preparations take place a day or two before departure. They obtain horses for travel, and take only what can fit in saddlebags or be tied to a saddle: toasted beans and maize, *cañihua* flour, and sugar to eat, a drinking cup, and blankets, coca, cigarettes, and liquor for the cold nights. The rustlers wear dark clothing, taking scarves to cover their faces.

Individual rustlers may pray and make offerings to San Antonio, the patron saint of *abigeato*, and to the *apus*, or mountain spirits, of the area. These preparations are very similar to those made by other groups in the southern highlands that take long overland trips, such as donkey and llama drivers (Centeno Zela, 1953:37–53) and puna peasants going to trade their products for agricultural foodstuffs (Flores, 1968:129–37). The only differences are that rustlers do not take beasts of burden and are more likely to be armed.

Travel

It takes the rustlers between one and three days to reach the place they have selected to raid. They travel during the day or at night, depending on how serious they judge the risk of discovery to be. They set camp in sheltered, isolated places where they are unlikely to be found. The steep, glaciated countryside of the *alturas* provides them with many such sites.

Theft

Only one species of animal is stolen at a time, to make driving them easier. On the haciendas, animals are usually kept in herds of only one species, both in pasture and in corrals, though llamas and alpacas are frequently herded together. There are two locally recognized methods of theft, known as *asalto* and *pakaylla*. The former term in this simple ethnocriminological scheme means "assault" in Spanish; it is an open attack, usually a charge of the entire group of rustlers on the place where the animals are kept, with threatened or actual violence. The owner or herder is tied up or otherwise confined in order to permit a successful escape. *Pakaylla* is furtive theft committed at night without alerting anyone; the word is Quechua, and means "merely in a hidden manner." Bits of bread or meat are thrown to the dogs so that they will not bark. The stolen animals are secreted away.

There may be collusion with hacienda herders. To further cooperation, they are offered money, as much as S/1000–3000 (at the period under discussion, U.S. $1.00 equals S/43.38). In the case of *asalto*, the herder may absent himself to allow the rustlers additional time in the attack. In the case of *pakaylla*, the aid of the herder can clearly be crucial in permitting an undiscovered raid. Since the hacendados visit their properties so infrequently, the complicity of the herders is difficult to prove. The money that they receive from the rustlers often compensates for the *daños* that the hacendados might charge. In other cases, the hacendados are unable to insist on collecting these fines.

Escape

A rapid escape is frequently important, since the owner of the animals, his administrator, or his foreman will often pursue the rustlers when he discovers the theft, if he is present. A route with several alternatives is planned. The animals are driven at night. Hideouts are occasionally established in caves or unfrequented parts of the mountains. In most cases, rustlers arrange to stay with individuals known as *amistades*, or friendships. These *amistades* provide lodging, mix the stolen animals with their own, and may also lend horses to make capture by identification of the horses or of their tracks more difficult. The owners or administrators, if present, set out after the rustlers on horseback, with arms. Sometimes they call out the police from the stations in the valley towns and in Santa Bárbara, although this tactic involves a delay of a day or two. Nevertheless, groups of rustlers, especially larger ones, are sometimes located. The rustlers scatter, so that it is rare for more than one to be captured. Rustlers almost never inform on each other, even under considerable pressure and repeated beatings, so that the other members of the group remain free. The animals, however, are recovered.

Conditions in highland jails are extremely bad, with inadequate food, sleeping quarters, and sanitary facilities. However, being in jail is not an unmitigated misfortune for a rustler. Contacts with other rustlers are made, and much of the information gathering described above takes place.

Disposal

The animals are, virtually without exception, destined for sale. They are usually sold live, sometimes at annual fairs or weekly *tabladas* in the valley, but more often to buyers in Sicuani, known as *agentes*, who ship them live by railroad to Arequipa. The railroad is faster than trucks. However, its main advantage is that police do not regularly inspect freight shipped by rail, as they do freight shipped by road. The prices that they receive vary from 50 to 80 percent of those given in normal commercial channels for legally obtained animals.

The railroad employees find a profitable sideline in failing to notice that animals are being loaded at night; they receive bribes of several hundred *soles*. Stolen animals are frequently mixed with legally purchased ones. The necessary documents (bill of sale, vaccination certificate, Agriculture Ministry registration) can be forged, if the employee insists on seeing them. With no organization to register brands, few animals are marked in a way that serves to distinguish them; bills of sale, in any case, do not refer to the brands. There is little inspection of documents in the Arequipa slaughterhouses.

In other cases, the animals are killed, especially if they are few in number. The meat and skins can easily be sold to buyers in Sicuani or at the weekly markets. In general no questions are asked, particularly if the price offered is slightly lower than usual. The rustlers may consume small portions of the meat in town, but they would not delay to consume much on the trail.

The rustlers receive payment in cash, and the members of the group who committed the raid divide it in equal shares. An individual receives between S/8000 and S/20,000, with the average being about S/10,000 if cattle are stolen; he gets about half as much for sheep and alpacas.

Different rustlers make raids with greater or lesser frequency, some as often as eight or ten times a year, others as little as once or twice. Three or four trips seems common. As the frequency of raids increases, the danger of recognition, pursuit, and capture becomes greater, and the material rewards less tempting. Rustling is not a full-time activity in Canchis. Rustlers live as ordinary peasants, although there are a few cases of rustlers who are artisans and merchants living in Sicuani.

Rustlers generally steal hacienda animals rather than those owned by peasants, whether the herds of *comuneros* or the *waqchos* of the hacienda herders. One motive is the fact that more money can be made by stealing the former. Hacienda animals are located in larger concentrations. They tend to be healthier, fatter, and larger, and more of them are of pure-bred ancestry. Rustlers constitute a major problem for the hacendados, rather than merely being an occasional nuisance. There are times when animals other than those belonging to a hacienda are stolen. A *comunero* who repeatedly leaves his animals unattended in a pasture at night is likely to find some missing one morning. Most such thefts are between fellow *comuneros*, though, and involve disputed inheritance, in which the party accused of *abigeato* takes an animal to which he feels he has a right. The "professional" rustlers might not pass by lost or abandoned animals, regardless of their ownership, but they would not take the animals of a *comunero* from herds that are in a corral or that are attended by a person. The question of why rustlers only rob haciendas will be taken up in more detail later in this chapter.

The Social Organization of Rustling

Rustlers are organized in bands with a recognized leader, or *kamachik* (Quechua: one who causes things to be). The members of a band refer to each other as *suwakmasi* (those who steal together) or *purikmasi* (those who travel together). Bands first form with a leader and several followers who go on a raid. They may have had experience in other bands which have ceased to operate. The leader has several criteria for choosing new members: loyalty to the band, likelihood of forming personal friendships with other members (if this is not already the case), and the ability to ride horses, drive animals, and prepare camp at night. The ability to use weapons is also important since rustlers travel armed. Peasants handle the sling with an accuracy that is surprising to those unfamiliar with such preindustrial weapons (Korfmann, 1973), and the *licenciados*, or men who have served in the army, can use firearms, which are easily smuggled in from Bolivia. As one might expect, rustlers are men, between eighteen and forty years old. They are usually of peasant origin, as the necessary skills imply, though some artisans and traveling wool and cattle buyers join bands.

A rustler rarely leaves his band to join another. Such a move would be interpreted as a sign that the individual creates conflict within a band, and that he is not accepted as a skilled rustler. Most individuals judge that they gain more from "accumulating seniority" in one band than from switching to another.

The *kamachik*, or leader, is generally the one who plans and organizes the raids, as well as the one who makes the contacts to dispose of the animals. It is rare for a leader to be directly challenged and replaced by another member of the band; rather the band dissolves. Bands go through periods of relative activity and inactivity and may remain dormant for several years. It is rare for a band to maintain a high level of raiding for more than ten years. If a leader is losing his authority, due to old age, discontent of the members of the band, or other reasons, the band is likely to go on raids less frequently. The arrest or illness of the leader will prompt a cessation of activity. The members may no longer go on raids, or they may join other bands. As word spreads in rustler circles that a band has stopped raiding, leaders of other bands may call on the former members to join them on raids. The former members may set themselves up as leaders of new bands.

An important point is that not all members of a band take part in every raid. For instance, in one band of five members, the leader and another member take part in all the raids, and a third member in most of them; the other two are called on less frequently, when additional members are needed. Though the band has five members, the size of the groups that perform the raids varies from two to five. One could infer that the first three members are core members and the latter two peripheral, though this distinction does not apply to all members of all bands. Thus, because the spoils of each raid are divided equally between participants, the leader and core members receive more than the peripheral members over a number of raids.

The processes of recruitment lead to a situation in which *suwakmasi* come from a relatively small geographical area, usually a district. They are often relatives, brothers, or a father and sons, and less frequently more distant relatives, such as cousins. A band may include two or more sets of relatives. However, friends, neighbors, and other nonkin also form bands. The social networks of nonkin are less likely to overlap; thus there are wider ties among the members of the band as a whole. The joint information and knowledge of a group of nonkin are also wider.

New members usually remain peripheral for several months to a year, in a sort of trial period or apprenticeship, before being either admitted to the core group or dropped. Others stay in the peripheral group for longer periods of time. Core members can also be dropped from the band, though they have a lower rate of turnover than peripheral members. This removal is a delicate process; rather than directly expelling a member, the leader calls on him less frequently to go on raids. He may be given some money after each raid, about S/300 to S/1000. In other cases, a member chooses to leave the band on his own. He may feel that he has earned enough money, or he may decide to set himself up as a leader, after a discreet waiting period to avoid gossip, suspicion, and bad feeling on the part of his former *suwakmasi*.

These processes of recruitment and expulsion allow the size of a band to change after its initial formation. Bands range in size between a lower limit of two and an upper limit of nearly fifteen, with a mode of four or five. Smaller bands rely on *pakaylla* more, and larger ones on *asalto*. In general, the earnings per individual per raid do not vary greatly with the size of the group committing the raid and with the size of the band. The most profitable raids are made by *asalto*, but they are also the riskiest ones, involving the possibility of having to abandon the animals. *Asalto* used to be practiced more in the past. With increasing police vigilance, *pakaylla* is becoming the predominant mode, and there are fewer large bands than in the past.

There is further flexibility in the size of groups that make raids, through the institution of partnerships between bands. It is not infrequent for two or three bands to join forces for a raid. The contacts for this arrangement are usually made by the leaders. The profits of the raid are divided equally among all the individuals who participate in it. Bands have partners that they prefer for joint raids, and there is more flow of information between such bands. These partnership ties do not form clearly bounded associations of bands. This institution of partnership between bands favors the distribution of the total rustler population of Canchis in a large number of small bands, while making it possible for larger groups to form to make raids by *asalto*. Thus a relatively large proportion of rustlers are leaders or core members, since the partnerships between bands allow a greater number of bands to exist.

There is an important territorial aspect to this partnership. Although bands draw their members from limited geographical areas, they have a close familiarity with the terrain and herds of a much wider area. It is common for links to be established between bands in different districts, provinces, or even departments. Rustlers plan joint raids with partners in other areas, which allows them to rob in the area of one band and sell the animals in the area of another. When a band makes a raid in its own area, it frequently relies on a distant partner to locate a buyer or *agente*, or even to act as one.

Just as an act of *abigeato* comprises more than the theft itself, the relations of rustlers to individuals outside their bands are also an integral part of their social organization. Reference has already been made to ties with hacienda herders, *amistades*, and information sources. Bands have such relations with a number of individuals. These three sorts of individuals, in turn, often have ties with more than one band.

The ties with the *agentes* are more complex. It is safer to dispose of stolen animals through a previously contacted *agente* than to look for a buyer after the theft. The leader often locates one before setting on a raid. It is also common for these *agentes* to contact a leader and request animals, offering a small cash advance. Some *agentes* dispatch as many as two or three railroad cars of stolen animals at a time, which requires the coordination of thefts by many bands. A number of simultaneous raids is an effective tactic, since the police cannot track all of them down. The risk is higher for the *agente*, though, since owners will alert railroad officials that stolen animals may be transported to Arequipa. But the *agente* also receives much higher earnings in this fashion, and may consider that the greater benefits outweigh the higher risk. With the great demand for meat in Arequipa, it is not difficult for the rustlers to dispose of the animals. There seems to be a certain degree of competition among the *agentes*, who try to maintain client bands as permanent suppliers. The leaders can use this fact to bargain with the *agentes* for higher prices, especially before starting a raid.

Rustlers are faced with a dilemma: as the number of contacts of a band increase, the band benefits from increased information and support, but it also faces greater risk of exposure and capture. It needs the silence of the people aware of its activities. At times an individual will threaten a rustler, usually the leader or a core member, with informing the police, and will receive a bribe of S/400 to S/1000 for his silence. This sort of blackmail is not very effective, however, since it is difficult to produce evidence against rustlers once the animals are sold. Rustlers also offer hospitality to their friends and acquaintances in the form of beer, alcohol, and meals. This largesse and other more explicit bribes and blackmail are similar; they are a form of redistributing the profits of the theft to a much larger group, which in turn provides the rustlers with information and support.

Rustling and Regional Society

The continued existence of rustlers in Canchis rests in part on the band organization and on the aid of individuals directly linked to it, such as *amistades* and *agentes*. However, it is the support of entire social sectors which allows them to steal such large numbers of animals with relative security. The complicity of the peasantry in helping the rustlers to escape is perhaps the crucial factor. The willingness of hacienda herders to enter into bargains with them has already been mentioned. When hacendados and policemen attempt to capture rustlers, the peasants claim not to have seen them, and offer no information on their movements. Similarly, rustlers can rely on most of the local populace to warn them of these pursuers, especially the police, and to conceal them if necessary. This support is not universal, but it is widely generalized. For instance, an hacendado can require one of his herders to accompany him on a search for a group of rustlers who have stolen his animals. However, the herder's participation is likely to be anything but enthusiastic and cooperative. The news of the police's presence in the countryside spreads quickly, since they impound unregistered firearms and, in the past, have rounded up people for unpaid labor on *faena* work projects and located young men trying to avoid military service.

The success of rustlers in Canchis comes from the assistance they receive from the peasantry. This support emerges from the rustlers' position in the extremely unequal *alturas* society, which is divided into the hacendados and the peasantry. There is strong conflict between these two groups. The roots of this conflict may be found in the recent large-scale expansion of haciendas in the uplands of Canchis. It began in the late nineteenth century, with rented church lands often serving as the nuclei for new estates (Ministerio de Agricultura, 1973a). It gained momentum during the 1920s, when the boom in wool prices made these lands more valuable (Piel, 1967: 395; Kapsoli, 1972). *Abigeato* also increased sharply during this period (*La Verdad*, 26.12.21; 7.4.22; 16.7.23; 8.9.23; 16.5.25; 12.3.27), taking place concurrently with the documented instances of hacienda appropriation of community land (23.12.20; 27.9.22; 5.12.22; 7.8.26; 13.11.29; 9.4.30). Hacendados made use of the recently formed Guardia Civil, a sort of national police (21.11.25; 14.10.26; 15.6.27; 21.6.27; 4.2.28) as well as of the army (14.10.26) to attempt repression. The rustlers received support from the local peasants, documented explicitly in only two instances (24.12.21; 7.4.22) but confirmed by personal accounts.

The peasants' loss of access to pasture was a long and complex process which is not yet complete. Hacendados attempt to increase their use of pasture land by reducing the number of *waqchos* and preventing the *comuneros* from grazing their animals on hacienda land. Both the *comuneros* working on haciendas during shearing season and the herders have personal experience with the hacienda labor system, with wages far below the legal minimum and humiliating treatment (beatings are not unknown).

There are other sources of conflict between the hacendados and the peasants. The road to Santa Bárbara is one example. Built by local peasant labor, it benefits the hacendados, who own pickup trucks. The peasants travel on foot and carry their goods on llamas, horses, and donkeys. They move on the trails which, though narrower and steeper than the road, are shorter. They maintain the road with unpaid *faena* labor (Kapsoli, 1972:9–11).

Similarly, the peasants are required to support the police in many ways. They built the police station in Santa Bárbara with *faena* labor, and other peasants, detained overnight on trumped-up charges, clean and maintain it. The police take food and lodging in the *cabañas* and *astanas* when they travel for long distances, and offer no payment or recompense.

The peasants, then, like the rustlers, see the hacendados and police as having interests in direct opposition to their own. The rustler-peasant ties run deeper than opposition to a common enemy. They are also based on class origin, reinforced in many cases by kinship and residence. The material benefits previously mentioned strengthen these ties further. The rustlers' choice to raid only haciendas is based not only on their preference for stealing from the largest and most valuable herds, but also on a conscious strategic alliance with the peasants.

The rustlers place small, but real, limits on hacienda expansion. The hacendados would prefer to end *comunero* incursion on their lands, take over remaining community lands, reduce the number of herders and size of *waqcho* herds, and install a system of wage labor, as was carried out in some other parts of the sierra. The peasants are opposed to these changes and have the rustlers as allies. The rustlers are one force that limits the hacendados' power and maintains the balance between different sectors of *alturas* society.

Rustlers continue to offer some small measure of control over the hacendados. Certain haciendas are raided several times a year, while others are not raided at all. Geographical location and size make certain haciendas tempting targets. Even taking these variables into consideration, the haciendas that consistently lose a high portion of their animals (such as the Meza and Guerra estates) are the ones where the herders are most poorly paid and most discontent. The rustlers form an integral part of a society in which the peasants, though poor, are better off than others in many areas in the sierra.

As the previous discussion shows, the organization of rustling in Canchis depends on several specific features: the ownership of the upper section of the uplands by hacendados, the lack of roads and police stations in the same area, and the proximity of the railroad in the Río Vilcanota valley. In other provinces in the southern highlands where these conditions do not exist, rustling is quite different in character. A brief discussion of these other areas serves to highlight the specificity of conditions in Canchis.

The eastern portion of the province of Cailloma in the department of Arequipa is similar to the *alturas* of Canchis in terms of high elevation, lack of roads and villages, and relative ease of transport of stolen animals to the markets of the city of Arequipa. However, it offers a sharp contrast in terms of land tenure, since most of the land is held by localized groups of peasants known as *parcialidades*. They have traditional grazing rights in these high grasslands, but they do not form officially recognized communities. There are very few haciendas in the area.

In this region, rustlers operate in bands, much as they do in Canchis. However, they tend to come from neighboring provinces rather than from Cailloma itself, and they steal from the peasants. They do not have ties to local dwellers. They hide their stolen animals in remote areas, rather than relying on *amistades* to conceal them. In short, the success of the rustlers is based on speed and secrecy, rather than on elaborate social networks.

Other provinces in the department of Cuzco, such as Chumbivilcas, represent the third pattern. In many portions of the province, elevations range from 3700 to 4300 meters; more cultivation can be practiced than in the *alturas* of Canchis or in the eastern portion of Cailloma. Population densities are somewhat higher, and there is a greater number of small villages and roads. The landholding pattern also is different. There are haciendas, although they do not own all the land of the region. Absentee ownership of haciendas, though common, is not universal, as it is in the uplands of Canchis. The hacendados spend more time on their properties and are more important politically, holding posts such as mayor and justice of the peace.

The social position of the rustlers and of the people from whom they steal is different than in the previous two cases. Many hacendados regularly participate in *abigeato*. Peasants as well as hacendados are robbed. There also appear to be more frequent cases of direct collusion of local political authorities with certain rustlers. The organization of rustlers is somewhat different. Bands not only have core and peripheral members; on occasion the leaders hire individuals to accompany them on particular raids. They receive a much smaller share of the spoils than would a full-fledged member of the band (Baca Mogrovejo, 1973).

There is also much more rivalry between individual bands. They inform on each other to the police and other authorities, and aid in capture. There are also fights between them. Rival bands are often involved in land disputes. *Abigeato* is only one aspect of the more fragmented and factionalized political life of Chumbivilcas. In many ways it resembles the conditions in the arid northeast of Brazil (Singelmann, 1975). It represents a less extreme version of the generalized civil disorders of much of the nineteenth century, in which rival groups of hacendados with armed followers vied for power throughout much of the highlands, where the central government was unable to exercise control (Favre, 1977).

Conclusions

The rustlers in Canchis resemble Hobsbawm's social bandits in many ways. They steal from the hacendados rather than from the peasants, they violate national laws rather than local norms, and they rely on the peasants for support. They operate in a region in which capitalist penetration has increased in the recent past. Their personal characteristics, such as their generosity, their band organization, and their methods of stealing, also fit closely with Hobsbawm's general descriptions (1959:1-29). They deviate from the model with regard to the issue of social protest. The motivation of the rustlers and their *amistades*, *agentes*, and other contacts can best be described as self-interest. They have found a successful way of augmenting their income that is less risky than it would initially appear to be. The rustlers ally themselves with one class against another, but these ties seem to be pragmatic rather than ideological, even though they have certain political consequences. Although rustlers do appear occasionally in folk songs, they do not seem to generate a myth of popular resistance to the oppression of landlords, in part because such a position may be better filled by the leaders and participants in the peasant rebellions that took place in earlier decades.

Blok's discussion of the "interdependencies between lords, peasants, and bandits" (1972:496) has proved instructive for this discussion of rustlers, but it is difficult to claim in the case of Canchis that the bandits have become oppressors of the peasants. The rustlers in the province of Chumbivilcas fit Blok's analysis more closely. Canchis may thus be one of the cases which Blok admits as an exception to his view of bandits as a conservative force (1972:500). However, it is difficult to assess his argument that banditry weakens class solidarity. He shows that class solidarity is weakened when bandits fight on the side of their powerful protectors and provide a channel of upward mobility. These effects presumably outweigh the strengthening of class solidarity that occurs through offering an ideological model for peasant action and through attacking the rich. The contrafactual pitfalls that haunt functionalist explanation appear in this context as well. To argue his case, Blok would have to demonstrate that peasants would be stronger if banditry were absent, rather than noting the frequent coincidence of banditry, weak peasantries, and powerful landlords.

Singelmann's approach seems the most useful, despite a few problems. It is not clear how one is to decide whether action that one observes is an "adaptation to" circumstances or a "reaction against" them. Two possible criteria are the consequences of the action (whether or not it changes the society in which the actor lives) and the author's subjective orientation (whether or not he desires to change the society in which he lives). Both of these seem difficult to apply in concrete cases, in the former because of the problems of contrafactual argument, and in the latter because of the complexities inherent in establishing an individual's motivation. The evidence in the case of Canchis is mixed; the "reaction against" position is weakly confirmed by the first criterion and the "adaptation to" case by the second. The strength of Singelmann's analysis is his examination in detail of the constraints under which individuals must make choices; his use of the term "rational life strategy" (1975:81) indicates this tendency. He dissects the political system of the Brazilian Northeast with insight and demonstrates its influence on the decisions of bandits.

One can find support both for Hobsbawm's view that rustling marks the unwillingness of peasants to accept oppression passively and for Blok's concern that rustlers will not provide a significant basis for change. It seems most useful to follow Singlemann, however. The rustlers in Canchis, much like the *cangaçeiros* in the Brazilian Northeast, build critical support networks around themselves. They attempt to construct viable lives for themselves in a hierarchal and oppressive society. The rustlers are faced with many decisions—whether to seek an additional member in the band, which hacienda to rob, whether to raid by *asalto* or *pakaylla*. Their choices can be seen as rational, as adaptations to the society in which they live, although they can also bear some influence in changing this society. The comparisons to other cases are instructive because they show that what bandits have in common is not simply their tendency to protect peasants or to exploit them; instead it is their need for support and the great extent to which this fact shapes their choice of allies and opponents.

CHAPTER 11

The Place of Ritual in Andean Rural Society

Glynn Custred

This paper will examine the social and the religious systems of the peasant population of the highlands of southern Peru in order to (1) demonstrate that a correlation exists between different ritual activities and the different groups and coalitions which constitute peasant society; and in order to (2) show how these rituals operate within their corresponding social contexts in two interrelated ways: first, as a means of establishing and maintaining groups and alliances, and second, as a means of expressing, in the language of religious symbols, the nature of these social entities. In the latter case, ritual activity may be seen as a kind of statement, made at the social level, on how the social system is constituted. In dealing with ritual activities, we are therefore dealing with both the semantics and the mechanics of social interactions, which are both fundamental to agrarian society.

The Nature of Ritual

Ritual, among all the other symbolic elements constituting a religious system, is particularly important in both aspects of social interactions since it consists not only of concrete symbolic objects, but also of the acting out of routine, conventional actions by laymen and specialists. It is this dramaturgical aspect, this involvement of people with one another in a highly prescribed manner and under special and constrained conditions, which makes ritual a forceful and a vivid means of expression. In this sense, ritual may be seen as a kind of language. Furthermore, ritual performances, like speech acts, signify and mark social differences, and identify and affirm the existence of social groups. Unlike language, however, the internal symbolism of ritual is highly polysemous. That is, a single form may have quite different meanings to the various groups participating in its performance; therefore people may perceive agreement even where it may not exist.

The Repertoire of Rituals in the Andean Countryside

There are two separate sets of rituals performed by the peasants of the region. Each set is based on a separate category of spiritual beings and involves different religious specialists. Furthermore, the rituals from the two sets complement one another within the daily and the yearly routine of peasant activity.

The first of these ritual sets is based on the preconquest Andean belief in spirits of the hills and the arable land, and is centered on a single symbolic motif involving the symbolic elements of corn, coca, and llama or alpaca fat. Such rituals are performed on the occasion of routine agricultural and herding activities and for healing, divining, and sorcery. The latter three activities are within the semisecret realms of a few peasant specialists. No formal cult organization is connected with these rites and beliefs.

The second ritual set deals with Catholic belief, primarily belief in Catholic saints, and involves a highly complex organization in the form of the established Catholic Church. Religious specialists within the church are nonpeasant priests whose status, authority, and prestige parallel those of government officials, and whose social position constitutes an important part of the elite stratum of local society. In fact, the church, in the person of the priest, was until the Agrarian Reform often the administrator of a hacienda employing peasant labor. Official priestly intervention within a number of peasant activities thus serves to legitimate those activities within both peasant and nonpeasant circles. Occasions on which church ritual is appropriate are rites of passage such as baptism, weddings, and funerals, and community- and regional-level feasts of patron saints which involve the interaction of a number of peasant households with one another and with members of local elites.

In sum, belief in the traditional nature spirits and the burning of offerings involve peasant interactions with the *physical environment* and belief in some degree of control over physical forces, as seen in agricultural and herding activities and in individual health. On the other hand, church rites deal with interactions within the *social environment* in which peasants must operate. It is in the former realm, that of the physical environment, that ritual functions as a means of environmental control and as an expressive system, while its signifying, marking, and legitimating functions prevail in the latter realm, or that of social involvements and interactions.

The peasant sector of the population consists of a number of local groups and coalitions, but it also forms an integral part of regional and national systems as articulated within economic and political institutions. For example, both the market system and the government create trading and administrative areas which are, by and large, coterminous with one another and which function to maintain definable regional entities, while at the same time linking the rural population with larger towns and cities. Every local peasant group, therefore, has its regional, economic, and political reference which is marked by periodic regional-level ritual events.

The local groups and alliances within such regions, which constitute the peasant segment of the population, are (1) households; (2) inter-household alliances; (3) various types of relations between households and local elites; and (4) some form of peasant community organization which is encountered in one form or another in most parts of the countryside, though not everywhere. The relationship of these social groups to the repertoire of rituals observed in the southern highlands of Peru is illustrated in the accompanying chart. The rest of the paper will elaborate on this information and will examine the role of ritual performance in each of these categories of social interaction.

The Household

Perhaps the most important of the peasant rituals is the burnt offering, called variously *alcanzo* (Spanish for offering), *werachurana* (Quechua for placing the fat), and *werakana* (Quechua for burning the fat) (see Flores, 1977b; Custred, 1979a). The most revealing of the various names for this ritual, however, is the Spanish term *pago* (payment), since the offering is considered by all peasants as a proper payment to the nature spirits in return for a reasonable level of agricultural production and peasant health. This ritual is considered by the peasants as playing just as important a role in production activities as the role played by the technologies of agriculture and herding. For this reason, the *alcanzo* may be regarded as one means by which peasants attempt to control their physical environments.

The offering consists of kernels of corn, the leaves and seeds of coca, and lumps of llama or alpaca fat. These elements represent corn, coca, and animal products (meat and wool), which are resources of high value in peasant production and exchange activities. These ingredients are mixed in a fixed order, followed by the addition of flower petals, flakes of soapstone, and incense. Invocations are made to specific hill spirits by name and to the spirit of the earth, and finally the entire offering is wrapped in a cloth and burned. Libations of *chicha* (a drink made of corn or barley) and sometimes of *aguardiente* (cane alcohol) are then poured to the hills and the earth by everyone present.

In the high-altitude herding zones these offerings are made on fixed animal days (in August for cattle, in July for horses, in June for sheep, and during carnival time in the month of February for llamas and alpacas). In many of the high-altitude potato- and barley-growing zones, such offerings are made before any agricultural activity, such as plowing, planting, or harvesting, is performed. And elsewhere, especially in the middle-elevation corn zones, the ritual is performed only twice, once in August, the time of year when the earth and the hills "come alive" in advance of the new agricultural season, and once in February at carnival, which is the month of the birth of llamas and alpacas in the production zones of higher elevations.

The smoke from the burning offering is believed to nourish the hill spirits and the earth. Failure to provide such nourishment leads directly to peasant misfortune. There are at least two variations on this theme. In the province of Chumbivilcas, department of Cuzco, it is believed that the hill spirits, like humans, must eat to survive, and that if the peasants do not provide them with nourishment in the form of the offering, the hill spirits have no other recourse

Table 11-1
Relation of Social Groups and Ritual Activity Among the Peasants of the
Southern Peruvian Andes

Social Group	Environmental Context	Ritual Activity	
		"spiritual" focus	cult organization
household	physical environment (agriculture, herding, long-distance trading trips)	hill spirits and earth mother	
interhousehold coalitions and ties to local elites	social environment (forging social alliances)		church ritual with priest
local groups (communities and subcommunities)	social environment (internal community cohesion, external articulation with other social classes)	Catholic saints	church ritual with priest
regional populations	social environment (politically and economically determined regional entities)	Catholic saints	church ritual with priest

than to feed directly on the "hearts" of the peasants or the "hearts" of their animals, thus causing peasant illness and accident and the loss of animal and agricultural production (Custred, 1979b).

The second regional variation has been observed in the province of Calca, department of Cuzco, by Nuñez del Prado (1974: 238–251). In this version, the hill spirits are said to protect the peasants from malignant spirits who bring ill fortune and disease. If the payment, in the form of the ritual offering, is not made to the hill spirits, this protection is withdrawn and peasants are left vulnerable to the demons. In both cases, the offering provides a modicum of control in a realm where peasant technology proves inadequate, and thus forms an essential part of peasant life.

Besides the manifest function of environmental control, this ritual also operates to express the nature of the entire social system as viewed from the peasant perspective. In fact, the conceptual component of the ritual is in reality the projection of social categories onto the physical world, and the transference of the logic of social relations, as understood by the peasants, to the relationships holding between the peasant and his physical environment. This logic thus makes it possible for the peasant to employ in his dealings with the physical world the same strategies which he knows from long experience give positive results in his world of social interaction.

In this conceptualization, hill spirits parallel local elites, and the ritual offering parallels the taxes, tributes, and services traditionally exacted by the elites from the peasantry. In the Chumbivilcas variation cited above, the emphasis is on the dependence of the elites on peasant production, symbolized in the offering, and on the power of the elites to punish and harass the peasants if services and goods are not forthcoming. The latter is symbolized by belief that ritual lapses cause ill fortune and ill health. In the example reported from Calca, the focus is on the peasant-client relationship holding between the hill spirits and the peasants; this is seen in the protective role played by the spirits and in the specialization of services rendered by individual hill spirits to their peasant clients. This symbolizes the most frequent positive relationship which holds between peasants and local elites. In both cases, the peasants and the hill spirits, like the peasants and local elites, stand in an asymmetrical relationship to one another, a relationship which can be maintained with minimal harm to the peasant households only through stipulated ritual offerings.

In the case of the earth, the offering represents the sharing of resources with a kinsman since the earth is the mother of all peasants. The same kinds of reciprocities which hold between members of a nuclear family and between close kinsmen, especially in inter-household labor exchanges, are thus actualized in the ritual offering between the peasant and his mother, the earth. It is clear, therefore, that the principles of symmetry and asymmetry underlying peasant social forms are also the principles upon which peasant-spirit interactions are based.

The entire symbolic system thus forms a vivid and a particularly elegant means of social expression. What is expressed in this symbolic action is no less than the irreducible structural principles upon which all peasant society is based, as seen by the peasants themselves. Or, to paraphrase Geertz (1966), the ritual performance expresses the peasants' most comprehensive ideas of order, the picture peasants have of the way they operate in sheer actuality.

The peasants themselves recognize the analogic nature of their spiritual world, thus indicating further that, on one level at least, ritual is a means of "saying" something about the way the social world is understood to work. This is revealed in specific comparisons of hills to elites and of the earth to kinsmen when discussing agricultural rituals, and in the application of the terms *pago* (payment), and *alcanzo*, (offering), when referring to the ritual offering. This recognition by the peasants of the social logic of their environmental interaction, and the periodic reiteration of this logic in the dramaturgical language of ritual, further serve to transmit and support the underlying belief that the ritual is indeed an effective means of environmental control. The ritual, therefore, not only "says" something about the world of peasant experience, but it also plays a role in maintaining the ritual-technological complex as it is currently utilized.

This ritual, considered necessary for continued peasant well-being, is the responsibility of the household, which forms the primary social unit of peasant society and the primary unit of peasant production, consumption, and management. In fact, no other group within the society bears so much responsibility for meeting basic human needs as does the household. It is not surprising, therefore, that the *alcanzo* is offered by this group, without the participation of religious specialists, and at those times most closely associated with production activities.

Interhousehold Coalitions and Ties to Local Elites

No household, however, can perform alone all the tasks required for its production activities. For that reason, coalitions are formed for agricultural and pastoral work. These cooperative labor groups change in membership from task to task, but the nuclear families of siblings show the highest long-term frequency of cooperation. Equal labor exchange is called *anyi*. *Mink'a* refers to situations where work is not exchanged for an identical amount of work, but rather where some other form of compensation is involved. Furthermore, no single household can remain isolated from local elites, just as no household can remain uninvolved with other households throughout the countryside. Stable, advantageous relationships with nonpeasants are therefore as highly desirable as are such relations with other peasant households. For that reason, arrangements of differing degrees of stability and symmetry are to be found throughout peasant communities and extending into the nonpeasant strata of society. These arrangements are highly important in the operation of a peasant enterprise and form one of the important aspects of Andean rural society.

One way of reinforcing interhousehold relationships among unrelated families and of strengthening and stabilizing patron-client ties is to extend the ties of kinship outward from the network of the consanguineal and affinal relations which constitute the system of kinship. The highly flexible institution of *compadrazgo*, or godparenthood, is used for this purpose. *Compadre* relations are not kin relations; however, they do involve mutual rights and obligations analogous to those of kinship, and thus serve to assure long-term cooperation between the parties involved, just as kinship provides the basis of such cooperation among kinsmen. We may regard *compadrazgo* then as a "social metaphor," in that certain features of kinship are extended outward to another social domain to create a new category of "relations," just as linguistic metaphor involves the extension of semantic features outward to other lexical domains to create new words and expressions. Even though such relationships tie together individuals, they in fact operate to unite households, since the individuals involved represent not just themselves in economic cooperation, but also their primary kin groups.

Godparent relations are initiated on the occasions of baptism and marriage. In the former case a suitable godparent, usually a well-to-do peasant or someone from the local elite, is asked to serve as godfather or godmother of the child. When someone agrees, he or she pays for the baptism and presents a gift to the parents. After this, a formal "coparent" relationship exists between the child's parents and its godparents, a relationship which becomes the channel for cooperation between the two.

On the occasion of marriage, a couple will ask someone of higher status to stand with them as godparent at their wedding. It is the responsibility of the godparent to pay for the wedding and the wedding feast, and to act as counselor and patron to the couple throughout their married life. In both of these cases, the parties entering into coparent and godparent-godchild relations gain some benefit from the arrangement. The higher-status person may call upon his *compadre* or his godchild for labor service, while the person of lower status may expect his *compadre* or his godfather to act as protector or advocate when necessary. In those cases where social equals enter into such arrangements, the advantages gained may be in the form of equally favorable goods or labor exchanges, which are received by the formal kinlike arrangements of the alliance.

Compadrazgo may operate in different ways depending on the needs of the people entering into such relationships, and the context in which the relationships are agreed upon. However, in order to operate as the vehicle for important social alliances at all, some legitimating agent must be active when these ties are made, and it is precisely at this point that ritual enters. The rituals here are those of baptism or marriage, as performed by authorized priests within the context, and with the full weight of authority, of the church. The ritual itself marks the relationship as a solemn event in contrast to less formal alliances. These alliances are further invested with the necessary legitimacy to allow the relationship to be binding through (1) the authority of the priest, which parallels the authority of state officials; and (2) the recording of the event in official ecclesiastical records, which parallels legal formalization in legal documents.

In sum, peasant *compadres*, like brothers and brothers-in-law, cooperate more among themselves in *anyi* and *mink'a* than do neighbors not related through blood, marriage, or godparenthood. And *compadres* outside the peasant sphere extend peasant contacts into realms where the peasant would otherwise have no influence at all. Church ritual, therefore, acts to seal these important social contracts both through the authority of the Church and through the solemnity of sacred ritual, and thus plays an important role in establishing and maintaining different kinds of social alliances.

Local Groups

The next set of rituals observed in the southern highlands of Peru is centered on Catholic saints, which are manifest in statues housed in churches and chapels not only in the countryside of Peru, but also in every town and city of all the Andean republics. These rituals are in the form of celebrations honoring the saints and are held on the saints' special days as stipulated in the official Catholic calendar. The primary features of the celebrations are: (1) a mass said by a priest; (2) the participation of members of all social classes in the celebration; and (3) a system of sponsorship in which the responsibility for financing the lavish festivities that constitute the feast is placed each year on different members of the community. Furthermore, such feasts are celebrated by groups of people ranging from peasant subcommunities to entire regions containing members of all social classes.

The feasts which have received the most attention in the ethnographic and folkloristic literature are those celebrated by peasant communities. Let us begin, therefore, with an analysis of community-level fiestas.

The most visible and the most elaborate of strictly peasant social organizations are communities. These consist of peasant households, and are characterized by specific names, clear territorial boundaries, land-use rights to recognized community members, internal prestige ranking that forms the basis for internal political organization, and mechanisms for mobilizing the labor of community members for community projects. All communities are recognized de facto by people of all social classes, and many such communities are recognized de jure by the state. Application by peasants for such legal status has, in fact, constituted one of the major dealings peasants have had with the state for a good part of this century. It should be pointed out, however, that not all rural areas are characterized by such peasant communities, but may instead be inhabited by households in much looser forms of cooperation. Also, there are a number of different kinds of peasant communities depending on the degree of internal cohesion, size, and population composition.

Preparations for community feasts begin with the selection of sponsors, known in southern Peru as *alferez*. This takes place a full year before the realization of the feast. The sponsor is selected from those within the community who can afford to bear the financial burden, and selections are made by a council of prestigious community members made up of former *alferez*. This constitutes one of the major community-level decisions made during the year. The *alferez* then mobilizes aid within his network of friends and kinsmen. The entire year is then spent in amassing the cash and the goods which will be lavishly expended in the one- to three-day celebration. In some communities, land is permanently set aside for the patron saint, and is worked in communal labor by community members. Proceeds from these lands then go to finance the community feast. In such cases the sponsor is in charge of organizing the work and providing food and drink for the work parties.

The celebration itself consists of a mass and a holy procession led by the officiating priest, and of the participation of a band especially hired for the occasion. Afterwards, traditional festive dances are often performed in rented costumes, fireworks are ignited, and clowns perform antics throughout the community. Eating, drinking, dancing, and general merrymaking round out the event.

The preparation for and the celebration of feasts in honor of community patron saints have definable results, both internally, within the territorial and the social boundaries of the community, and externally, between the community and its broader social context. Internal results of such celebrations vary from community to community, and even from year to year within a single community. Generalizations, therefore, are difficult to make.

Perhaps the safest generalization that can be made in this respect is that such sponsorship provides a means of establishing and of signifying social ranking within the community. This is, of course, expressed primarily in the selection of the *alferez*, but it is also revealed in the fixed proportions of food and drink the sponsor must dispense to the community members according to rank. Former sponsors are high in prestige within this ranking system. In some communities this is an unambiguous signifier of internal ranking, while in others, ranking is more subtly signified, not through traditionally fixed proportions of distribution, but rather through exclusion from invitations, toasts, and the like.

Such ranking may become the vehicle for other forms of social action within the local community. The most obvious of these is the influence which may accrue to community members by virtue of their sponsorship. In some communities this is translated directly into political terms, as seen in the requirement that men pass through degrees of festival sponsorship before they may hold various community offices. In such cases, there exists a parallel between degrees of sponsorship and hierarchies of political authority. Another internal effect the feast may have is that of economic leveling, as suggested by Eric Wolf. In such cases, the feast may function to inhibit the amassing of wealth among those peasants in the best position to do so. By sponsoring the feast, these peasants trade wealth for prestige. A low economic level is thus maintained throughout the community, by drawing resources from the highest economic ranks, and thereby maintaining community homogeneity. Such leveling, if it does occur in the southern Peruvian countryside, takes place only in especially close-knit communities of a certain type.

Since the varying social forms and internal operations, and even the very existence of community-level organization, depend on a host of highly fluctuating external factors such as geographic location, population density, state policies, and marketing opportunities, the investigator in the Andean countryside observes a great deal of change in the political and in the social structures of individual communities over time. In fact, community-level organization is highly mutable. Therefore, rituals associated with it are likewise fluid in the range and in the intensity of their social, political, and economic results (Orlove, 1979).

The most uniform of the social results of such community celebrations, however, are not those internal, but rather those external to community organization. De facto recognition of communities by other peasants and by local elites is an important factor in maintaining the claims on land and water resources made by those individual households comprising communities. Without a community name, traditional boundary markers, and a community level of organization to support them, individual households within the community would find it difficult to exert these claims and to protect their resources from encroachments, both from other peasants and from members of local elites. Furthermore, community officials, selected and maintained by internal political institutions, are more effective representatives of the constituent households of the community before state officials, public service agencies, and the courts than individual peasant families would be. In fact, community identity and community organization play important mediating roles between households and the broader society.

Community feasts parallel and support in the ritual sphere what community organization does in the social and the political realms. First, they are centered on a saint that is not only a local spirit but is also recognized as a legitimate spiritual entity by all members of the society. This recognition is further supported by the official Catholic Church, whose spiritual authority parallels the political authority of the national state. By organizing and celebrating the recognized feast of a community saint (a saint accepted with reverence throughout society), the community is asserting its identity to all concerned through ritual action, while at the same time supporting its own internal organization and its territorial claims. This is done in a public manner, with open participation. Most importantly, the entire ritual event is legitimated by the presence and the participation of a Catholic priest.

So important is the community feast in this respect that with the creation of new communities, corresponding cults develop with their own annual ritual celebrations. One example of this is the splitting up of Surimana in the province of Canas, department of Cuzco, into six officially recognized peasant communities (Orlove, 1976).

Surimana was, in the early part of the century, a distinct social and land-use entity consisting of the town of Surimana and five outlying hamlets. Due to a number of economic and political factors, the ties that held the town and its hamlets together weakened and finally dissolved, resulting in the development of six separate communities: Surimana, now having declined from a town to a village, and its five former hamlets. Each of these communities now has a lieutenant governor, and each has been recognized by the state as a legal entity. Moreover, schools have been built in each of the former hamlets, thereby supporting the separate identities of each community by focusing community attention and activity inward.

Before the dissolution of "greater" Surimana, the festival of the patron saint of the town of Surimana formed the central feast of the entire community. Each hamlet had its own chapel and its own saint, but these saints remained ritually subordinate to that of the town. As the hamlets evolved into separate communities, however, the feast at Surimana became weaker and more sporadic in response to the diminishing position of the town, while the patron saints of the evolving communities became the focal points of more elaborate fiestas in response to their growing autonomy and, ultimately, their status as separate communities. Ritual in this case functioned to assert and to press the claims of emerging community status by each hamlet, and now it operates as a signifier of community autonomy.

Regional Populations

Feasts honoring patron saints are not only celebrated by peasant communities, but by a wide range of social groups within regional contexts throughout the entire society. In many parts of the southern Peruvian Andes, community organization as so far described is nonexistent. This is especially true in the high-altitude zones above the upper limits of agriculture, where there is a highly dispersed population. In these zones, state administrative areas (*anexos* and *distritos*), which have corresponding civil officials, form the only generally recognized bounded territories. In these zones, peasant activity is focused more on kin-based lineagelike groups of households than is the case in the territorially based peasant communities in the more densely populated lower-elevation agricultural lands. Patron saints in these high-altitude herding zones tend to be associated with such districts rather than with peasant community organizations. Ritual celebrations there are more of a regional nature than are the closeknit affairs of the classic peasant community further down. These feasts, in fact, often reveal more of district stratification than of the identity assertion of strictly peasant entities.

Regional feasts of Catholic saints vary in size and composition throughout the southern highlands of Peru, yet they all play important roles within the annual ritual calendar. Very little attention has been paid to regional systems of all kinds in the southern highlands; therefore, the close relationship of political, social, economic, and ritual interactions within definable regions is a fertile and little-known field for investigation. The following three examples will serve to illustrate the great variability encountered in this realm of ritual activity, and to demonstrate how present interactions within broader social and economic contexts are paralleled by ritual activities. The first example is from the city and province of Cuzco, and the second and third are from the remote province of Chumbivilcas in the southern end of the department of Cuzco.

Cuzco is a city of over a hundred thousand and serves as (1) the capital of the department of Cuzco, a political entity comparable to that of a state of the United States or a province of Canada; (2) the seat of the archdiocese of Cuzco; and (3) the center for a large market area of the southern highlands. On a local level, it is the capital of the province of Cuzco, the seat of the diocese, and the headquarters for a number of provincial-level national public service agencies, such as the ministries of agriculture and public education. Furthermore, two daily markets within the city serve as primary markets for an area that more or less follows the political boundaries of the province. Political, religious, and market areas, therefore, are roughly coterminous, and form a region defined by the city of Cuzco and its immediate hinterland.

The significant ritual event of this region is that of Corpus Cristi. This is primarily an urban festival since most of the parishes of the diocese are located within the city of Cuzco itself. The diocese does, however, include the nearby town of San Sebastian and a rural hinterland. Ritual associations within the peasant communities are organized to represent their communities within their respective parishes. The members of such associations remove the community's patron saint from the local chapel and bear it on their shoulders to the parish church. At this point the peasants join the procession of the patron saint of the parish, which is carried through the streets of Cuzco to the cathedral. Thus representatives of all sections of the greater Cuzco region participate in the festival of Corpus Cristi.

Peasant participation in the Corpus Cristi festival is quite visible, first in the lodging of community saints in the parish church, and secondly in the participation of community contingencies within the procession in which the parish patron saint is transported from the parish church to the cathedral. In these processions, the peasants march alongside nonpeasants and play their traditional music alongside bands representing more prestigious parish groups. Such participation on a regional basis and within the emotion-packed drama of ritual thus marks the community as an entity with its proper place within regional society as seen in the representation of all other social classes, each with their own saints and their own cult organizations.

The focal point, and perhaps the most important single feature of both community and regional level feasts, is the statue of the Catholic saint, since it acts as a symbol on which ritual activity of different social classes is articulated. No matter what underlying "meanings" peasants and other classes within the society may attach to these symbols, that is, no matter what place saints may hold within the greatly differing conceptualizations of different groups, they nonetheless represent a common symbolic form. In this sense, the saint is polysemous since it has different value for different groups. In responding to this polysemous symbol with a common ritual response the illusion of agreement is created, thus masking the different currents of belief and social and economic functions which underlie both the symbol and its corresponding ritual. Conversely, regional level participation in regional rituals signifies the real interdependence of different social classes, according to their stations, within a definable interaction sphere.

The example of the Corpus Cristi feast illustrates how political and religious regions define a sphere of interaction which is further strengthened by market interactions and marked by ritual activity. In the southern portion of the province of Chumbivilcas the feasts of the Holy Cross illustrate how ritual activity is correlated only with market activity and with periodic market service areas.

A single motor road penetrates the province of Chumbivilcas. It enters at the town of Velille where it forks, one branch passing through the village of Esquina and terminating in the provincial capital of Santo Tomás, the other extending to the town of Colquemarca, where it ends. Traffic, in the form of trucks from Arequipa, Cuzco, and Sicuani, begins on Saturday, bringing goods into the province, as well as entrepreneurs to do the buying and selling at the provincial markets. Sunday markets are held at Santo Tomás and Colquemarca. As the trucks leave the province on Monday, smaller markets are held in Esquina and Velille. Complementary market service areas are therefore created by the motor roads and the weekly traffic patterns on them.

The feast of the Holy Cross is celebrated in the month of May only in the market towns. Sponsors of the feasts are chosen from the residents of these towns (with the exception of Santo Tomás), and responsibility for the various events which constitute the feasts remains with the townsmen. Peasants from the market hinterland come into these settlements to enjoy the festivities, just as they come to participate in the weekly market. They have no stake in the prestige system the ritual expresses, just as their participation in market exchanges is that of low capital consumer and primary seller rather than that of business specialist. Their ritual participation therefore corresponds to their participation within the local periodic market areas.

The Holy Cross feast of Santo Tomás has more prestige than those of the other market centers, as is commensurate with its superior market status. It differs from the smaller festivals, however, in another important respect. Unlike the sponsors of the small feasts, the *alférez* of the Santo Tomás celebration are not selected from the local townsmen, but rather from the truckers who maintain the market link between the province of Chumbivilcas and the market centers of the rest of the southern Peruvian market region. In this way, transportation specialists, so important to the market system as it now exists, are ritually integrated into the sedentary provincial population they serve. The Holy Cross feasts of the southern portion of the province therefore parallel in ritual activity both internal market districts and the vital link with the outside which has created and which maintains them.

Regional feasts may also provide a means of asserting regional identity while at the same time expressing in the dramaturgical language of ritual the social stratification of rural society. Such expression may further provide a means of moderating to some degree the latent conflicts inherent in such stratification. An excellent example of this is the patron-saint feast of the capital of Chumbivilcas, Santo Tomás, a feast which functions as a province-wide festival event.

The sponsors of this feast are chosen from the elites of Santo Tomás, thus marking the degree of importance of the town within Chumbivilcas, and the status of its citizens within provincial society. The festival routine is similar to that elsewhere in the southern highlands; however, one feature of the Santo Tomás festival stands out in contrast to festivals in all but a few adjacent provinces. This feature is the two days of bullfighting that conclude the celebration.

Two separate *toreros*, or organizers, are selected from different constituencies to borrow bulls and to arrange the bullfights in the municipal ring. One of these sponsors is a member of the local elites, called in Quechua *mistis*. The other is a peasant. Bulls for the first day are borrowed by the *misti torero* from among *misti* herds. Bulls for the second day come only from peasant herds. The bullfights are performed by volunteers who face the bulls with nothing but courage and their own native deftness at evading the horns, rather than with any learned skills. A great deal of bravado by the combatants accompanies the bullfights, and since the bullfighters are amateurs, and since much alcohol is consumed throughout the fiesta, several bullfighters each year are injured or even killed.

There is an idealized regional identity found among Chumbivilcanos, even among the peasant population. This is associated with the trappings and glamour of a herding way of life reminiscent of *vaqueros* in Mexico, *gauchos* in the pampas, and cowboys in the United States Southwest. Horses, chaps, bolos, guns, the myth and the reality of local cattle rustling, and of bullfighting, are all parts of this mystique. The important position of bullfights in the Santo Tomás festival serves to emphasize the uniqueness of Chumbivilcas, and to express the traits of the idealized Chumbivilcan character. Participation in the bullfights, therefore, provides the Chumbivilcano with, among other things, a means of expressing his regional identity in a striking manner consonant with the stereotype of the province and its people.

The bullfights also provide a vivid means of social expression. This is done by dichotomizing the population into *misti* and peasant within the bullring, where one of the most central and emotion-packed events of the festival takes place. This opposition is then mediated by (1) providing equal status to the two events that correspond to the two social groups; and (2) by means of certain reversals of ordinary behavior. That is, the peasants are excluded from the *misti* event, and likewise the *mistis* are excluded from the peasant event. If a peasant attempts to take part in the *misti* bullfight, he is forcefully ejected, and more importantly, if a *misti* attempts to enter the ring on the peasant day, peasants will eject him in the same manner.

In this way, the boundaries are symbolically drawn between *misti* and peasant. Furthermore, two separate spheres are created within the festival context, in which members of each group, without interference from outside their respective social spheres, may prove their manliness and their regional affinities on equal but separate terms.

Besides the forceful ejection of *mistis* from peasant bullfights, another reversal of normal behavior is also observed. This is seen in the labels given by peasants to each bullfight. *Alqo toro*, "bulls of the dogs," is used to refer to the *misti* event, while the peasant bullfight is called *runa toro*, "bulls of the people." These apparent affronts are not only tolerated by the local elites, but are pointed to with pride as features of their own distinctive provincial ritual.

This sharp symbolic dichotomizing of social classes and its accompanying reversal of normal behavior ritually express the conflict latent in the more complex, but nonetheless stratified, society of Chumbivilcas. Moreover, this social rivalry is symbolically played out within the danger-charged atmosphere of the bullfights, which is invariably punctuated with bloodshed and sometimes even with sudden death. The opposition of the normally subdued society with the blood and the conflict of the ritual complements both the opposition of *misti* and peasant as well as the further opposition of men (both *misti* and peasants) contending separately against a hostile nonhuman force. The bullfight therefore not only dramatizes an idealized vision of regional society, but also serves to reduce to some degree the tension latent within it.

Conclusion

This chapter has attempted to demonstrate the correlation between different rituals and the different social contexts in which peasants interact within the contemporary highlands of southern Peru. It has further attempted to show how these rituals operate in two interrelated ways: first as a means of expressing social identity and the nature of social relations, and second as a means of establishing and maintaining social groups. In this way we have tried to show how ritual, along with economic, political, and other forms of social activities, plays an important role in the structure and in the dynamics of the agrarian system of the southern Peruvian highlands.

CHAPTER 12

Peru's Invisible Migrants:
A Case Study of Inter-Andean Migration

Stephen B. Brush

The orderly, overly idyllic, characterization of the Latin American peasant communities presented by social scientists in the tradition of Redfield and the *Indigenista* movement has been disputed by later generations of iconoclasts. Issues which have received critical attention are the supposed native, pre-Hispanic roots of the indigenous communities and the nature of the indigenous community as an isolated and clearly bounded entity (Fuenzalida, 1970b; Adams, 1962). This article will discuss an aspect of Andean communities which has received little attention: the migration between smaller towns, villages, haciendas, and communities. The extent of this migration, which is internal to the Andes, belies two former images: (1) that the relationships between the various social units of the Andean region are generally confined to economic (trade) and institutional (political-administrative) spheres; and (2) that the only significant migration which concerns the Andean area is emigration to the coast.

The mobility of the Peruvian highland population is well established. The results of this mobility are highly visible in many parts of the country, especially in Lima and other major urban-industrial centers on the coast, such as Chiclayo, Trujillo, and Chimbote. In terms of the magnitude of the number of people involved, the westward movement from the Andes to the coast is the predominant flow in the country. There is a growing body of literature concerned with this migration, and a number of topic areas have emerged: (1) the source of migration (Preston, 1969; Dobyns and Vazquez, 1963); (2) the impact of migration on coastal cities (Mangin, 1967); and (3) the impact of urban life on the lives of migrants (Patch, 1967; Mangin 1970). A second type of migration in Peru is in an easterly direction from the central Andes to the eastern slopes of the Andes (Martínez, 1969, 1970; Díaz Martínez, 1969). The literature on this type of migration is considerably smaller than that on the westward movement.

A third type of migration is one which is internal to the Andes. In

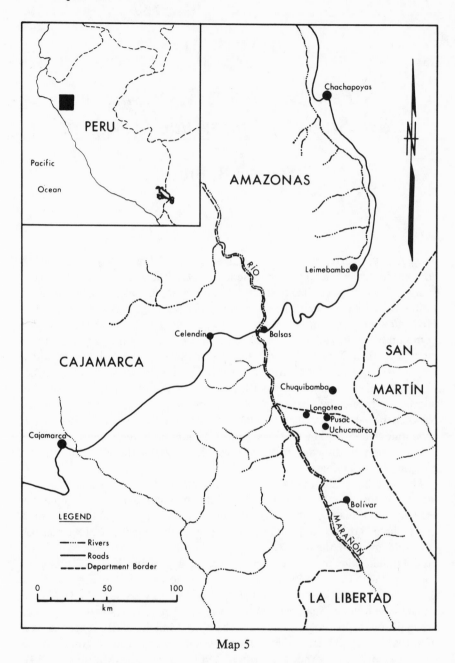

Map 5

comparison to the first two types mentioned above, this third type has received very little attention in the social scientific literature on Peru. Field work in the northern Andes of Peru indicates that this is an important and pervasive type of migration, although the migrants may be indistinguishable from the locally born population to an outside observer. Unlike migration from the highlands to the coast, where differences in language, dress, and cultural backgrounds often require major changes in the migrants' behavior, interprovincial migration within the Andes usually does not demand such changes. The cultural differences between the immigrants and the local population are usually minor. On the other hand, interprovincial migration requires a specific set of adaptive strategies on the part of the migrant, and it may require a concomitant response on the part of the town receiving the migrants. This migration will be described for one province, Bolívar, in the far northeastern corner of the department of La Libertad. The description will focus on the district of Uchucmarca, which is in the province of Bolívar (Brush, 1977).

Uchucmarca and the Province of Bolívar

The province of Bolívar is among the most isolated in the department of La Libertad (Map 5). Local residents stress that they are separated from the rest of La Libertad by two other departments, Amazonas and Cajamarca.[1] There are six districts in the province, all comparable in size and geographic orientation, and the ethnic composition of each district is similar. Each district contains valley complexes which run from the hot and dry Marañón Valley to the cold, wet eastern slopes of the Andes. The only road which penetrates the province reaches only one of the six district capitals, Longotea. It takes three to four days to traverse the province on horse or foot.

Uchucmarca is a large village which serves as the administrative center of both the district of Uchucmarca and the *comunidad campesina* of Uchucmarca (peasant community). Three of the other districts of Bolívar (Ucuncha, Condormarca, and Bambamarca) are also officially recognized peasant communities. Uchucmarca lies some six to eight hours (thirty-three kilometers) from the terminus of the road at Pusac at the base of the Uchucmarca Valley. Travel to the provincial capital (Bolívar) takes six hours by horse, and Trujillo, the department capital, is two or three days from the town. The isolation of Uchucmarca, and of the rest of the province, may be described as both economic and political. The economic isolation of Uchucmarca is attributable in part to the fact that the peasant community of Uchucmarca controls a single valley system with adequate land in all of the major Andean crop zones. Included here are:

1. The *temple* zone at the base of the valley (1,000–1,500 meters), where sugar cane, coca, fruit, and vegetables are cultivated on irrigated lands.
2. The *kichwa fuerte* zone (1,500–1,900 meters) in the lower valley, where maize and wheat are grown in small quantities in nondrought years and where firewood is gathered.
3. The *kichwa* zone (1,900–2,450 meters) in the central valley, where maize and wheat are grown in considerable quantity.
4. The *templado* zone (2,450–3,000 meters) immediately below the village, where field peas (*arvejas*), barley, lentils, maize, and some potatoes are cultivated.

5. The *jalka* zone (3,000–3,500 meters), where potatoes and other Andean tubers are cultivated and where limited grazing occurs.
6. The *jalka fuerte* zone (3,500–4,300 meters), where livestock is grazed on natural pastures.
7. The *ceja de montaña* (located on the Huallaga drainage below 2,500 meters), where lumbering and some hunting are done.

The major portion of the peasant community's land is in the valley of the Río Pusac, a small tributary of the Marañón. The community's lands run up to and over the watershed of the eastern Andean *cordillera* between the Marañón and Huallaga rivers. The village is located at 3,035 meters, between the *templado* and *jalka* zones.

The subsistence strategies of individual households in the village are centered on gaining access to *chacras* (plots) in as many of these zones as possible, through usufructuary rights granted by the peasant community or through other forms of land tenure such as renting or sharecropping (*sociedad*). Other strategies involve labor recruitment through reciprocal labor exchange (*huasheo*) or the hiring of labor for payment in either food or cash (*minga*). Deficits in household food production are made up through systems of exchange (*canje* or *trueque*), by purchases with cash (*compra*), and by working for payment in food items (*minga*). Although the resources in the valley appear adequate to meet the subsistence needs of the valley population, the distribution of these resources is uneven. Many of the subsistence strategies of individual households may be analyzed as an attempt to gain access to unevenly distributed resources. A primary technique, and one which this paper will return to later, is the *sociedad* system, in which relative inequalities of land and labor availability are balanced.

The nucleated settlement of Uchucmarca has a population of slightly over one thousand individuals, living in some two hundred separate households. The only other sizable town in the valley, Pusac, has five hundred inhabitants. Outside of these two nucleated settlements are some one thousand people living in small hamlets (*caseríos*) and on isolated homesteads. Each of the other five districts of the province of Bolívar is marked by a similar pattern of one major nucleated settlement and numerous small hamlets and homesteads. The largest town, Bolívar, has 1,100 inhabitants. The population of the entire province was 13,307 in 1972 (Instituto Nacional de Planificación, 1972).

Migrants in Uchucmarca

Like most other Andean villagers, the people of Uchucmarca are involved in different types of migration. One is away from the valley to larger cities in the highlands, such as Cajamarca, and another more common form is to the urban-industrial centers on the coast, particularly Lima and Trujillo. Virtually every person in the village has at least one close relative who has emigrated to the coast on either a temporary or a permanent basis. There are 178 adult

Uchucmarquinos who have migrated permanently. Thirty-eight percent of the households in the village have immediate kin who have emigrated permanently, and 31 percent have members who have emigrated temporarily but who have returned to the village. Temporary migration is especially prevalent among young adults (twenty to thirty years old), who go to the coast as an adventure before settling down to raise a family in the village. Many people who establish a permanent residence away from the village return periodically for festive occasions and for major family events such as a funeral or a wedding.

The other major type of migration affecting Uchucmarca is immigration to the valley. There are some 280 adult immigrants in the district, comprising roughly 46 percent of the adult population. The impact of this immigration is strongly felt by all local residents, but the relative density of migrants varies considerably in different parts of the district.

Immigration to Uchucmarca has occurred in two waves. The first, occurring between 1930 and 1960, was comprised of immigrants who moved into the town of Uchucmarca and the upper part of the Uchucmarca Valley. The second wave of migration began in the late 1950s and continues now. The second migration is very different from the first in that these immigrants have tended to remain in and around the town of Pusac, whereas the former immigrants settled predominantly in the higher zones. Immigration to Pusac was greater than that to Uchucmarca. Above Pusac, 35 percent of the males and 25 percent of the females are immigrants to the Uchucmarca Valley. In Pusac, 78 percent of the males and 82 percent of the females are immigrants. Pusac, a new town, was thus formed mainly by immigrants. The immigration to these two areas varies also in terms of source and integration into the existing valley community of Uchucmarca.

Migrants in the first wave, that is, those who came to the upper valley between 1930 and 1960, came predominantly from districts that are adjacent to Uchucmarca. Sixty-two percent of the immigrant males and 60 percent of the immigrant females during this period were from adjacent districts. This migration slowed considerably after 1961, as indicated by the fact that only 5 percent of the immigrant families in the upper valley arrived after that year (Figure 12-1). The remaining immigrants came from the adjacent department of Amazonas and from the department of Cajamarca, on the other side of the Marañón River. The two sources which figure predominantly here are Chuquibamba, in the department of Amazonas which is adjacent to Uchucmarca, and the area around Celendín in Cajamarca. Table 12-1 presents a breakdown of the specific sources of the first wave of migration to the upper Uchucmarca Valley.

Specific reasons for this migration differ with individual cases, but most of the migrants refer to regional economic differences as being the general cause of their decisions to move to the Uchucmarca Valley. These differences include a low population density and a relative abundance of arable land in Uchucmarca compared to a shortage of land in the districts from which the

Table 12-1
Immigrants to Uchucmarca (Upper Valley Areas)

Place of Origin		Number	
Department	District	Males	Females
La Libertad	Bolívar	36	24
	Longotea	2	2
Amazonas	Chuquibamba	5	5
	Other	9	9
Cajamarca		16	11
Total		68	51

migrants came. A clear example of this regional economic difference can be seen in a comparison between the districts of Bolívar and Uchucmarca. As Table 12-1 indicates, Bolívar was the most important source of migrants to the Uchucmarca Valley during the first wave of migration.

The most important difference between the districts of Bolívar and Uchucmarca is the fact that Bolívar contains a number of large haciendas, while Uchucmarca, since colonial times, has been a "free" community. In 1946 this status was officially recognized when Uchucmarca became a

Figure 12.1   Immigration to Uchucmarca (Upper Valley Area).

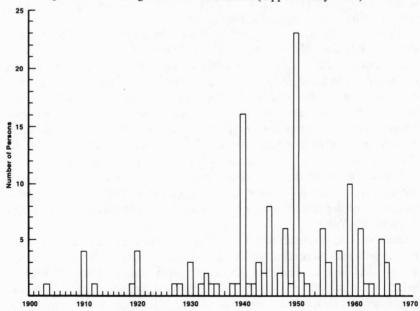

comunidad indígena (indigenous community). In 1969 this title was converted to the present *comunidad campesina* (peasant community). According to local municipal archives, haciendas have been a feature of the land tenure of Bolívar since colonial times, whereas Uchucmarca has been defending its lands as a community free from large estates since the early seventeenth century. Two features of the haciendas of Bolívar are significant in terms of regional economics of migration. The first is their size, and the second is their relative location in the district of Bolívar.

The size of the haciendas of Bolívar is small in comparison to coastal haciendas and to some of the large estates west of the Marañón, such as La Pauca in the district of San Marcos. Within the district of Bolívar, however, they dominate the local area, covering 65 percent of the district. The two largest haciendas, Cujibamba and Pana, with 19,625 and 16,300 hectares respectively, occupy 38 percent of the land within the district. The size of these holdings is particularly impressive when compared to the average land-holdings in free communities such as Uchucmarca, where the average household cultivates only 1.58 hectares per year. Although landholdings are actually more extensive because of fallowing, no family in the peasant community of Uchucmarca claims more than ten hectares of land.

Although single-family ownership of the estates in Bolívar does not mean single-family occupation, the population size and density of haciendas tends to be far lower than in nonhacienda areas. The presence of haciendas tends to increase the population pressure on peasant lands within the same district; districts such as Uchucmarca, where large estates are prohibited by the existence of peasant communities, also become more populated due to the presence of haciendas in nearby areas. Virtually all migration into Uchucmarca came from districts which had haciendas, while there has been very little immigration from other free communities.

Although specific figures for this difference in densities were unobtainable, many migrants from Bolívar as well as actual residents in Bolívar point to this condition. They note that the population density in the nonhacienda areas of the district of Bolívar were raised because the hacendados have attempted to hold down population on their estates. The limiting of population began in the early 1940s and coincided with the first wave of migration to Uchucmarca. Beginning in 1940, three of the largest haciendas in the district were purchased by one family from Trujillo who owned several other haciendas both on the coast and in the highlands of the department of La Libertad. Two of these haciendas had been previously owned by two kin-related families in Bolívar. The Trujillo family purchased the largest hacienda in 1940 and the others in 1950. The largest two were sold again in 1964 to a family from Celendín, while the third was sold in parcels to six different local families in 1970. Former residents of the haciendas now living in Uchucmarca report that at each of these land transfers between hacendado families, pressure was placed on peasant tenants to leave their hacienda plots and to move to Bolívar. In the first case, the family from Trujillo purchased the haciendas in Bolívar for the specific purpose of livestock production. The owners of these haciendas apparently hoped to take advantage of new and projected highways connecting the western flank of the Marañón River to Cajamarca and Trujillo. Before road links to the towns of San Marcos and Celendín were completed, cattle drives from the eastern flank of the Marañón were uneconomic. In order to increase the amount of grazing lands, they forced a number of tenants to abandon potato plots in the *jalka* crop zone. Furthermore, both tenants and nontenants were discouraged from grazing livestock on hacienda land by the imposition of rent on grazing land. Both the limiting of subsistence plots and the imposition of rents on grazing land are common features of twentieth century Andean haciendas (Horton, 1974). Both strongly influenced emigrants to leave the district.

These haciendas control the major portion of grazing land in the district of Bolívar. Many persons see this condition as the most significant single factor in the land tenure situation in the district prior to the Agrarian Reform Law of 1969. They point out that the haciendas of the district controlled, almost exclusively, one of the four crucial production zones in the traditional Andean complex. The significance of this grazing zone (known locally as the *jalka fuerte*) to subsistence peasant farmers is two-fold. First, it provides primary products such as meat (mutton and some beef), which supplement the potato and grain diet, and wool for blankets and essential articles of clothing. More importantly, the natural pastures of the *jalka fuerte* support livestock (cattle, sheep, horses, and mules), which represent the most reliable and largest source of cash for many peasant households. The pastures of the province of Bolívar today support over twenty thousand animals. Cattle (ten thousand to twelve thousand head in the district) are produced almost exclusively for sale outside of the province. Each town and village in the province is visited regularly by cattle traders from the towns of Celendín, San Marcos, and Cajabamba on the other side of the Marañón. The cattle are driven to markets in Celendín and San Marcos. In the generally cash poor economy of the province, pastures and livestock assume an important place in the subsistence strategies of many households. It is often difficult to find work that pays cash, and few peasants produce enough agricultural surplus to be sold locally or in the one weekly market in the district. Livestock represent a relatively secure and productive means of earning cash. As capital goods, they increase both in value (through growth and appreciation) and in numbers. In most years, cattle prices inflate faster than other commodity prices. Moreover, the nearest interest-paying bank is two-days travel from the district. Because they can be easily converted into a sizable amount of cash, livestock may be thought of as a living bank account, and this is indeed the way the people of the region view livestock. The fact that the haciendas of Bolívar closed or curtailed the use of this production zone to both tenants and nontenants of the district of Bolívar played a central role in the decisions of most immigrants to Uchucmarca in the late 1940s. It is important to note that Uchucmarca followed the traditional practice of granting community members grazing rights to these lands, rather than charging them rents as was done in Bolívar.

The sale in 1964 of the two large haciendas in Bolívar had smaller repercussions for migration within the district. Most former tenants had already been forced off the haciendas. At the time of that sale there were growing pressures for an effective agrarian reform in Peru. The family that bought the two haciendas apparently decided that its best strategy in avoiding the reform was to maintain the limited number of tenants on each hacienda and to parcel the haciendas among family members. The first step was seen as a means of reducing the possibility of tenants becoming politicized and organized enough either to invade hacienda property or to bring legal pressure. The second step was seen as a legal means of avoiding government parceling of the haciendas. At the time of the author's most recent visit, in July 1974, neither of the haciendas had yet been affected by the Agrarian Reform Law of 1969.

Thus the general condition of unequal densities between the districts of Bolívar and Uchucmarca was brought into focus by the sales of large haciendas in the late 1940s and 1950s. The first sale occurred at the time when Uchucmarca received official recognition from the national government as a *comunidad indígena*. The legal guarantees accorded to the members of *comunidades indígenas* added to the attractiveness of the perceived abundance of land in the Uchucmarca Valley for those who chose to leave Bolívar.

Migrants to Pusac

The district of Uchucmarca experienced its second wave of migration from the late 1950s through the late 1960s (Figure 12-2). This wave differed from the first both in terms of the origin and of the final destination of the immigrants. The focus of this second wave was the hot lower valley around the hamlet of Pusac. Until the mid-1950s, this area, like many other intermontane valleys of the Andes, was considered uninhabitable because of malaria.[2] Between 1957 and 1959, this disease was eradicated by a joint Unesco-Peruvian campaign to fumigate the area with DDT. There is still a full-time government agent in Pusac who fumigates and dispenses antimalaria medicine. Prior to the eradication of malaria, the lower valley was only sparsely occupied by a very few families who grew sugar cane, coca, and fruit, which they traded for grains and tubers from the higher crop zones. This pattern was similar to migrations into the *montaña* from the central and southern highlands (Burchard, 1974; Mayer, 1971; Webster, 1971). After the introduction of DDT into the lower valley, a few families from Uchucmarca and the surrounding districts of Bolívar and Chuquibamba began to settle there. Concurrently, the Pusac area also began to receive immigrants from the region around Celendín on the other side of the Marañón. These migrants soon

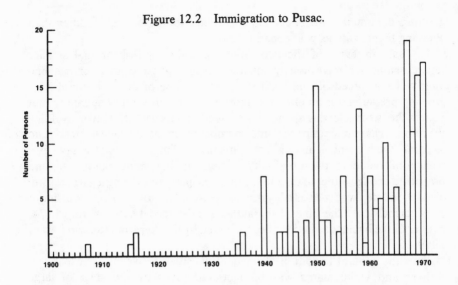

Figure 12.2   Immigration to Pusac.

became the most numerous type in the area, and they have dominated Pusac ever since.

One incentive for this migration was the fact that a hacienda in the district of Longotea, adjacent to Uchucmarca, parceled and sold land which it had previously held in the lower valley of Uchucmarca. This hacienda was also the property of the Trujillo family who had purchased the three haciendas in Bolívar. Some of the established residents of the lower valley had previously been tenants of this hacienda, and several of these residents purchased plots of their own from the hacienda.

Another factor which made the Pusac area more attractive was the completion in 1965 of a road which connected to Balsas and Celendín. Until this link was completed, the province of Bolívar was roughly eighteen hours by horse to Celendín. The road brought increasing numbers of immigrants from the other side of the Marañón River, especially from the province of Celendín.

Like the people who migrated to the upper Uchucmarca Valley from the district of Bolívar, these migrants from Celendín came from an area which contained a number of large haciendas. The immigrants to Pusac, however, maintained that it was the poverty of the soil of the Celendín Valley which was the major factor in their decision to migrate to Pusac. In addition to the opportunity to obtain a small plot of land, the appeal of Pusac consisted in the fact that there was wage labor available in the fruit orchards and in the sugar cane and coca fields of the area. Many of the migrants complained of their inability to find regular cash-paying work in Celendín and of the low pay they received when they did find work. A causal relationship between the existence of haciendas and the conditions of exhausted soil and depressed wage labor conditions is neither recognized by the immigrants from Celendín nor demonstrated by statistical measures. It is relevant to note, however, that

Hobsbawm (1969a) has been able to demonstrate the role of haciendas in depressing the wage level in southern Peru.

The Migrant Experience in Uchucmarca

Interdistrict and interregional relationships in the Andes may be seen in a number of contexts. One is the administrative hierarchy, involving the district and the province and such national institutions as the judicial system. Another is the vast network of interprovincial and interregional trade relationships. Primary trade networks in the central Marañón region involve cattle, hats, salt, the products of sugar cane (*chancaca* and *aguardiente*), coca, and a limited number of manufactured goods such as cloth and metal tools. Less important trade networks involve potatoes, grains, wool, and pottery. These trade networks may be analyzed according to such variables as regional economic differences or Andean energy flow systems (Mayer, 1971; Thomas, 1973).

Migrants and migration provide a third context in which to view interdistrict and interregional relationships. The migrants themselves provide a wide network of social ties between the towns, villages, and hamlets of the region, and these ties transcend the normal ties of the administrative hierarchy and often encompass the economic links involved in the trade networks. The impact of immigrants on the villages of Uchucmarca and Pusac may be observed and measured in different ways. The receptiveness of locally born Uchucmarquinos toward migrants may be traced to three factors: (1) a slight demographic imbalance in the village; (2) a relative abundance of land in the valley; and (3) the ability of locals to use the labor of migrants.

Within Uchucmarca there is a slight demographic imbalance of females over males. Although more males are born, there is a greater infant mortality rate for males than females. Added to this natural differential is the fact that adolescent and young adult males tend to emigrate from the village at a higher rate than females. The result of these two factors is that for the fifteen to thirty-nine-year age group, there is an 8 percent deficit of males. This is the age group which is most concerned with finding spouses, and immigrant males may help to correct this demographic imbalance. Such an imbalance tends to lessen the competition for wives. From Table 12-1, it may be derived that 14 percent more migrant males than females settled in the village. The demographic imbalance may also be noted in the preponderance of single female households in Table 12-2. With so many single females, the marriage pool remains open and accessible to immigrant males.

Migrants to Uchucmarca are incorporated into the village in two formal ways: marriage and membership in the peasant community of Uchucmarca. The first is often seen as a precondition to the latter. Marriage to a native of the village automatically incorporates a stranger into the kinship system of the village, the matrix of social interaction. Although affines and affinal networks are generally not as important as consanguineal ones, they are indispensable to a migrant without consanguines in the village. An immigrant to the village who

Table 12-2

Immigration and Marriage in Uchucmarca (by household)

	Locally born		Mixed		Immigrant	
	Number	Percent	Number	Percent	Number	Percent
Single Adults						
Male	17	7			4	2
Female	23	10			10	4
Nuclear Families						
Male local/female local	92	41				
Male immigrant/female immigrant					21	9
Male local/female immigrant			19	9		
Male immigrant/female local			42	18		
TOTAL	132	58	61	27	35	15

marries a member may immediately petition the *comité de administración* (executive committee) for membership. It is common, however, for such a person to wait one or two years before making his appeal. A fee of S/200 must accompany an appeal by such a migrant. Those immigrants who do not marry natives have a more difficult time in attaining the status of members in the peasant community. There is a minimum residency period of five years, although most such immigrants do not appeal for membership until after a considerably longer period. The average is closer to ten years, and the executive committee has discussed raising the residency requirement to ten years. The fee for immigrants who do not marry natives is double that for those who do.

Table 12-2 presents a summary of immigration to the village, showing that immigrants who marry into the village outnumber those who do not. There are no formal rules of endogamy in Uchucmarca, but for practical reasons it is advantageous to marry within the community if possible. Endogamous marriages offer far greater potential for kin-based reciprocal relationships than exogamous marriages.

In petitioning for membership in the community, there is a strong element of good faith which the immigrant must demonstrate. He is expected, for instance, to participate in the periodic projects called by the communal organization, and he is expected to pay occasional fees levied by the communal organization. Finally, he must demonstrate his commitment to the village by participating in such things as the sponsorship of the religious activities. There is a certain amount of reticence on the part of the communal organization toward granting membership to immigrants, pertaining more to immigrants without affinal or other kinship ties to the village. This may relate to the long history of legal conflicts over boundaries between Uchucmarca and neighboring haciendas and communities (Brush, 1974a). Several immigrant families with permanent residence of ten years or more feel that the peasant community is not ready to accept their application for membership.

Given its population, Uchucmarca has a relative abundance of land. This is especially true in the upper zones of the valley, the *templado, jalka,* and *jalka fuerte.* According to archaeological and air photograph surveys,[3] there was more land under cultivation in these zones in pre-Hispanic times than today. Thus the valley has the potential to absorb migrants into these higher crop zones. As the community's population grows, however, the villagers are becoming more aware of an increasing strain on the land base. So far, this pressure is confined to the lower grain-producing zones, where many members have not been able to obtain land and must work as sharecroppers. The perception by Uchucmarquinos of a potential threat to their land base from the landless peasantry of nearby haciendas is a source of tension. As in southern Peru, the pattern of migration from districts controlled by haciendas to those in which communities predominate has put considerable demographic stress on the land base of communities which are adjacent to haciendas (Martinez, 1970). Although the migration to Uchucmarca has not caused the serious demographic stress found in the southern highlands, the Uchucmarquinos are aware of the potential danger posed by their relation to nearby haciendas.

In the upper zones of the Uchucmarca Valley and in the village of Uchucmarca itself, there is very little apparent friction between migrants and natives. The reasons most often cited by the people of the valley for this harmony are the length of residence in the village by the first wave of migrants, and the fact that the large majority of them have made a determined effort to integrate into the life of Uchucmarca. The majority of them are married to native spouses, and virtually all of them are members of the peasant community. One of the clearest signs of the integration of immigrants into the village is the fact that they regularly fill various positions in the administrative hierarchy of both the district and the peasant community of Uchucmarca. In the contemporary administration of the peasant community, three out of the eight positions, including the presidency, are filled by immigrants.

Immigrants are, however, clearly distinguished from natives in one important aspect, the ownership and use of land. Tables 12-3 and 12-4 present a comparison of the production of various crops under different types of land tenure according to whether a household is composed of immigrants, natives, or a combination of both. Two types of land tenure are predominant: ownership and sharecropping (*sociedad*). Under the latter, the owner of a given plot provides the plot, oxen, and seed, while the partner (*socio*) provides his labor. The harvest is divided equally, after payments are made to extra labor.

It is clear from Table 12-3 that households composed of natives fare better in terms of direct ownership of fields that produce the variety of crops which constitute the diet of the region. Those households that include immigrants tend to rely more heavily on the system of sharecropping in their subsistence agriculture. This is apparent in Table 12-4. As one might expect, that category which owns the least number of plots of all crops, namely, households comprised entirely of immigrants, relies most heavily on *sociedad* as a means of obtaining plots. The specific reason for this difference appears to rest not with overt discrimination but rather with the fact that immigrants have a more limited set of kinship networks, and they do not have equal access to plots through inheritance. The result, however, is that immigrants and their families work for natives far more frequently than vice versa. In other words, this migration tends to produce laborers rather than land owners.

The pattern of relative pressure on different crop zones, and its effect of limiting the access that immigrants have, is also demonstrated here. In the cereal-producing zones of the *kichwa* and the *templado*, immigrants have a much smaller percentage of plots than do natives in such crops as wheat, maize, and field peas. The fact that males who marry outside of the village generally have more land than other immigrant households is also demonstrated here. Finally, the fact that mixed households did better than immigrant couples testifies to the importance of having either affinal or consanguineal links, or both. As the households of Uchucmarquino couples show, those

Table 12-3

Ownership of Plots According to Immigration and Marriage

(percentages of household in each category that owned crop in 1971)

| | Households Involving Immigrants | | | Households of Natives Only | | | |
Crop	M-Immigrant* F-Immigrant*	M-Immigrant F-Native	M-Native F-Immigrant	Both M and F in Household	Single M Only	Single F Only	Village Average
Potatoes	76	67	84	90	56	30	75
Maize	24	41	53	77	31	39	51
Wheat	05	29	47	41	25	44	37
Field Peas	14	36	42	36	25	13	33
Barley	14	29	47	32	19	09	29
Ocas	31	29	74	54	31	13	40

*M = male; F = female

Table 12-4

Sociedad According to Immigration and Marriage

(percentages of households in each category that were Socios (not owners) for certain crops in 1971)

	Households Involving Immigrants			Households of Natives Only	
Crop	M-Immigrant* F-Immigrant*	M-Immigrant F-Native	M-Native F-Immigrant	M-Native F-Native	Village Average
Potatoes	14	12	05	13	13
Maize	33	17	10	26	24
Wheat	38	12	21	18	19
Field Peas	19	17	05	14	14
Barley	24	14	05	20	12
Ocas	10	02	—	07	07

*M = Male; F = Female

households with the maximum number of linkages have a better performance in owning plots than those households which have either consanguines or affines, but not both. There are only a very few households of single immigrants, and the land ownership by these was too marginal to report.

The Migrant Experience in Pusac

The experience of immigrants to Pusac provides a sharp contrast to that of immigrants to Uchucmarca in several aspects. First, the relative percentage of immigrants in Pusac is far higher than that in Uchucmarca, so that each migrant coming to Pusac has fewer opportunities to find a native spouse. Second, the arable land base of Pusac is small and controlled by relatively few families. Most of the immigrants to the area do not own land, and only a few of them are *socios* of persons who do. Instead, the majority of migrants are wage laborers in the sugar cane, fruit, and coca fields of the valley. This majority of landless immigrant laborers has had little incentive to join the peasant community of Uchucmarca. Only 40 percent of the adults in Pusac are members of the peasant community.

The town of Pusac has taken on a very independent political and economic life from that of the central village of the district, Uchucmarca. It is more strongly oriented toward Celendín, where the majority of the immigrants came from. In comparison to the immigrants to Uchucmarca, those to Pusac show little interest in adjusting their behavior to patterns set by the native residents of Uchucmarca. There is active interest in Pusac in seceding from Uchucmarca to form an independent district. The people of Uchucmarca refer to Pusac, somewhat wryly, as a rebel annex (*anexo rebelde*). The population of Pusac refused to participate in any of the normal activities, such as communal work projects, which have been called by the community officials.

Conclusion

I have described here some aspects of the interrural migration which is an important fact in one highland Peruvian district. Similarities in the cultures of the places of origin and destination of the migrants may obscure the fact that they are migrants. In order to understand this migration, I have examined the regional economic differences which arise from the presence of haciendas in some districts and their absence in others. In order to evaluate the importance of this "invisible" migration the material presented here should be compared to that on other regions of the Andes. Social scientists engaged in community studies might also observe the effects of the agrarian reform on this migration. It should become evident by the end of the decade whether this type of migration will be stopped, or even reversed, as people move back to the expropriated haciendas.

Notes

1. Similar patterns of isolated provinces are found in other parts of the Peruvian Andes, notably Castrovirreyna in Huancavelica, Marañón in Huánuco, and Parinacochas in Ayacucho.

2. On similar conditions elsewhere in Peru, see Gade, 1973.

3. Personal communication with Donald E. Thompson and Dale McElrath, who have done archaeological survey and excavation in the upper Uchucmarca Valley.

Glossary

Agregado: An individual who cannot claim rights to membership in an Indian reservation (Colombia), but who has been granted temporary privileges in it.

Aguardiente: Strong alcohol, usually rum or some other sugarcane liquor.

Ahijado: Godson.

Alcalde: The mayor of a town or an Indian community.

Alguila: The obligation of a *colono* to transport hacienda produce to a town, market, or railroad station.

Avíos: Monthly food allotment to *colonos* on a hacienda.

Ayllu: 1. A pre-Columbian form of social organization, based on kinship and residence. 2. An Indian community. 3. A kinship group that may vary in size and lineality.

Ayni: Reciprocal labor exchange.

Cabaña: The dwelling of a *colono* on a hacienda.

Cabildo: The governing council on Indian reservations (Colombia).

Canje: Barter or nonmonetarized exchange, usually involving foodstuffs.

Cargo: 1. A political or religious office in a town or community. 2. The tasks and responsibilities assigned to a *colono* on a hacienda.

Casa hacienda: The central complex of buildings on a hacienda including dwellings of the owner and employees, storeroom, offices, and other administrative facilities.

Caserío: 1. Hamlet. 2. Settlement of *colono* households on a hacienda. 3. See *casa hacienda*.

Chacra: Plot for cultivation.

Chancaca: Brown, noncentrifuged sugar.

Coca: The leaf of the *Erythroxylon coca* plant, which is chewed for its mild narcotic effect in both work and ritual contexts.

Comité de Administración: The committee which represents the internal government of a variety of corporate bodies (Indian communities, agricultural production cooperatives, etc.). The head of the committee acts as the official spokesman for the entire corporate body.

Compadrazgo: The set of ties of ritual kinship established between the parents and godparents of a child, between a couple and their matrimonial sponsors, and between participants in several other rituals.

Compadre, comadre: The reciprocal terms used between individuals linked by *compadrazgo*.

Compra: Monetarized exchange transactions.

Comunero: Member of a *comunidad*.

Comunidad campesina: 1. Any peasant community. 2. A peasant community which has received official recognition from the central government and is registered with the Dirección de Comunidades Campesinas, or Bureau of Peasant Communities.

Comunidad indígena: 1. Any native community. 2. Prior to 24 June 1969, any native community which had received official recognition from the central government and was registered with the Dirección de Comunidades Indígenas, or Bureau of Native Communities.

Concuñado: The reciprocal term used between an individual and his sibling's spouse's sibling or his spouse's sibling's spouse.

Conquistador: One of the Spanish conquerors of the native societies in sixteenth-century America.

Corregimiento: Subunit of a large municipality (Colombia), with certain attached officials.

Decreto: A political or administrative ruling or order.

Encomienda: During the colonial period, a territory assigned to a Spaniard who collected tribute from its inhabitants.

Faena: A form of collective labor for public works in towns, in haciendas, and in communities.

Fiesta: 1. The public celebration of a holiday, particularly a saint's day. 2. Any festivity or celebration.

Gamonal: A powerful landowning member of the rural elite, who usually holds an administrative or judicial office.

Guardia Civil: The national police force (Peru).

Hacendado: Owner of a hacienda.

Hacienda: A landed estate with a resident work force.

Huasheo: Reciprocal labor exchange: see *mink'a*.

Indigenismo: Intellectual movements which sought to improve the living conditions of the Indian population. *Indigenismo* exalted the Indian customs and cultural heritage.

Jalka: Production zone where tubers (principally potatoes) are grown.

Jalka fuerte: The highest production zone: an area of natural pastures the limits of cultivation.

Juez de paz: Justice of the Peace.

Junta de Administración: See Comité de Administración.

Junta de Vigilancia: The committee whose duty it is to oversee the operation of the Junta de Administración.

Kichwa: Production zone where grains (principally maize and wheat) are cultivated.

Kichwa fuerte: Production zone between the *kichwa* and the *temple* zones. Areas of maize and wheat cultivation frequently affected by drought.

Mayordomo: Foreman on a hacienda.

Mestizo: A person superior to an Indian because of fuller participation in national culture, greater wealth, or higher social status.

Minga, minka, mink'a: A labor arrangement in which workers are paid in crops, other goods, or cash, and in which food, alcohol, and *coca* are provided.

Montaña: The mountainous tropical forest region of the eastern foothills of the Peruvian Andes.

Panela: See *chancaca*.

Patrón: Employer, landlord, boss.

Pongo: Domestic servant in a *casa hacienda* or elite household.

Promotor: A field or extension agent.

Puna: High-altitude grasslands where extensive pastoralism is practiced. Cultivation with long-term fallowing possible in certain areas. Similar to the *jalka*.

Representante: The direct representative of a hacendado.

Reservation: The land grants given by the Spanish crown to communities of Indians in Colombia: many of them have survived to the present.

Rodeante: Hacienda overseer.

Sierra: 1. The Peruvian, Ecuadorian, and Bolivian highlands. 2. Any mountain range.

Sanitario: Health worker, particularly government employee.

Selva: The low moist tropical forest in the Amazon basin.

SINAMOS: Acronym for Sistema Nacional de Apoyo a la Movilización Social, or National Social Mobilization Agency. A government agency which was composed of a number of subagencies dealing directly with local-level groups; it was dismantled in the mid 1970s.

Sociedad: A sharecropping arrangement where land, seed, and oxen are given by one partner (*socio*) and labor is given by the other. The harvest is divided equally. Also known as *a medias* and *waki*.

Socio: Partner in a sharecropping arrangement (*sociedad*).

Sol: The unit of Peruvian currency. S/43.38 = U.S. $1.00 during the period when much of the ethnographic research was conducted.

Solicitud: A formal request or petition, often written on official stationery, normally required in transactions with public agencies.

Templado: An intermediate crop zone between the *kichwa* and the *jalka*.

Temple: The hot, dry intermontane valleys where tropical crops such as sugar cane and *coca* are cultivated using irrigation.

Teniente gobernador: An appointed official who represents the national government in a community.

Trapiche: Animal-powered sugar mills.

Trueque: See *canje*.

Varayoc: An individual who has a *cargo* in the political-religious structure of many communities associated with religious *fiestas*.

Vereda: Rural neighborhoods or postal routes, which may or may not constitute territorially defined political units.

Bibliography

Adams, Richard N.
1962 The Community in Latin America. *Centennial Review of Arts and Sciences* 6:409–434.
1970 *Crucifixion by Power: Essays on Guatemalan National Social Structure 1944–1966*. Austin and London: University of Texas Press.
Aguirre Beltrán, Gonzalo
1957 *El proceso de aculturación*. México: Universidad Nacional Autónoma de México.
1967 *Regiones de refugio*. México: Instituto Indigenista Interamericano.
Alberti, Giorgio and Enrique Mayer, eds.
1974 *Reciprocidad e intercambio en los Andes peruanos*. Perú-Problema 12. Lima: Instituto de Estudios Peruanos.
Albó, Xavier
1972 Dinámica en la estructura intercomunitaria de Jesús de Machaca. *América Indígena* 32(3):773–829.
Alencastre, Andrés
1965 *Kunturkanki. Un pueblo del Ande*. Cuzco: Editorial Garcilazo.
Alencastre, Simeón
1967 *Aspector jurídico de la tenecia de la tierra en la provincia de Canas*. Universidad National de San Antonio Abad del Cuzco. Tesis para optar al grado de Bachiller en Derecho.
Andrews, David Henry
1963 *Paucartambo, Pasco, Peru: An Indigenous Community and a Change Program*. Ph.D. dissertation, Cornell University.
Aparicio Vega, Manuel Jesús
1971 *Cartografía histórica cuzqueña. Mapas del Cuzco existentes en el Archivo General de Indias*. Cuzco: Editorial Pozas.
Arguedas, José María
1968 *Las comunidades de España y del Perú*. Lima: Universidad National Mayor de San Marcos.

Baca Mogrovejo, Zenovio M.
1973 El abigeato en el campo económico en Velille. Universidad Nacional de San Antonio Abad del Cuzco, programa académico de antropología. Cuzco: unpublished manuscript.
Balandier, Georges
1955 *Sociologie actuelle de l'Afrique noire*. Paris: Presses Universitaires de France.

Barnes, J.A.
1954 Class and Committees in a Norwegian Island Parish. *Human Relations* 7:39–58.

Barnes de Marshall, Katherine
1970 Cabildos, corregimientos y sindicatos de Bolivia después de 1952. *Estudios Andinos* 1(2):61–78.

Barnett, Clifford Robert
1960 *An Analysis of Social Movements on a Peruvian Highland Hacienda*. Ph.D. dissertation, Cornell University.

Barraclough, Solon L.
1970 Agricultural Policy and Strategies of Land Reform. *In* Irving Louis Horowitz, ed. *Masses in Latin America*, pp. 95–117. London and New York: Oxford University Press.

Barrette, Christian
1972 Aspects de l'ethno-écologie d'un village andin. *Canadian Review of Sociology and Anthropology* 9(3):255–267.

Barth, Fredrik
1966 *Models of Social Organization*. Royal Anthropological Institute, Occasional Paper no. 23.

Baudin, Louis
1928 *L'Empire socialiste des Inka*. Paris: Institut d'Ethnologie.

Bauer, Arnold J.
1972 The Hacienda "El Huique" in the Agrarian Structure of Nineteenth Century Chile. *Agricultural History* 46:455–470.
1975 *Chilean Rural Society from the Spanish Conquest to 1930*. Cambridge University Press.

Blok, Anton
1972 The Peasant and the Brigand: Social Banditry Reconsidered. *Comparative Studies in Society and History* 14(4):494–503.

Bollinger, William
1977 The Bourgeois Revolution in Peru: A Conception of Peruvian History. *Latin American Perspectives* 4(3):18–56.

Bolton, Ralph, and Enrique Mayer, eds.
1977 *Andean Kinship and Marriage*. Washington, D.C.: American Anthropological Association.

Bonilla, Heraclio
1973 Islay y la economía del sur peruano en el siglo XIX. Lima: Instituto de Estudios Peruanos. Mimeographed.
1974 *Guano y burguesía en el Perú*. Lima: Instituto de Estudios Peruanos.
1977 *Gran Bretaña y el Perú: los mecanismos de un control económico*. Tomo V. Lima: Instituto de Estudios Peruanos y Fondo del Libro del Banco Industrial del Perú.

Bourque, Susan C., Leslie Ann Brownrigg, Eileen Maynard, and Henry F. Dobyns

1967 *Factions and Faenas: The Developmental Potential of Checras District.* Ithaca, New York: Cornell University, Department of Anthropology.

Brush, Stephen B.

1974a Conflictos intercomunitarios en los Andes. *Allpanchis Phuturinqa* 6:29–41. Cuzco.

1974b *El lugar del hombre en el ecosistema andino. Revista del Museo Nacional del Perú* 40:277–299.

1976a Introduction to the Symposium on Cultural Adaptations to Mountain Ecosystems. *Human Ecology* 4(2):125–133.

1976b Man's Use of an Andean Ecosystem. *Human Ecology* 4(2): 147–166.

1977 *Mountain, Field, and Family: The Economy and Human Ecology of the Andean Valley.* Philadelphia: University of Pennsylvania Press.

Buitrón, Aníbal

1966 *Cómo llegó el progreso a Huagrapampa: guía práctica para los trabajadores del desarrollo de la comunidad.* México: Instituto Indigenista Interamericano.

Burchard, Roderick

1974 Coca y trueque de alimentos. *In* Giorgio Alberti and Enrique Mayer, eds., *Reciprocidad e intercambio en los Andes peruanos*, pp. 200–251. Perú-Problema 12. Lima: Instituto de Estudios Peruanos.

Burga, Manuel

1976 *De la encomienda a la hacienda capitalista: el valle del Jequetepeque del siglo XVI al XX.* Estudios de la Sociedad Rural 4. Lima: IEP ediciones.

Calero y Moreira, Jacinto

1792 Descripción corográfica de la provincia de Canas y Canches, conocida generalmente por el nombre de Tinta. *Mercurio Peruano de historia, literatura y noticias públicas que de a luz la sociedad académica de Amantes de Lima.* Tomo V, pp. 3–6, 9–14, 17–22.

Caravedo Molinari, Baltazar

1978 La historia en el Perú, siglos XIX y XX. *In* Bruno Podestá, ed., *Ciencias sociales en el Perú: un balance crítico.* Lima: Universidad del Pacífico.

Carter, William

1964 *Aymara Communities and the Bolivian Agrarian Reform.* Gainesville: University of Florida Press.

Casagrande, Joseph and Arthur Piper

1969 La transformación estructural de una parroquia rural en las tierras altas del Ecuador. *América Indígena* 29(4):1039–1064.

Castillo Ardiles, Hernan

1970 *Pisac: estructura y mecanismo de dominación en una región de refugio.* México: Instituto Indigenista Interamericano.

Castro Pozo, Hildebrando
1924 *Nuestra comunidad indígena*. Lima: Editorial El Lucero.
1936 *Del ayllu al cooperativismo socialista*. Lima: P. Barrantes Castro.

Celestino, Olinda
1972 *Migración y cambio estructural: la comunidad de Lampián*. Lima: Instituto de Estudios Peruanos.

Centeno Zela, Antonio
1953 *La arriería en Antabamba: una contribución a la etnología peruana*. Universidad Nacional del Cuzco, Facultad de Letras. Tesis para obtar al grado de Bachiller en Letras. Cuzco: unpublished manuscript.

Chayanov, A.V.
1966 *The Theory of Peasant Economy* [1925]. Homewood, Ill.: Richard D. Urwin.

Cheung, S.N.S.
1969 *The Theory of Share Tenancy*. Chicago: University of Chicago Press.

Chevalier, François
1963 *Land and Society in Colonial Mexico: The Great Hacienda*. Berkeley: University of California Press.
1966 Témoignages littéraires et disparités de croissance: l'expansion de la grande propriété dans le Haut-Pérou au XXe siècle. *Annales: économies, sociétés, civilisations* 21(4):815–831.

Chonchol, Jacques
1965 Land Tenure and Development in Latin America. *In* Claudio Veliz, ed., *Obstacles to Change in Latin America*, pp. 75–90. London and New York: Oxford University Press.

Colby, Benjamin N., and Pierre L. van den Berghe
1969 *Ixil Country: A Plural Society in Highland Guatemala*. Berkeley: University of California Press.

Compañía Nacional de Recaudación
1924 Tasación de los bienes de Don Manuel Guillermo de Castresana. Lima.

Concha Contreras, Juan de Dios
1975 Relaciones entre pastores y agricultores. *Allpanchis Phuturinqa* 8:67–101. Cuzco.

Cornblit, Oscar
1970 Society and Mass Rebellion in Eighteenth-Century Peru and Bolivia. *In* Raymond Carr, ed., *Latin American Affairs*, pp. 9–44. St. Antony's Papers no. 22. Oxford University Press.

Costa, Joaquín
1915 *Colectivismo agrario en España*. Madrid: Biblioteca Costa.

Cotler, Julio
1969 La mecánica de la dominación interna y del cambio social en el Perú.

In Matos Mar, José, ed. *Perú Problema*, pp. 145–188. Lima: Moncloa-Campodónico.

1970 Haciendas y comunidades tradicionales en un contexto de movilización política. *Estudios Andinos* 1(1):127–148.

1978 *Clases, estado y nación en el Perú*. Lima: Instituto de Estudios Peruanos.

Cunow, Heinrich

1927 *Allgemeine Wirtschaftgeschichte: eine Ubersicht über die Wirtschaftsentwicklung von der primitiven Sammelwirtschaft bis zum Hochkapitalismus*. Berlin: J.H.W. Dietz.

Custred, Glynn

1979a Symbols and Control in a High Altitude Andean Community. *Anthropos* 74:379–392.

1979b Inca Concepts of Soul and Spirit. *In* Bruce Grindal and Dennis Warren, eds., *Essays in Humanistic Anthropology: A Festschrift in Honor of David Bidney*, pp. 277–302. Washington, D.C.: University Press of America.

Dandler, Jorge

1969 *El sindicalismo campesino en Bolivia: los cambios estructurales en Ucureña*. México: Instituto Indigenista Interamericano.

Davies, Thomas M., Jr.

1974 *Indian Integration in Peru: A Half Century of Experience, 1900–1948*. Lincoln: University of Nebraska Press.

Davis, L. Harlan

1970 The Structure and Operation of Rural Local Government, *In* A. Eugene Havens and William L. Flinn, eds., *Internal Colonialism and Structural Change in Colombia*. New York: Praeger.

Degregori, Carlos, and Jurgen Golte

1973 *Dependencia y desintegración estructural en la comunidad de Pacaraos*. Lima: Instituto de Estudios Peruanos.

Dew, Edward

1969 *Politics in the Altiplano: The Dynamics of Change in Rural Peru*. Austin, Texas: University of Texas Press.

Díaz Martínez, Antonio

1969 *Ayacucho: hambre y esperanza*. Ayacucho: Ediciones Waman Puma.

Dobyns, Henry

1960 *The Religious Festival*. Ph.D. dissertation, Cornell University.

1964 *The Social Matrix of Peruvian Indigenous Communities*. Ithaca, New York: Cornell University Press.

———— and Paul L. Doughty

1976 *Peru: A Cultural History*. New York: Oxford University Press.

————, Paul L. Doughty, and Harold D. Lasswell, eds.

1971 *Peasants, Power and Applied Social Change: Vicos as a Model*.

Beverly Hills, Cal.: Sage Publications.
_____ and Mario Vásquez
1963 *Migración e integración en el Perú*. Lima: Editorial Estudios Andinos.
Doughty, Paul L.
1963 *Peruvian Highlanders in a Changing World: Social Integration and Culture Change in an Andean District*. Ph.D. dissertation, Cornell University.
1968 *Huaylas: An Andean District in Search of Progress*. Ithaca, New York: Cornell University Press.
1970 Behind the Back of the City: Provincial Life in Lima, Peru. *In* William Mangin, ed., *Peasants in Cities*, pp. 30–46. Boston: Houghton Mifflin.
Duncan, Kenneth, and Ian Rutledge, eds.
1977 *Land and Labour in Latin America: Essays on the Development of Agrarian Capitalism in the Nineteenth and Twentieth Centuries*. Cambridge Latin American Studies 26. Cambridge: Cambridge University Press.

Escobar, Gabriel
1970 Interacción de la economia y la política en dos comunidades andinas. *América Indígena* 30(1):205–212.
1973 *Sicaya: cambios culturales en una comunidad mestiza andina*. Lima: Instituto de Estudios Peruanos.
Escobar, María Elvira
1972 Analyse diachronique d'un conseil traditionnel, Colombie, *Canadian Review of Sociology and Anthropology* 9(3):268–287.
Espinoza Soriano, Waldemar, comp.
1978 *Los modos de producción en el imperio de los Incas*. Lima: Editorial Mantaro.

Fals Borda, Orlando
1955 *Peasant Society in the Colombian Andes: A Sociological Study of Saucio*. Gainesville: University of Florida Press.
1957 Indian Congregations in the New Kingdom of Granada: Land Tenure Aspects, 1595–1850. *The Americas* 13:331–351.
Favre, Henri
1977 The Dynamics of Indian Peasant Society and Migration to Coastal Plantations in Central Peru. *In* Kenneth Duncan and Ian Rutledge, eds., *Land and Labour in Latin America: Essays on the Development of Agrarian Capitalism in the Nineteenth and Twentieth Centuries*, pp. 253–267. Cambridge: Cambridge University Press.
_____, Claude Collin-Delavaud, and José Matos Mar
1967 *La hacienda en el Perú*. Lima: Instituto de Estudios Peruanos.
Fawcett, Brian
1963 *Railways of the Andes*. London: George Allen & Unwin.

Fiorivanti-Molinié, Antoinette
1978 La communauté aujourd'hui. *Annales: économies, sociétés, civilisations* 33(5–6):1182–1196.
Flores, Jorge A.
1968 *Los pastores de Paratía. Una introducción a su estudio.* Mexico: Instituto Indigenista Interamericano.
1975 Sociedad y cultura en la puna alta de los Andes. *América Indígena* 35(2):279–319.
1977a *Pastores de puna: uywamichiq punarunakuna.* Lima: Instituto de Estudios Peruanos.
1977b Aspectos magicos del pastoreo. *In* Jorge Flores, ed., *Pastores de puna: uywamichiq punarunakuna.* Lima: Instituto de Estudios Peruanos.
1978 Organización social y complementaridad económica en los Andes centrales. *Actes du XLIIe Congrès International des Américanistes* 4:9–18.
Fonseca, Martel César
1966 La comunidad de Cauri y la quebrada de Chaupiwaranga. *Cuadernos de Investigación* 1:22–33. Huánuco, Perú.
1972a La economía vertical y la economía de mercado en las comunidades alteñas del Perú. *In* John V. Murra, ed., *Visita de la Provincia de León de Huánuco en 1562.* Tomo II, pp. 317–338. Huánuco, Perú: Universidad Nacional Hermilio Valdizán, Facultad de Letras y Ciencias.
1972b *Sistemas económicos en las comunidades campesinas del Perú.* Ph.D. dissertation. Universidad Nacional Mayor de San Marcos, Lima.
Friedlander, Judith
1975 *Being Indian in Hueyapan: A Study of Forced Identity in Contemporary Mexico.* New York: St. Martin's Press.
Fuenzalida, Fernando
1970a Poder, raza y etnía en el Perú contemporáneo. *In* Fernando Fuenzalida et al., *El indio y el poder en el Perú,* pp. 15–87. Perú-Problema 4. Lima: Moncloa-Campodónico.
1970b La estructura de la comunidad de indígenas tradicional: un hipótesis de trabajo. *In* R. Keith et al., *La hacienda, la comunidad y el campesino en el Perú,* pp. 61–104. Perú-Problema 3. Lima: Instituto de Estudios Peruanos.
Furnivall, J.S.
1948 *Colonial Policy and Practice.* London: Cambridge University Press.
Furtado, Celso
1970 *Economic Development of Latin America.* Cambridge: Cambridge University Press
Gade, Daniel W.
1972 Bridge Types in the Central Andes. *Annals of the Association of American Geographers.* 62(1):94–109.

1973 Environment and Disease in the Land Use and Settlement of Apurimac Department, Peru. *Geoform* 16:37–45.

García, Antonio
1952 *Legislación indigenista de Colombia*. México: Instituto Indigenista Interamericano.

Geertz, Clifford
1966 Religion as a Cultural System. *In* Michael Banton, ed., *Anthropological Approaches to the Study of Religion*. A.S.A. Monographs 3. London: Tavistock Publications.

Goins, John
1967 *Huayculi: los indios quichua del valle de Cochambaba, Bolivia*. México: Instituto Indigenista Interamericano.

Gómez, Tomás
1977 Indiens et terre en Nouvelle-Grenada (1539–1843). Les *resguardos*: structures de protection ou spoliation déguisée? *Cahiers du Monde Hispanique et Luso-Brésilien* 28:11–31.

Grieshaber, Erwin P.
1979 Hacienda-Indian Community Relations and Indian Acculturation: An Historiographical Essay. *Latin American Research Review* 14(3): 107–128.

Guillet, David
1974 Transformación ritual y cambio socio-político. *Allpanchis Phuturinqa* 6:143–159. Cuzco

Gutiérrez Galindo, Blas.
1967a El área de Langui-Layo, Cuzco. In *Cuatro estudios*, pp. 41–70. Lima: Ministerio de Trabajo y Comunidades, Instituto Indigenista Peruano.
1967b Agua potable de Chectuyoc, Cuzco. In *Cuatro estudios*, pp. 117–126. Lima: Ministerio de Trabajo y Comunidades, Instituto Indigenista Peruano.
———— and Aurelio Miranda Rocha
1967 La comunidad de Ccochapata. *Las comunidades de Ccochapata y Llocllora, Cuzco*, pp. 3–63. Lima: Ministerio de Trabajo y Comunidades, Instituto Indigenista Peruano.

Halperín Donghi, Tulio
1972 *Revolución y guerra: formación de una élite dirigente en la Argentina criolla*. Buenos Aires: Siglo XXI.

Hammel, Eugene A.
1969 *Power in Ica. The Structural History of a Peruvian Community*. Boston: Little, Brown.

Harris, Olivia
1978 Kinship and the Vertical Ecology of the Laymi Ayllu, Norte de Potosí. *Actes du XLIIᵉ Congrès International des Américanistes*. 4:165–177.

Hindess, Barry, and Paul Q. Hirst
1975 *Pre-capitalist Modes of Production*. London: Routledge Kegan Paul.
Hobsbawm, Eric J.
1959 *Primitive Rebels: Studies in Archaic Forms of Social Movement in the Nineteenth and Twentieth Centuries*. Manchester: Manchester University Press.
1969a A Case of Neo-Feudalism: La Convención, Peru. *Journal of Latin American Studies* 1:31–50.
1969b *Bandits*. London: George Weidenfeld and Nicolson.
1972 Social Bandits: Reply. *Comparative Studies in Society and History* 14(4):503–505.
Horton, Douglas E.
1973 *Haciendas and Cooperatives: A Preliminary Study of Latifundist Agriculture and Agrarian Reform in Northern Peru*. Research Paper Number 3. Madison, Wisconsin: Land Tenure Center.
1974 *Land Reform and Enterprises in Peru*. Madison, Wisconsin: Land Tenure Center.
Houdart-Morizot, Marie-France
1976 *Tradition et pouvoir à Cuenca, communauté andine*. Lima: Institut Français d'Etudes Andines.
Hsaio, J.C.
1975 The Theory of Share Tenancy Revisited. *Journal of Political Economy*. 83(5):1023–1032.
Hunt, Eva, and June Nash
1967 Local and Territorial Units. *In* Manning Nash, vol. ed., *Social Anthropology*, vol. VI, pp. 253–282. *Handbook of Middle American Indians*, Robert Wauchope, series ed., Austin: University of Texas Press.
Hurtado G., Hugo
1974 *Formación de las comunidades campesinas en el Perú*. Lima: Editorial Tercer Mundo.

Instituto Indigenista Peruano
1968 *Tres estudios en la zona Canas-Canchis*. Ministerio de Trabajo y Comunidades. Sub-proyector de Investigación. Proyecto de Desarrollo e Integración de la Poblacíon Indígena del Concejo Nacional de Desarrollo Comunal. Zona: Canas-Canchis.
Instituto Nacional de Planificación
1972 *Población del Peru: resultados provisionales del censo de 1972*. Lima.
Isbell, Billie Jean
1977 No servimos más: un estudio de los efectos de disipar un sistema de la autoridad tradicional en un pueblo ayacuchano. *Actas y Memorias del XXXIX Congreso Internacional de Americanistas*. 3:285–298. Lima.

1978 Introduction to Andean Symbolism. *Actes du XLIIe Congrès International des Américanistes* 4:259–268.

1979 *To Defend Ourselves: Ecology and Ritual in an Andean Community.* London and Austin: University of Texas Press.

Jacobsen, Nils

1979 Desarrollo económico y relaciones de clase en el sur andino (1780–1920). *Análisis* 5:67–81. Lima.

Johnson, Allen W.

1971 *Sharecroppers of the Sertão.* Stanford: Stanford University Press.

Kapsoli, Wilfredo

1972 *Los movimientos campesinos en Cerro de Pasco 1880–1963.* Lima. Mimeographed.

Kay, Cristobal

1974 Comparative Development of the European Manorial System and the Latin American Hacienda System. *Journal of Peasant Studies* 2(1):69–98.

Keating, Elsie B.

1973 Latin American Peasant Corporate Communities: Potentials for Mobilization and Political Integration. *Journal of Anthropological Research* 29:37–55.

Keith, Robert G.

1971 Encomienda, Hacienda and Corregimiento in Spanish America: A Structural Analysis. *Hispanic American Historical Review* 51(2): 431–46.

1976 *Conquest and Agrarian Change: The Emergence of the Hacienda System on the Peruvian Coast.* Cambridge: Harvard University Press.

Korfmann, Manfred

1973 The Sling as a Weapon. *Scientific American* 229(4):34–42.

Kubler, George

1952 *The Indian Caste of Peru, 1795–1940. A Population Study Based Upon Tax Records and Census Reports.* Smithsonian Institution. Institute of Anthropology publication no. 14. Washington: United States Government Printing Office.

Kula, Witold

1970 *Théorie économique du système féodal. Pour un modèle de l'économie polonaise 16e-18e-siècles.* Paris and the Hague: Mouton.

Kuper, Leo, and M.G. Smith

1969 *Pluralism in Africa.* Berkeley: University of California Press.

La Barre, Weston

1948 *The Aymara Indians of the Lake Titicaca Plateau, Bolivia.* Memoir 68, American Anthropological Association. Menasha, Wisconsin.

Lambert, Bernd

1977 Bilaterality in the Andes. *In* Ralph Bolton and Enrique Mayer, eds., *Andean Kinship and Marriage,* pp. 1–27. American Anthropological

Association publication no. 7. Washington: American Anthropological Association.

Lanning, Edward P.
1967 *Peru Before the Incas*. Englewood Cliffs, New Jersey: Prentice-Hall.

La Verdad
1915–1960 Newspaper. Sicuani, Perú.

Leeds, Anthony
1973 Locality Power in Relation to Supralocal Power Institutions. *In* Aidan Southall, ed., *Urban Anthropology. Cross-Cultural Studies of Urbanization*, pp. 15–42. New York and London: Oxford University Press.

LeGrand, Catherine
1977 Perspectives for the Historical Study of Rural Politics and the Colombian Case: An Overview. *Latin American Research Review* 12(1):7–36.

Lenin, V.I.
1939 *Imperialism: The Highest Stage of Capitalism. A Popular Outline*. [1916] New York: International Publishers.

Lewin, Bolseslao
1957 *La rebelión de Tupac Amaru y los orígenes de la emancipación americana*. Buenos Aires: Editorial Hispanoamericano.

Lockhart, James
1969 Ecomienda and Hacienda: The Evolution of the Great Estate in the Spanish Indies. *Hispanic American Historical Review* 49(3):411–29.

Long, Norman
1975 Structural Dependency, Modes of Production and Economic Brokerage in Rural Peru. *In* Ivan Oxaal et al., eds., *Beyond the Sociology of Development*, pp. 253–282. London: Routledge and Kegan Paul.

Long, Norman and Bryan R. Roberts
1978 Peasant Cooperation and Underdevelopment in Central Peru. *In* Norman Long and Bryan Roberts, eds., *Peasant Cooperation and Capitalist Expansion in Central Peru*, pp. 297–218. Austin: University of Texas Press.

Lowenthal, Abraham F., ed.
1975 *The Peruvian Experiment: Continuity and Change Under Military Rule*. Princeton: Princeton University Press.

Macera, Pablo
1968 *Mapas coloniales de haciendas cuzqueñas*. Lima: Universidad Nacional Mayor de San Marcos.
1977 Feudalismo colonial americano: el caso de las haciendas peruanas. *In* Pablo Macera, *Trabajos de historia*, volume III, pp. 139–228. Lima: Instituto Nacional de Cultura.

Mangin, William
1967 Squatter Settlements. *Scientific American* 217(4):21–29.

1970 Tales from the Barriadas. *In* William Mangin, ed., *Peasants in Cities*, pp. 55–61. Boston: Houghton Mifflin.

Mariátegui, José Carlos
1928 Regionalismo y centralismo. *In* José Carlos Mariátegui, *7 ensayos de interpretación de la realidad peruana*. Lima: Biblioteca Amauta.
1965 *7 ensayos de la interprectación de la realidad peruana.* Tenth edition [1928]. Lima: Biblioteca Amauta.

Martínez Arellano, Héctor
1963 La hacienda Ccapana. *Perú Indígena* 10(24–25):37–64. Lima.

Martinez, Héctor
1969 *Las migraciones altiplánicas y la colonización del Tambopata.* Lima: Centro de Estudios de Población y Desarrollo.
1970 *Migración en las comunidades indígenas del Perú antes de la Reforma Agraria.* Lima: Centro de Estudios de Población y Desarrollo.

Martinez-Alier, Juan
1972 Relations of Production in Andean Haciendas: Peru. *In* Kenneth Duncan, and Ian Rutledge, eds., *Land and Labour in Latin America: Essays on the Development of Agrarian Capitalism in the Nineteenth and Twentieth Centuries,* pp. 141–164. Cambridge: Cambridge University Press.

Marx, Karl
1947 *The German Ideology* [1845–46]. New York: International Publishers.
1963 *The Eighteenth Brumaire of Louis Napoleon* [1852]. New York: International Publishers.
1964 *Pre-Capitalist Economic Formations.* E.J. Hobsbawm, ed. New York: International Publishers.

Matos Mar, José, ed.
1969 *Dominación y cambios en el Perú rural.* Lima: Instituto de Estudios Peruanos.
1970 Comunidades indígenas del área andina. *In* José Matos Mar, comp. *Hacienda, comunidad y campesinado en el Perú*, pp. 219–263. Peru Problema 3. Lima: Instituto de Estudios Peruanos.

Matrículas de Castas
1841 Matrícula de Castas de la Provincia de Andahuaylas. Archivo Nacional del Perú, Seccion Histórica, Documentos del Antiguo Archivo de Hacienda.
1851 Matrícula de Castas de la Provincia de Quispicanchis. Archivo Nacional del Perú, Sección Histórica, Documentos del Antiguo Archivo de Hacienda.

Mayer, Enrique
1971 Un carnero por un saco de papas: aspectos de trueque en la zona de Chaupiwaranga: Pasco. *Actas y Memorias del XXXIX Congreso Internacional de Americanistas* 3:184–196. Lima.

1974 Las reglas del juego en la reciprocidad andina. *In* Giorgio Alberti and Enrique Mayer, eds., *Reciprocidad e intercambio en los Andes peruanos*, pp. 37–65. Perú-Problema 12. Lima: Instituto de Estudios Peruanos.

1977 *Tenencia y control comunal de la tierra: el caso de Laraos (Yauyos)*. Lima: Pontificia Universidad Católica del Perú, Departamento de Ciencias Sociales.

McEwen, William J.

1969 *Changing Rural Bolivia: A Study of Social and Political Organization and the Potential for Development in Six Contrasting Communities.* New York: Research Institute for the Study of Man.

McGreevey, William Paul

1971 *An Economic History of Colombia, 1845–1930.* Cambridge: Cambridge University Press.

Métraux, Alfred

1959 The Social and Economic Structure of the Indian Communities of the Andean Region. *International Labour Review* 79:225–243.

1969 *The History of the Incas.* New York: Random House.

Miller, Frank C.

1973 *Old Villages and a New Town: Industrialization in Mexico.* Menlo Park, Cal.: Cummings Publishing Company.

Ministerio de Agricultura

1973a Zona Agraria XI. Expedientes de Afectación (Canchis). Cuzco.

1973b *Datos oficiales del II Censo Nacional Agropecuario.* Lima: Oficina Nacional de Estadística y Censos.

Mintz, Sidney W.

1966 The Caribbean as a Socio-Cultural Area. *Journal of World History* 9(4):912–937.

Miranda Rocha, Aurelio

1967 Las artesanías en la provincia de Canchis. *In Cuatro estudios*, pp. 5–39. Lima: Ministerio de Trabajo y Comunidades, Instituto Indigenista Peruano.

Mishkin, Bernard

1947 The Contemporary Quechua. *In* Julian H. Steward, ed., *Handbook of South American Indians*, vol. 2, pp. 411–470. Washington, D.C.: United States Government Printing Office.

Montoya, Rodrigo, M.J. Silveiria and F.J. Lindoso

1979 *Producción parcelaria y universo ideológico: el caso de Puquio.* Lima: Instituto de Estudios Peruanos.

Morner, Magnus

1973 The Spanish American Hacienda: A Survey of Recent Research and Debate. *Hispanic American Historical Review* 53(2):183–216.

1978 *Perfil de la sociedad rural del Cuzco a fines de la colonia.* Lima: Universidad del Pacífico.

Moseley, Michael E.

1974 Organizational Preadaptation to Irrigation: The Evolution of Early Water Management Systems in Coastal Peru. *In* T.D. Downing and M. Gibson, eds., *Irrigation's Impact on Society*, pp. 72–82. Tuscon: University of Arizona press.

1975 *The Maritime Foundations of Andean Civilization*. Menlo Park, California: Cummings Publishing Company.

Moss, David

1979 Bandits and Boundaries in Sardinia. *Man* (n.s.) 14:477–496.

Murra, John V.

1964 Una apreciación etnológica de la visita. *In Visita hecha a la provincia de Chucuito por Garci Diez de San Miguel en el año 1567. Documentos Regionales para la Etnología y Etnohistoria Andinas*, tomo 1, pp. 419–442. Lima: Ediciones de la Casa de la Cultura del Perú.

1967 *La visita de los Chupachu como fuente etnológica. In* John V. Murra, ed., *Visita de la Provincia de León de Huá*nuco en 1562, tomo 1, pp. 383–417. Huánuco, Perú: Universidad Nacional Hermilio Valdizán, Facultad de Letras y Educación.

1968 An Aymara Kingdom in 1567. *Ethnohistory* 15:115–151.

1970 Current Research and Prospects in Andean Ethnohistory. *Latin American Research Review* 5(1):3–36.

1972 El "control vertical" de un máximo de pisos ecológicos en la economía de las sociedades andinas. *In* John V. Murra, ed., *Visita de la Provincia de León de Huánuco en 1562*, tomo II, pp. 429–476. Hermilio Valdizán. Facultad de Letras Y Ciencias.

1975 *Formaciones económicas y políticas del mundo andino*. Lima: Instituto de Estudios Peruanos.

Nachtigall, Horst

1966 *Indianische Fischer, Feldbauer und Viehzüchter: Beiträge zur peruanischen Völkerkunde*. Marburger Studien zur Völkerkunde, Band 2. Berlin: Dietrich Reimer Verlag.

Newberry, D.M.G.

1975 Tenurial Obstacles to Innovation. *Journal of Development Studies*. 11(4):263–277.

Núñez del Prado, Oscar, with William Foote Whyte, coll.

1973 *Kuyo Chico: Applied Anthropology in an Indian Community*. Chicago: University of Chicago Press.

Núñez del Prado, Juan

1974 The Supernatural World of the Quechuas. *In* Patricia J. Lyon, ed., *Native South Americans*. Boston: Little, Brown.

O'Brien, Philip J.

1975 A Critique of Latin American Theories of Dependency. *In* Ivar Oxaal et al., eds., *Beyond the Sociology of Development: Economy and*

Society in Latin America and Africa. London: Routledge & Kegan Paul, pp. 7–27.

Orlove, Benjamin S.
1973 Abigeato: la organización social de una actividad ilegal. *Allpanchis Phuturinqa* 5:65–81. Cuzco.
1975 Surimana: decaimiento de una zona, decadencia de un pueblo. *Antropología Andina* 1:75–110. Cuzco.
1976 Molloccahua 1931: A Peasant Uprising in Southern Peru. Paper presented at the XLI International Congress of Americanists. Mexico.
1977a *Alpacas, Sheep, and Men: The Wool Export Economy and Regional Society in Southern Peru*. New York: Academic Press.
1977b The Decline of Local Elites: Canchis in Southern Peru. *In* Raymond D. Fogelson and Richard N. Adams, eds., *The Anthropology of Power: Ethnographic Studies from Asia, Oceania and the New World*, pp. 337–348. New York: Academic Press.
1977c Inequality among Peasants: The Forms and Uses of Reciprocal Exchange in Andean Peru. *In* Rhoda Halperin and James Dow, eds., *Studies in Peasant Livelihood*. New York: Saint Martin's Press, pp. 201–214.
1979 Two Rituals and Three Hypotheses: An Examination of Solstice Divination in Southern Highland Peru. *Anthropological Quarterly* 52:86–98.

Ortiz, Sutti
1967 Colombian Rural Market Organization: An Exploratory Model. *Man* (n.s.), 2:393–414.
1973 *Uncertainties in Peasant Farming: A Colombian Case*. London: Athlone Press.

Ossio, Juan
1973 *Ideología mesiánica del mundo andino*. Lima: Edición de Ignacio Prado Pastor.
1978 El simbolismo del agua y la representación del tiempo y el espacio en la fiesta de la acequia de la comunidad de Andamarca. *Actes du XLIIe Congrès International des Américanistes* 4:377–398.

Paige, Jeffery M.
1975 *Agrarian Revolution: Social Movements and Export Agriculture in the Underdeveloped World*. New York: The Free Press.

Palomino Flores, Salvador
1971 La dualidad en la organización socio-cultural de algunos pueblos del área andina. *Revista del Museo Nacional del Perú* 37:231–260.

Parsons, James J.
1949 *Antioqueño Colonization in Western Colombia*. Ibero-Americana 32. Berkeley: University of California Press.

Patch, Richard
1959 How Communal are the Communities? *American Universities Field*

Service Reports. (West Coast South America) 6(5):1–18.
1967 La Parada, Lima's Market, Parts 1, 2, 3. *American Universities Field Service Reports.* (West Coast South America) No. 14.

PEIFEDER
1971 *Estudio socio-económico cultural y pedagógico de las provincias de Canas y Canchis (Cuzco).* Sicuani: Proyecto Especial Integrado sobre la Función de la Educación en el Desarrollo Rural.

Perú, República del
1898 *Resumen del Censo General de habitantes del Perú hecho en 1876.* Lima.

Piel, Jean
1967 A propos d'un soulèvement rural péruvien au début du vingtième siècle: Tocroyoc (1921). *Revue d'Histoire Moderne et Contemporaine* 14:374–405.

Pinto, Edmundo
1971 Ecos de Huarochirí en la comunidad de Tomanga. *Revista del Museo Nacional del Perú* 37:261–284.

Platt, Tristan
1975 Experiencia y experimentación: Los asentamientos andinos en las cabeceras del Valle de Azapa. *Chungara* 5:33–60. Arica, Chile.
1976 *Espejos y maíz: temas de la estructura simbólica andina.* Cuadernos de Investigación No. 10. La Paz: Centro de Investigación y Promoción del Campesinado.

Preston, David
1969 Rural Emigration in Andean America. *Human Organization* 28(4): 279–286.

Primov, George P.
1975 *Ethnicity in Highland Peru.* Ph.D. dissertation, University of Washington, Seattle.

Pulgar Vidal, Javier
1964 *Geografía del Perú: las ocho regiones naturales del Perú.* Lima: Editorial Universo.

Redfield, Robert
1956 *The Little Community.* Chicago: University of Chicago Press.

Revilla Corrales, Arcenio
1967 Las comunidades de Ocobamba y Llallahui. *In Cuatro estudios,* pp. 71–116. Lima: Ministerio de Trabajo y Comunidades, Instituto Indigenista Peruano.
_____ and Ana Báez de Revilla
1967 La comunidad de Llocllora. *In Las comunidades de Ccochapata y Llocllora, Cuzco,* pp. 65–128. Lima: Ministerio de Trabajo y Comunidades, Instituto Indigenista Peruano.

Rhoades, Robert and Stephen I. Thompson
1975 Adaptive Strategies in Alpine Environments: Beyond Ecological Particularism. *American Ethnologist* 2(3):535–551.

Rivet, Paul
 1949 Les langues de l'ancien diocèse de Trujillo. *Journal de la Société des Américanistes de Paris*, v. 38 (n.s.):1–53.
Rodríguez, Humberto
 1969 Progresismo y cambios en Llica. *In* José R. Weisse, ed. *La comunidad andina*, pp. 73–147. México: Instituto Indigenista Interamericano.
 1969 *Caqui: estudio de una hacienda costeña.* Lima: Instituto de Estudios Andinos.
Romero, Emilio
 1928 *Monografía del departamento de Puno.* Lima.
Rowe, John Howland
 1957 The Incas under Spanish Colonial Institutions. *Hispanic American Historical Review* 37:155–199.

Saénz, Moíses
 1933 *Sobre el Indio peruano y su incorporacion al medio nacional.* México: Secretaria de Educación Pública.
Sahlins, Marshall
 1972 *Stone Age Economics.* New York and Chicago: Aldine-Atherton.
Sánchez, Rodrigo
 1978 The Model of Verticality in the Andean Economy: A Critical Reconsideration. *Actes du XLIIe Congrès International des Américanistes* 4:199–212.
Scorza, Manuel
 1972 *Redoble por Rancas.* Barcelona: Editorial Planeta.
Scott, James C.
 1972 The Erosion of Patron-Client Bonds and Social Change in Rural Southeast Asia. *Journal of Asian Studies* 37(1):5–37.
Sempat Assadourian, Carlos
 1972 Integración y desintegración regional en el espacio colonial. Un enfoque histórico. *EURE* 4:11–23. Santiago.
Simmons, Roger
 1974 *Palca and Pucara: A Study of the Effects of Revolution on Two Bolivian Haciendas.* University of California Publications in Anthropology, volume 9. Berkeley: University of California Press.
Simpson, Lesley Byrd
 1966 *Many Mexicos.* 4th ed. rev. Berkeley: University of California Press.
SINAMOS
 1974 *Directorio de Comunidades Campesinas.* Lima: Sistema Nacional de Apoyo a la Mobilización Social. Oficina Nacional de Apoyo a la Mobilización Social. Dirección General de Apoyo a Empresas.
Singelmann, Peter
 1975 Political Structure and Social Banditry in Northeast Brazil. *Journal of Latin American Studies* 7(1):59–83.

Snyder, Joan
   1960 *Group Relations and Social Change in an Andean Village*. Ph.D. dissertation, Cornell University.
Sofri, Gianni
   1971 *El modo de producción asiático. Historia de una controversia marxista*. Barcelona: Ediciones Peninsula.
Spalding, Karen
   1974 *De indio a campesino: cambios en la estructura social del Perú colonial*. Lima: Instituto de Estudios Peruanos.
   1975 Hacienda-Village Relations in Andean Society to 1830. *Latin American Perspectives* 2(1).
   1977 Clases sociales en los Andes peruanos, 1750–1920. *Análisis* 1:25–35. Lima.
Squier, Ephriam
   1877 *Peru: Incidents of Travel and Exploration in the Land of the Incas*. London: Macmillan.
Stavenhagen, Rodolfo
   1975 *Social Classes in Agrarian Societies*. Garden City, New York: Doubleday.
Stein, William W.
   1955: *Hualcan: An Andean Indian Estancia*. Ph.D. dissertation, Cornell University.
Steward, Julian H. and Louis Faron
   1959 *Native Peoples of South America*. New York: McGraw-Hill.
Symanski, Richard
   1971 *Periodic Markets of Andean Colombia*. Ph.D. dissertation, Syracuse University.

Thomas, Brooke
   1973 *Human Adaptations of a High Andean Energy Flow System*. Occasional Papers in Anthropology No. 7. University Park: Pennsylvania State University.
Tschopik, Harry, Jr.
   1947 *Highland Communities of Central Peru: A Regional Survey*. Smithsonian Institution Institute of Social Anthropology, Publication No. 5. Washington, D.C.: United States Government Printing Office.
Tuma, Elias H.
   1965 *Twenty-Six Centuries of Agrarian Reform: A Comparative Analysis*. Berkeley and Los Angeles: University of California Press.

Urbano, Henrique Osvaldo
   1974 La representación andina del tiempo y del espacio en el fiesta. *Allpanchis Phuturinqa* 7:9–48. Cuzco.

Vallée, Lionel
   1971 La ecología subjetiva como elemento esencial de la verticalidad.

Revista del Museo Nacional del Perú 37:167–173.
1972 Cycle écologique et cycle rituel: le cas d'un village andin. *Canadian Review of Sociology and Anthropology* 9(3):238–254.
van den Berghe, Pierre L.
1974a The Use of Ethnic Terms in the Peruvian Social Sciences Literature. *International Journal of Comparative Sociology* (3–4):132–142.
1974b *Class and Ethnicity in Peru*, ed. Leiden: E.J. Brill.
1974c Pluralism. *In* John J. Honigmann, ed., *Handbook of Social and Cultural Anthropology*, pp. 959–977. Chicago: Rand McNally.
1974 *Class and Ethnicity in Peru*. Leiden: E.J. Brill.
———— and George P. Primov
1977 *Inequality in the Andes: Class and Ethnicity in Cuzco*. Columbia, Missouri: University of Missouri Press.
Vargas Calderón, Cesar
1967 Síntesis de la flora de las provincias de Canas, Espinar y Chumbivilcas. *Revista Universitaria. Organo de la Universidad Nacional de San Antonio Abad del Cuzco*. Años LIII–LIV (1964–1965), nos. 126–129, pp. 55–76.
Villasante, Marco
1978 El problema mercantil simple y la economia campesina de Espinar. *Crítica Andina* 1:77–111. Cuzco.
von Tschudi, Juan Jacobo
1966 *Testimonio del Perú (1932–1942)*. Lima: no pub.

Wachtel, Nathan
1973 *Sociedad e ideología: ensayos de historia y antropología andinas*. Lima: Instituto de Estudios Peruanos.
Webster, Steven
1971 An Indigenous Quechua Community in Exploitation of Multiple Ecological Zones. *Actas y Memorias del XXXIX Congreso Internacional de Americanistas* 3:174–183. Lima.
1973 Native Pastoralism in the South Andes. *Ethnology* 12(2):115–133.
1974 *Factors of Social Rank in a Native Quechua Community*. Mimeographed.
Whyte, William Foote
1975 Conflict and Cooperation in Andean Communities. *American Ethnologist* 2(2):373–392.
———— and Giorgio Alberti
1976 *Power, Politics and Progress: Social Change in Rural Peru*. New York: Elsevier Scientific Publishing Company.
Winther, Paul
1977 Contemporary Dacoity and Traditional Politics in South Asia. *University of Oklahoma Papers in Anthropology* 18(2):153–166.
Wolf, Eric
1956 Aspects of Group Relations in a Complex Society: Mexico. *Ameri-*

can Anthropologist 58:1065–1078.

1957 Closed Corporated Peasant Communities in Mesoamerica and Central Java. *Southwestern Journal of Anthropology* 13:1–18.

1966 *Peasants.* Englewood Cliffs, New Jersey: Prentice Hall.

1967 Levels of Communal Relations. *Handbook of Middle American Indians,* Robert Wauchope, ed., vol. 6, pp. 299–316. Austin and London: University of Texas Press.

1969 *Peasant Wars of the Twentieth Century.* New York: Harper and Row.

———— and Edward Hansen

1972 *The Human Condition in Latin America.* London and New York: Oxford University Press.

Womack, John Jr.

1969 *Zapata and the Mexican Revolution.* New York: Alfred A. Knopf.

Zuidema, Tom

1964 *The Ceque System of Cuzco: The Social Organization of the Capital of the Inca.* Leiden: E.J. Brill.

————, and Ulpiano Quispe

1967 Un viaje a Dios en la communidad de Warkaya. *Wamani* 1:109–116. Ayacucho, Perú.

List of Contributors

STEPHEN B. BRUSH received his Ph.D. in anthropology from the University of Wisconsin. His research on a highland peasant community in northern Peru has resulted in a book (*Mountain, Field and Family: The Economy and Human Ecology of an Andean Valley*) and several articles. He has recently conducted field research on traditional potato cultivation in the Andes. He is an associate professor of anthropology at the College of William and Mary.

GLYNN CUSTRED received his M.A. in Latin American history and his Ph.D. in anthropology from Indiana University. He has done ethnographic field work in the high-altitude zones of southern Peru, and has published articles on the environment, the religion, the economy, and the kinship arrangements of the Quechua-speaking peasants of those regions. Dr. Custred is an associate professor of anthropology at California State University at Hayward.

LAURA MALTBY (A.B. Harvard 1972, M.Ed. Temple 1976) is currently a lecturer in the English Program for Foreign Students at the University of Pennsylvania. She spent the 1972–73 year in Peru on a Fulbright fellowship researching early twentieth-century Indian rebellions in the Department of Puno.

BENJAMIN ORLOVE (Ph.D., University of California at Berkeley) conducted field research on the wool export economy and regional society in southern highland Peru. He is the author of *Alpacas, Sheep, and Men* and has published several articles on economics, politics, and related topics. At the present he is engaged in anthropological and ecological research in the Lake Titicaca region of Peru and Bolivia. He is associate professor of environmental studies and anthropology at the University of California at Davis.

SUTTI ORTIZ received her Ph.D. from the London School of Economics. Her research in Colombia includes a monograph (*Uncertainties in Peasant Farming*) and a number of articles. She has taught and been a research scholar at the London School of Economics, Oberlin College, and Case Western Reserve University.

GEORGE PRIMOV was born in Bulgaria and raised in Venezuela. He received his Ph.D. in sociology from the University of Washington. He is currently doing research on the economic and social problems of Amerindian groups in Amazonia. He is assistant professor of sociology at the University of Missouri at Columbia.

KAREN SPALDING is associate professor of history at the University of Delaware. She received her Ph.D. degree in 1968 from the University of California at Berkeley, and has taught at Rutgers University (1967–70) and Columbia University (1970–75). She has done most of her work in the area of Peruvian ethnohistory, and has published various articles as well as a book, *De Indio a Campesino* (Lima, 1974) in that field. Her work on the nineteenth and twentieth centuries is not so much a departure from her other research, as an outgrowth of an effort to comprehend the origins and characteristics of Peru today by tracing the road that Peruvian society has traveled.

PIERRE L. VAN DEN BERGHE is professor of sociology and anthropology at the University of Washington. He has done field work in South Africa, Nigeria, Mexico, Guatemala, and most recently in the Cuzco region of Peru. His books on Latin America include *Race and Racism, Ixil Country* (with Benjamin N. Colby), and *Inequality in the Peruvian Andes* (with George P. Primov).

KARL A YAMBERT is a doctoral candidate in social anthropology at the University of California at Davis. He is currently engaged in dissertation research in the lower Piura valley of Peru, where he is studying cotton export agriculture and agrarian reform.

Index

Index